TAKING FUNNY MUSIC
SERIOUSLY

COMEDY & CULTURE
NICK MARX AND MATT SIENKIEWICZ, *series editors*

TAKING FUNNY MUSIC
SERIOUSLY

LILY E. HIRSCH

INDIANA UNIVERSITY PRESS

This book is a publication of

Indiana University Press
Office of Scholarly Publishing
Herman B Wells Library 350
1320 East 10th Street
Bloomington, Indiana 47405 USA

iupress.org

© 2024 by Lily E. Hirsch

All rights reserved

No part of this book may be reproduced or utilized in any form or by any means, electronic or mechanical, including photocopying and recording, or by any information storage and retrieval system, without permission in writing from the publisher. The paper used in this publication meets the minimum requirements of the American National Standard for Information Sciences—Permanence of Paper for Printed Library Materials, ANSI Z39.48-1992.

Manufactured in the United States of America

First printing 2024

Library of Congress Cataloging-in-Publication Data

Names: Hirsch, Lily E., author.
Title: Taking funny music seriously / Lily E. Hirsch.
Description: Bloomington : Indiana University Press, 2024. | Series: Comedy & culture | Includes bibliographical references and index.
Identifiers: LCCN 2023058721 (print) | LCCN 2023058722 (ebook) | ISBN 9780253069948 (hardback) | ISBN 9780253069955 (paperback) | ISBN 9780253069962 (ebook)
Subjects: LCSH: Humor in music. | Humorous songs—History and criticism. | BISAC: SOCIAL SCIENCE / Media Studies | PERFORMING ARTS / Comedy
Classification: LCC ML65 .H57 2024 (print) | LCC ML65 (ebook) | DDC 780.2/07—dc23/eng/20240119
LC record available at https://lccn.loc.gov/2023058721
LC ebook record available at https://lccn.loc.gov/2023058722

CONTENTS

Acknowledgments vii

Introduction *1*

PART I. *The Setup*

1. Live from Largo *19*
2. Staying Demented *38*
3. Bad Singing *52*

PART II. *Jesting by Genre*

4. Tapping into Movie Music *73*
5. Classical Music Is Comedic (Again) *91*
6. Hip-Hop Meow *108*
7. Banter, Banjo, and Bumpkins *126*
8. Heavy and Hilarious (Metal) *143*
9. Funny Girls *157*

PART III. *Humorous Music by Topic*

10. Humor about Humor *177*
11. Silly Love Songs *195*
12. Poisoning Pigeons *210*
    Conclusion: Comedic Music in Crisis *229*

Selected Bibliography *239*
Index *251*

ACKNOWLEDGMENTS

I MUST FIRST THANK SEVERAL individuals who contributed to this book in conversation and correspondence about funny music and related topics or with awesome examples of humorous song: Ted Gizmo, Lauren Mayer, Paul W. Hankins, Bruce Triggs, David J. Buck, Robert Fink, Dr. Demento, Taylor Roelofs, Daniel Goldmark, and Jake Johnson. I am also especially grateful to those I interviewed for individual chapters—all of whom challenged and pushed up against conventional thinking about funny music: Katie Goodman (March 2, 2020), Insane Ian (March 30, 2020), Jess McKenna (March 11, 2020), Tom Lehrer (July 9, 2020), Kate Micucci and Riki Lindhome (August 15, 2020), Peter Schickele (October 17, 2019), Theodore Shapiro (April 4, 2020), Fred LaBour (or Too Slim) (July 18, 2019), and Tim Stafford (April 26, 2019). In this respect, I want to thank "Weird Al" Yankovic as well, who spoke with me as I wrote my first study of humor in music: *Weird Al: Seriously*. The fun and challenge of that project, as well as the wonderfully supportive Weird Al fan community, encouraged me to continue to explore comedic music of all types while further highlighting funny music's significance.

The editors of this new series at Indiana University Press, the Comedy and Culture series, deserve special mention—Matt Sienkiewicz and Nick Marx. I am so pleased that they are heading up a serious series focused on hilarity. I would also like to thank the acquiring editor Allison Chaplin and the peer reviewers, who took the time to thoughtfully respond to the manuscript. I was lucky to work with people who recognize the importance of comedy.

I want to dedicate this book to all the people who have needed funny music as well as the funny musicians who have satisfied this need. One musician mentioned in this book, Logan Whitehurst, was my husband's childhood friend—the two grew up in Los Banos, California. Together, in this small Central Valley town, Logan and Austin amused themselves and others through music. Austin explained to me the process of writing funny songs, describing it as "doubly creative"—the fun of creating a good song and a good joke that work in combination—a lovely take on one aspect of the overlooked exceptionality of humorous music. As a young adult, Whitehurst embarked on a successful music career, one that included funny songs. Though Whitehurst died in 2006, his music has continued to inspire and entertain, sometimes with important lessons (like, "Monkeys are bad people"). I am grateful Austin introduced me to Logan's music well before I had any idea that I might write about funny music. I am also thankful that my kids, Grant and Elliana, continue to remind me that humorous music is significant in so many ways. Their love of humor and funny music has kept laughter alive around me, even during difficult times. And that laughter, quite frankly, has been a lifeline.

TAKING FUNNY MUSIC
SERIOUSLY

INTRODUCTION

ONE DAY IN APRIL, MY son's kindergarten class gathered on the colored carpet squares in front of me, and together we sang:

> Happy birthday to you
> Happy birthday to you
> You look like a monkey
> And you smell like one too.[1]

The song, I told them, is a parody—an existing song made new, changed in some way, often humorously. The parody lesson was part of my class visit, some extracurricular play approved by the class's regular teacher with the school year almost over. And I had come prepared, armed with recordings of "Weird Al" Yankovic and a box full of crayons. I was sure my experience teaching college students would easily translate, and I was not wrong. What do university kids and a bunch of five- and six-year-olds have in common? Well, everything. No punchline. Both groups generally need more sleep than full-grown adults and can eat pizza for all meals. They can also be somewhat squirrely and easily distracted, especially when they sense weakness, a chance to misbehave without consequence. But, in my case, there was no weakness. On that day, with my experience interviewing Weird Al himself for my book *Weird Al: Seriously* (2020), I was feeling pretty confident. Funny music was my new jam (hold the peanut butter, though; it's a nut-free classroom).

Over lunch two months before, I had discussed humor in music with one of my favorite musicologists, professor Robert Fink at the University of California, Los Angeles. Why has so little been written about funny music? First off, musicians, we agreed, might not want the coverage, especially those who use comedy as a musical tool among many, more traditional techniques. Humorous music, after all, is often seen as frivolous and unworthy, casually dismissed as inconsequential. As Iain Ellis observed in *Rebels Wit Attitude* (2008), it's typically "underappreciated" and "underestimated," unfairly judged to be irrelevant and light. In comparison to so-called serious music, funny music will supposedly never be true art. It's neither lofty nor sublime. As artists, musicians typically want to be taken seriously, and a comical rep simply doesn't help.

Talking about humor, the words we use often make matters worse. It's *just* a joke. Nothing important here, *just joking*. Humor is somehow minimized, less than something, though that something is left unsaid. I was *only kidding*. It's another easy means of diminishment. And in the word *kidding*, humor is further connected to children and play—a youthful world without weight. Weird Al himself is well aware of the associated bias. In 2017, he told Randy Lewis of the *Los Angeles Times*, "Humor is such an important part of the human experience. I just don't know why showcasing it makes people think, 'You're not a real artist.'"

Writers and those who study music, including musicologists, may not be able to afford the associated bias. Writing about funny music is no way to gain prestige or some sort of respect. Concerned about a comedic musician's transferred standing, they may wisely sidestep humor in music. Apart from vanity, that choice has basic merit in job placement and security. Writing about funny music, I told Fink, might not be the best way for an academic to get that job and then keep it, tenure and beyond, especially given the pitiful crop of academic jobs each year—part-timers adjuncting from their cars (which really only works if the topic is Donna Summer's "Bad Girls": "Toot toot, hey, beep beep"). Sociologist Cate Watson came to a similar conclusion. Academics who write about humor or, yikes, employ humor in their writing, she maintains, "may find themselves dismissed as lightweight and trivial."[2] No surprise, then, that the field of humor studies is relatively young, with its first rumblings in the mid-1970s.[3]

In a new book, *The Routledge Companion to Popular Music and Humor* (2019)—one that finally addresses funny music in a scholarly way—it's one step forward, one step stuck. Though the breadth of coverage is impressive, from comedy in punk music to humor in K-pop, the editors recycle the same old musical hierarchies, keeping funny music on the defensive. In the introduction, Thomas M. Kitts and Nick Baxter-Moore write, "Less cerebral than the work of Tom Lehrer, Flanders and Swann, or the Danish musical humorist Victor Borge, is the comedy novelty record." Such novelties, they continue, "are lightweight, often the epitome or nadir of 'low comedy.'" Even in a significant book on humorous music, they still had to take sides, picking a humorous-music loser. That loser comes up short based on the very values that help dismiss funny music in the first place.

Fink offered yet another take. Maybe musicologists just aren't that funny. You write what you know. But wait, what about the professors who don whimsical musical-note ties or jewelry—Dr. Howard Bannister's bow tie in the movie *What's Up, Doc?* Does kooky couture count as a sense of humor? Even with that exception, I agreed, Fink may have a point. Thank goodness, for the purposes of this book, I am a musicologist gone rogue. And I like to joke and am sometimes funny (or, well, I think I am), though women are often assumed to be the opposite, at least historically—unless, that is, they are unattractive (pretty women apparently don't need a sense of humor) or Jewish (according to

Linda Mizejewski, author of *Pretty/Funny*). Alessandra Standley believes that that way of thinking is changing, but not necessarily for the better. In "Who Says Women Aren't Funny?" (*Vanity Fair*, April 2008), she writes, "Now a female comedian has to be pretty—even sexy—to get a laugh." Either way, it's a hard road for funny ladies. Obviously, these ideas rely on inherent and evolving prejudice—based in gender and race—which science occasionally attempts to support for no discernible reason (I'm looking at you, October 2019 issue of the *Journal of Research in Personality*). There are also so many counterexamples: Mindy Kaling, Natasha Leggero, Tig Notaro, Claudia O'Doherty, Maya Rudolph, Amber Ruffin, Kristen Schaal, Amy Schumer, Jessica Williams, and so on and so on. So what now?

Writing about both humor and music is tricky for anyone. As E. B. White famously wrote, "Humor can be dissected, as a frog can, but the thing dies in the process." This commonly held pseudo wisdom, according to Mark Evans and Philip Hayward (editors of *Sounding Funny*, 2016), is part of the problem for the rare academic willing to engage with comedy: "Developing a definition is necessary for our work but it can also be seen as threatening the experience we wish to explore." The same is true in music, which has much in common with comedy. (Both are sonic arts, similarly marked by sound in response—laughter or applause; and both involve rhythm, timing being important in music just as it is in comedy, the pause before the punchline.) Romantic composer Robert Schumann believed, "The best way to talk about music is to be quiet about it."[4] Music is thought to exist beyond words. Any attempt to describe music is then inevitably wrong, a sort of betrayal.

This conclusion in comedy and music is fear-based and misplaced, motivated by a desire to protect something that does not exist. A pure, unfiltered joke or musical score is a myth; comedy and music depend on performance. And, in performance, an entertainer must interpret the joke or music in some way. Not only that, but this thinking supports a no-win cycle. We do not always take comedic music seriously because we aren't supposed to consider and discuss it seriously. And we cannot consider and discuss it seriously because it's funny music—unless, of course, the comedy crosses a certain line. Then, suddenly, we take comical music *very* seriously. Earlier, as off-color comic Lenny Bruce learned in the 1960s, the government performed a comparable service, with legal ramifications. At court, Bruce would plead his case: "Don't lock up these six thousand words. That's what you're doing—taking away my words, locking them up."[5]

There's also more to White's quote: "Humor can be dissected, as a frog can, but the thing dies in the process *and the innards are discouraging to any but the pure scientific mind* [emphasis added]." In his book *Poking a Dead Frog* (2014), Mike Sacks suggests that discussing humor may then be "fascinating to a certain type of person." That may be true. But I wouldn't be writing this book if I didn't think the subject of humor, what it is and how it works, could appeal to anyone. With explanation of music, any listener can better appreciate and enjoy a piece of music. The same goes for comedy, especially humorous music, which can pack punchlines aplenty in a single song, sometimes requiring repeated listening to get the joke in full. Making that effort can be rewarding and worthwhile, despite the frog-related warnings (and the risks I'm assuming here by becoming *that* person, the person who explains jokes, *ugh*). Even the explanation itself can be entertaining or funny, the "explanation-as-joke."[6] It can forge connections—between those who get it and those who don't. And quite frankly, with that in mind, the frog excuse smacks of a strange sort of elitism or snobbishness, a desire to distinguish oneself as better in a very specific way. *I get the joke, and you don't. And there's no way to change that or help you because, well, frogs.*

For the scientific mind and everyone else too, then, *Taking Funny Music Seriously* examines humor in music in a variety of genres and contexts—from bad singing to rap, classical music to country, the Broadway musical to film music, and even love ballads to songs about death. It's a big task. Humor is everywhere in music. Music is in some ways one big joke or multiple jokes. And that's not an insult. That's impressive. Humor in music is creative and dynamic, and it serves multiple aims from celebration to rebellion. Humor is also slippery, reliant on a variety of factors surrounding any one joke. Nothing is funny without a conducive context, the situation being "keyed," including the right people, place, and time. And the intended joke isn't always what gets the laugh. With a bad joke, for example, the joke teller can inadvertently become the punchline. Believe me, I know.

When I taught music appreciation classes at Cleveland State University, in my former life as a serious scholar, I devoted one class period to funny music, starting with classical composer Joseph Haydn. It was in part an homage to legendary conductor and composer Leonard Bernstein, who did so as well in episode 6 of his *Young People's Concerts*, originally broadcast from Carnegie Hall on February 28, 1959. In the episode, Bernstein made known the problem of funny music, in a variation on White. The "minute you explain" it, the music "isn't so funny anymore." Still, he ventured some explanation, citing incongruity—a generally accepted source of humor related to surprise and the unexpected, and one particularly significant in musical humor given its semantic makeup.[7] That is, humorists can generate comedic incongruity through meaning in a variety of ways, not just through verbal language. In my teaching, I told a joke to illustrate the point, relying on a linguistic model before moving toward the extralinguistic, toward music:

Q: Why did the monkey fall from the tree?

A: He was dead.

Some students would gasp; some would laugh. The initial line seemed rather innocent. Since they knew I was telling a joke, the morbid turn was a surprise. It's the same in music, I would say, playing Haydn's "Surprise" Symphony, no. 94. After the unexpected fortissimo chord in an otherwise sedate passage, I would pause the recording, looking at the students with my eyes wide—"Huh? Huh?" Many students then laughed, but Haydn's music may not have been the main reason. More likely, my over-the-top giveaway, my insistence that there had been a joke, was the real moment of humor. "That poor professor doesn't get out much," they no doubt thought. "She actually expects us to laugh at a loud chord." I would forge ahead, nonetheless, insisting that they had to think like audiences back then. The music set up certain expectations, expectations that Haydn's listeners during his lifetime would have known. The loud chord, to them, would have been a violation of established musical norms, and that incongruity could create humor. The students were unmoved. Nice try, their fixed expressions said. Compared to Aziz Ansari, that was just, well, sorry.

In contrast, the kindergarteners, sitting on their carpet squares, were primed to laugh—and at everything. Before I played Weird Al's parody song "Eat It," the 1984 hit extolling listeners to finish their dinner, I played the original, Michael Jackson's "Beat It" (a choice I would not make now, by the way, given the mountain of criminal evidence against Jackson). The kids couldn't stop laughing, some jumping up to dance. Over Jackson's music, I told them with a smile, "This isn't the funny one," though in a way it was.

Humor, in both classroom settings, was obviously subjective, and the setting had a significant impact. The kindergarteners knew I was going to talk about funny music—they were ready to laugh regardless of the particular song. They perhaps needed the release too—something both comedy and music provide. Humor was also specific to the individual. When I asked the kindergarteners to create their own parody of "Happy Birthday," that individuality was on full display. One boy with a mass of golden hair gleefully shared: "Happy birthday to you / You look like a ninja / And are awesome like one too." A small girl with dark eyes then sweetly raised her hand. She wouldn't sing her creation out loud, but I read off her paper, "Happy Butt-day." "Good job,"

I said. Both her word-hybrid *butt-day* and my positive response would no doubt be unique moments in her educational experience. I can't imagine either repeating, sadly.

To close the class, I had the kids choose a popular song that we could parody together. The winner, unfortunately, was "Baby Shark." And I don't write *unfortunately* as a commentary on the song's inanity or its overplay. No, there just aren't enough words in that song to do much creatively. But "Baby Owl" and "Baby Shake" proved me somewhat wrong. And, of course, the class was treated to "Baby Poop," courtesy of my son. Proud mama, #Blessed. In all the examples, the referential humor, playing on a song they all knew, proved irresistible.

We all want to be taken seriously, even me at times. But, from lyrical wordplay to funny performers (cats included), humor is part of music. And one particularly rich source of humor, as I argue throughout this book, is music. In fact, the various assumptions around music that diminish the import of funny music may make music particularly ripe for comedy. In funny music, for a laugh, expectations of music are often flipped or otherwise exploded, as in the Haydn example. There are so many expectations in music and in different musical genres—all at the ready for a comedic left turn. Supposedly, music should be serious, but rap should be hard, rock manly, and country music pro-gun. That's a great foundation for humor. What does the opposite look and sound like? Will it make you laugh? Music—or the cultural meanings we assign music—is a clear joke setup, with multiple potential punchlines. Indeed, this book raises the question, Is musical humor actually more creative and varied than other types of humor, given the remarkable comedic possibilities provided by musical traditions and customs as well as the related, wide semantic field of play?

In part 2, *Taking Funny Music Seriously* showcases humor by genre, spotlighting the hallmarks of various musical genres traditionally upended by the comedic musician, including country music, rap, film music, musicals, and heavy metal. Each genre, in fact, has distinct comedic traditions. Given the scope of those traditions, I cannot examine each history comprehensively in a single book. Instead, I explore these traditions in case studies, choosing certain examples—often examples based in the United States—that inevitably exclude other musicians and geographical contexts worthy of consideration.

Along the way, sociological associations with genre based in race and gender serve as comedic material—all fully exploited for a laugh. Humor itself has a long association with race. Comedy has been explained as "the intrusion of another reality in the everyday reality of a social group," based on its conventions of behavior and cultural beliefs.[8] Comedy in this way can be used to both subvert racial boundaries and support them. In regard to the latter, the superiority theory of humor comes into play—a theory that recognizes a cruelty in some humor, including comedy that depends on the identification of someone or some group as inferior. In this context, pronouncements like "it's just a joke" aren't only an easy dismissal of comedy; they also allow racist jokes to continue unchecked.[9]

In music, race is similarly significant, with various types of music connected to a hierarchical ranking of people. It is no surprise, then, that the history of music has its own pronouncements disguising that tie, including faulty romantic notions that music somehow transcends context as a universal language. Humor in music can both upend and cement those existing associations, extending that intrusion of another reality into realities of genre, or at least the perception of those realities.

Of course, it isn't just rules of or associations with genre that establish a joke's premise. In part 3, the chapters look at funny songs by topic, including love songs and songs about death, all with their own histories and customs ripe for comedic commentary and hijacking. Often, in this regard, fantasies around each topic collide with reality in the making of humor. Listeners laugh at the truth. And it takes special talent, on the part of a musician, to present that truth in clever and comical ways.

To establish some guiding principles for this core focus on genre and song, part 1 explores the basics of music's connection to comedy, the evaluation of funny music, and the many reasons we often miss the musical joke, additional explanations for funny music's general dismissal. To get musical humor in full, a listener often has to pay attention to music in a way we rarely do, and a little knowledge of music helps too. Funny music's dismissal, then, might say more about those who dismiss funny music than the music itself, including their hang-ups and prejudices as well as a basic unfamiliarity with music and how it works. This latter point is tricky in some ways—it may be perceived as almost a personal attack. If someone insists there is humor when listeners do not initially get it, as I did with my music appreciation class, those listeners might not react with amusement; they might actually be angry or otherwise resistant. How dare you insist that I, a smart person, didn't notice or understand the joke? As Salvatore Attardo observes in *The Linguistics of Humor* (2020), audiences tend "to aggressively deny the humorousness" of a joke they don't get. But perhaps with a little effort or a second listen, the world of funny music can open up—one richly layered with meaning, built around play with patterns in music, established associations with sound and categories of music, and surprising mash-ups of lyric and tone, sometimes with a visual element. In a way, music does comedy better, or at least in vastly varied ways, with hilarious potential and serious depth beyond traditional jokes, dependent as they often are on the verbal component alone. Humor might also make music better or more engaging, given the attention and knowledge required.

For argument's sake, let's take the fundamentals of music as illustration. These basic elements are loaded with sites of potential sonic disruption and surprise, incongruity in the making.

The basic major scale—all white notes on the piano starting on C and climbing eight notes up (*do re mi fa sol la ti do*)—has baked-in anticipation, tension in need of resolution. Once we hit ti, we expect, even require, the move a half step up to *do*. If that resolution never comes or is somehow delayed, depending on the context and effect, the surprise may be funny. Traditional patterns, arrangements of these notes, and large-scale musical organization provide the same promise. We expect a certain amount of repetition in many musical forms, conditioned through our hearing of those forms even if we aren't necessarily aware of the forms' specifics: the exposition or initial section in sonata form and the eventual recapitulation, or conclusion based on the same material we heard in the exposition, for instance. What happens when a composer deviates from the standard? Dynamics, or volume, can also factor into similar sonic disruption, like Haydn's loud chord in a quiet section. Then there's rhythm, another pattern potentially disturbed or delayed.

With these ingredients, Leonard Meyer likens a musical composition to a person, with an inferred character and behavior to match.[10] When those expectations are blocked or otherwise unsettled, we can no longer listen on autopilot. We are jolted awake and forced to take notice. In this way, a musical piece with some sort of interruption is especially "meaningful," Meyer argues, requiring us to make sense of something new or at least pay attention.[11] We may react in kind, responding with pleasure or upset but also humor, depending on the context and whether or not we regard the deviation as "benign," a precondition for humor.[12] With his conclusion about meaning in music, Meyer does not address humor specifically. But it is easy to make that move, especially for the purposes of this book. Exploding conventions of music through humor invites active participation in music and the information it communicates while underscoring how contingent that communication really is. Just as music might enrich comedy, comedy may expand and deepen the musical experience.

The musical performance is another site of expectation, with established traditions often differing by genre—where and how music is performed, by whom, and in what attire. A departure, again depending on the type and the situation, might seem incongruous and thereby funny. Sometimes silly concert attire is a cathartic release for the classical musician, who is often buttoned up and stiff, and for audiences as well, who also may dress up, convinced they should follow suit (pun intended). Comedic musicians may riff on these norms, sometimes raising interesting issues of race and prejudice in the process. And the deviation may transform audiences from passive listeners into full participants, perhaps involving them in necessary conversations about problematic traditions and histories.

Individual pieces of music often allude to other music, musically quoting another composition or taking a short melody from a separate song and placing it in a new musical context. That allusion has the potential to be funny as well, and when lyrics are involved, the combination of references can multiply—packing any number of jokes into a single musical line. Parody, in some ways, is allusion without the requirement of direct quotation, creating a conversation between old and new.[13] Sometimes, that conversation punches down, with derision or disparagement, but the joke or jokes may also be entirely innocent. As Linda Hutcheon makes clear, parody can have an array of intents and effects, including both homage and criticism.[14] Once more, listeners are invited into the discussion, this time one about past and present. Ultimately, the meaning of music expands.

Just as in humor in general, incongruity is a central device in comedic music, "an essential condition for humor," as long as it's benign.[15] And with so many patterns and established standards, the viable options are endless—from a resolution that never comes to lyrics that defy genre convention, from performers who don't look or act the part to instruments seemingly out of place. Often, music allows for more than one laugh—with a traditional pun in the lyrics alongside a vocal impersonation of another singer or a clever undermining of multiple musical expectations simultaneously.

We thus overlook a particularly remarkable area of comedy if we ignore music, and we cannot appreciate or understand music in full without acknowledging music's many connections to humor. In a related move, we do a disservice to comedic musicians by sidelining their art, art that is just as challenging as so-called serious art, if not more so. As we will see, that dismissal may have something to do with who's performing—women, for example, are often sidelined in both comedy and music. But comedic musicians have to know music, really know music, in order to turn it inside out. As "nerdy comedy" musician Insane Ian told me, "Anyone can write a love song. Only a comedy musician can write a love song—about a taco." Many of the humorous musicians featured in this book are extraordinarily accomplished and well schooled (for those who hold fast to education as a hallmark of serious musicianship). Their work, perhaps obscured by the levity of their comedy, is often far more difficult than we realize in execution and conception—sometimes requiring abilities that surpass those of many serious professional musicians. In execution, a musical joke often takes musical talent, a certain showmanship, and an ability to operate masterfully in multiple realms of thought and skill with put-on ease. The creation of that joke already requires intelligence. In fact, humor theorists have long linked intelligence and humor—both a concrete intelligence based on knowledge, especially of language and words, and a more fluid intelligence, an ability to manipulate "conceptual material that is distant or incompatible."[16] As comic novel author Marie Phillips told the BBC, "Humor is not just an example of intelligence but a *form* of intelligence."[17] The cleverness of funny musicians' craft may seem light, but it's complicated and creative, dense with meaning, and rich with multileveled humor. We laugh and are meant to laugh at the music of comedic musicians, but there is also a seriousness behind it and in it.

In the coming together of talent, craft, and multiple forms of intelligence, humorous music can make a serious point, upending categories in need of upending and even effecting political and social change. In short, comedic musicians are not impotent clowns but often music's rebels and mavericks, agitating for a better world in new ways. Laughter alone has serious benefits too—lowering stress, creating commonality and connection, and offering psychological uplift, especially in times of crisis. When humorous music is undervalued as art, people also dismiss its value as a coping strategy and source of health.

I combined *funny music* and *serious* in the title of this book because the match-up seems to have the makings of a humorous incongruity. But, clearly, funny and serious are not incompatible. "The opposite of funny," as Phillips says, "isn't serious; the opposite of funny is unfunny."

Several special informants will help in the making of these arguments: interviews with legendary parody songwriter Tom Lehrer; Peter Schickele, who performed as his own invented character, P. D. Q. Bach, the supposed lost son of the great J. S. Bach; the son of Jo Stafford, legendary '50s crooner, who also sang badly for laughs as Darlene Edwards; the current go-to funny film composer Theodore Shapiro; Kate Micucci and Riki Lindhome of the funny folk music duo Garfunkel and Oates; Too Slim of Riders in the Sky, who is integral to his group's ongoing country clowning; and Jessica McKenna, musical comedian on the podcast *Off Book* and another in a long line of funny girls. This book is uniquely informed by these invaluable participants as well as my previous experience writing about Weird Al, providing distinct insight into music, comedy, and what both can do together. It is also a pointed response to dismissals of funny music. *Taking Funny Music Seriously* reveals the serious musicianship, intelligence, and creativity behind humorous music as well as the comedic depth in the combination of music and comedy. And that in itself might be the book's last laugh. What if writers and academics have shied away from funny music because it seems inconsequential when it is in fact far richer and more profound than art accepted as serious? This question is meant to be provocative. It is not my intention to create new hierarchies of music, with comedic music on top. But, by stressing funny music's significance, I do hope to urge readers to reconsider the past division between serious and humorous music, a division in need of its own dismissal or, even better, a comic upending.

NOTES

1. I had wanted to perform comedian Maria Bamford's version of "Old MacDonald" for the class, but I was not sure I could pull off a pterodactyl shriek.

2. Cate Watson, "A Sociologist Walks into a Bar (and Other Academic Challenges): Towards a Methodology of Humor," *Sociology* 49, no. 3 (2015): 407.

3. See Salvatore Attardo, *The Linguistics of Humor: An Introduction* (Oxford: Oxford University Press, 2020), 21.

4. Quoted in Lydia Goehr, "'Music Has No Meaning to Speak Of': On the Politics of Musical Interpretation," in *The Interpretation of Music*, ed. Michael Krausz (Oxford: Clarendon, 1993), 177.

5. Quoted in Osita Nwanevu, "The 'Cancel Culture' Con," *New Republic*, September 23, 2019.

6. Sharon McCoy, "Is a Joke Really Like a Frog?," *Humor in America*, December 6, 2011, https://humorinamerica.wordpress.com/2011/12/06/is-a-joke-really-like-a-frog/.

7. See Attardo, *Linguistics of Humor*, 81.

8. Attardo, 313.

9. See Raúl Pérez, "Racism without Hatred? Racist Humor and the Myth of 'Color-Blindness,'" *Sociological Perspectives* 60, no. 5 (2017): 956–974.

10. Leonard B. Meyer, "Meaning in Music and Information Theory," *Journal of Aesthetics and Art Criticism* 15, no. 4 (1957): 413.

11. Meyer, 415.

12. A. Peter McGraw and Caleb Warren, "Benign Violations: Making Immoral Behavior Funny," *Psychological Science* 21, no. 8 (2010): 1141–1149.

13. Writing on the topic, John Thomerson defines parody as a new work "created through musical borrowing." John Thomerson, "Parody as a Borrowing Practice in American Music, 1965–2015" (PhD diss., University of Cincinnati, 2017), 19, 26.

14. Linda Hutcheon, *A Theory of Parody: The Teachings of Twentieth-Century Art Forms* (New York: Metheun, 1985), 16.

15. D. D. Perlmutter, "On Incongruities and Logical Inconsistencies in Humor: The Delicate Balance," *HUMOR* 15, no. 2 (2002): 155. See also McGraw and Warren, "Benign Violations."

16. See Alexander P. Christensen et al., "Clever People: Intelligence and Humor Production Ability," *Psychology of Aesthetics, Creativity, and the Arts* 12, no. 2 (2018): 137.

17. Quoted in John Self, "Why the Funniest Books Are Also the Most Serious," BBC, November 9, 2020.

PART I

THE SETUP

ONE

LIVE FROM LARGO

AS JULIE ANDREWS SINGS IN *The Sound of Music*, starting at the very beginning is indeed "a very good place to start." In a parody version, that's "a sore throat, and cough in Wuhan," but in this chapter, that place is Los Angeles. Described by émigré composer Eric Zeisl as "a sunny blue grave," Los Angeles is both nightmarish—especially in terms of its traffic—and hilarious, with a thriving comedy scene often compared in a winner-take-all competition of comedic supremacy to that of New York. In her dissertation on stand-up comedy (2015), Katja Elisabet Antoine helps distinguish LA from NYC: "Comics typically say that you go to New York to hone your skills and to LA to get on film and television." For my funny-musical money, however, New York can wait. LA, after all, hosts the innovative club Largo at the Coronet, which *Rolling Stone* dubbed in 2013 one of "the best clubs in America." Largo has featured and nourished musicians and comedians as well as their mutual admiration. As comedian Greg Proops observed (in the *Los Angeles Times*), "Comedians want to roll with musicians, and vice versa. That's been the most fantastic part of Largo, interfering with each other's worlds."[1] For the purposes of this book, it's the Carnegie Hall of funny music venues. In fact, despite conventional thinking, Largo might even top Carnegie

Hall, offering audiences an unrivaled sampling of comedy and music while supporting a complex blending of the two.

While the pandemic for a time challenged the future of live musical performance—with what philosopher Walter Benjamin called its irreplaceable "aura" ("The Work of Art in the Age of Mechanical Reproduction," 1935)—live performance has always been central to comedy as well as music, engaging audiences and performers in ways that more solitary experiences of both cannot. Talking about music, a representative for Alice Cooper, Toby Mamis, summed up the issue: "There is a special thing about the live music experience that cannot be replicated in a livestreamed event. The shared communal feeling of the crowd, the artist playing off the crowd's energy."[2] For comedians, stage time matters for other reasons, offering a chance to test out new material. In a 2018 interview with Dave Itzkoff of the *New York Times*, Bret McKenzie, of the funny music duo Flight of the Conchords, said something similar: "Playing live is such a quick editor. You just feel it—if the crowd goes quiet, or the song's not working or it's not connecting."

There is also an excitement in the live event, whether it's musical, comedic, or both: anything can happen. And that excitement goes both ways. As an audience member, I wonder what I might hear or see during a live concert, and as a performer, before stepping up to the microphone, I envision both my tremendous success and cataclysmic failure. The long-running television series *Saturday Night Live*, which began in 1975, has capitalized on that anticipation, making liveness central to its broadcast. In the recorded live show, which echoes variety performance of the past, there is a theatricality and expectation unusual on the small screen. In 1978, *SNL* creator and producer Lorne Michaels told *Rolling Stone*, "Live laughter from an audience is real, it's theater."[3] At Largo, that liveness has inspired unique collaborations between musicians and comedians—defined by some as "weird." It has also stirred consideration of the ties between music and comedy. Based on various existing interviews with Largo artists, this chapter offers a fast foundation (nothing slow about Largo) in the similarities between music and comedy as well as the differences, basics at the heart of our topic and part 1 as a whole. These connections and distinctions help make funny music seemingly inevitable but also potentially richer than either music or humor alone.

One of the many comedic-musical collaborations traced back to Largo involves singer Fiona Apple. Never in my wildest dreams would I have predicted Apple featuring up front in a book about music and comedy. With her debut album *Tidal*, released in 1996, she is the soulful singer of my angst-filled youth. With her waifish appearance and full-bodied voice, she offers up her own deceptive mismatch, tied together by naked lyrical confession. In her 2005 video for the song "Not about Love," she at first appears true to form: "This is not about love / 'Cause I am not in love." In the video, she looks despondent, alone in a room and then in her bed, until her voice enters, linked to another body—that of comedian and actor Zach Galifianakis, who expressively lip-synchs the tune. When I first hit play, I knew Galifianakis was somehow a part of the video. But his entrance still came as a shock. How did this happen?

Apple met Galifianakis at Largo, where she's a regular, as advertised in her ode to the club, a 2012 song with a simple chorus: "When over the rainbow's too far / Go to Lar-go to Lar-go to Largo." The club came into its own when Irish-born Mark Flanagan became its part owner in 1992, though Largo's history starts much earlier. Flanagan had moved to Boston as a student but eventually settled in Los Angeles to get away from the East Coast cold. In an interview with Rob Bell on *The Robcast* podcast (April 14, 2016), Flanagan describes driving cross-country hoping for a new start in a warmer climate. When he arrived in

Southern California, he thought, "I'll do more with my life if the weather's like this." He had only been in Los Angeles for a few weeks when he visited Largo and decided, along with several others, to purchase the club. When his partners chose to turn Largo into a sports bar, Flanagan left, booking his preferred artists at neighboring clubs. But in 1994, Largo's then owners went bankrupt, and Flanagan was able to buy the club, shaping it into Apple's second-best somewhere. In 2008, as its sole owner, Flanagan moved Largo from Fairfax Avenue to the Coronet Theatre on La Cienega, with its own storied musical history, including its opening in 1947 with the premiere of Bertolt Brecht's *Life of Galileo*. In a photograph from the theater's earlier days, Charlie Chaplin, Angela Lansbury, and Jimmy Stewart mingle in its crowded courtyard—truly a wonderful life.

In Largo's programming, an eclectic mix of comedy and music, Flanagan has let his own artistic taste and temperament dictate the roster of performers. But he also believes the pairing makes some sense. In 2002, he told the *Los Angeles Times*, "I have a lot of singer-songwriters who don't write about the happy things in life. I mean, there's a sense of humor in there, but you gotta dig for it. In Ireland, when I was growing up, a comedian or a magician would often open for an artist. So I thought it would be good to do that at Largo." The combination might have been unusual in Los Angeles at the time, but, as in Ireland, it had precedent in club programming across the United States before the 1970s and even earlier in vaudeville performance and the "chitlin' circuit," venues showcasing Black performers in a segregated South. In the club scene, the Copacabana, which opened in 1940 in New York, famously mixed comedy and music, along with Ciro's in Los Angeles, the glamorous night club of William Wilkerson. Los Angeles also had the Crescendo, another musical term as title, and Cocoanut Grove, at the Ambassador Hotel. Of the "four high Cs," as no one ever called these clubs, Cocoanut Grove came first in 1921. Up Highway 1, San Francisco had its own legendary setting for music and comedy: the Purple Onion and hungry i.

Typically, at these clubs, comics opened for the headliner, a musical star. Along with its iconic musical acts, the Copacabana featured the comedy team Martin and Lewis—singer Dean Martin and comedian Jerry Lewis—who collaborated on stage and screen in a wildly successful ten-year run. The Cocoanut Grove hosted famous bandleader Art Hickman, dance contests, and the very best jazz and swing bands as well as stars like Judy Garland, Ella Fitzgerald, and Louis Armstrong. In the 1950s, the Rat Pack were regularly in attendance, and Sammy Davis Jr., a triple threat—singer, dancer, and comedian—recorded a live album there. In San Francisco's North Beach, hungry i was Enrico Banducci's pioneering club from 1951 until its close in 1970. Some of its famous performers included music parodist Tom Lehrer, singer Barbra Streisand, and comedian Lenny Bruce. Unlike other club owners, Banducci didn't allow hecklers or other interruptions. Comedian Shelley Berman, who performed there, recalled, "Enrico was the most unique human being, not like any nightclub owner we'd ever met. You didn't get to talk to them much. They were too busy counting their money. Enrico really cared for the talent and watched out for them."[4] In this way, he treated his space a lot like those in charge of symphony concerts treat concert halls—with a certain respect for the serious artistic credentials on display.

In *Make 'Em Laugh: The Funny Business of America* (2007), Laurence Maslon and Michael Kantor chronicle the history of these venues as well as the coming division between music and comedy in the 1970s, which they credit to "the greater presence of comedy and television screens—talk shows, variety shows." The comedy club then came into its own, with stand-up comics the main attraction. One of the first of these sites, the Improv in New York, opened in 1963, under the leadership of Budd Friedman. Friedman described the change in terms of male-centric sexual prowess: "But, you know, stand-ups have become stars. Stand-ups get the women now. Except for a handful of Milton Berles and Sid Caesars, stand-ups were basically opening acts and the singers for the girls. Well, comics are getting the girls now." Ciro's became a stand-up joint in 1972, when it rebranded itself as the famed Comedy Store. The club combination of comedy and music was then no longer the norm—except, that is, at Largo.

From the beginning, Flanagan had the best in music and comedy perform at his club; many of them found the Largo atmosphere inviting and inspiring, returning again and again. Like Banducci, Flanagan does not tolerate extraneous audience noise or distracting photography—and will ask disrespectful patrons to leave. He too responds to comedy and music with a seriousness of purpose, his club a philharmonic for funny music. On stage, he'll announce, "If you want to talk, just go to the Coconut Teaszer,"[5] the Los Angeles club associated with Heidi Fleiss's onetime prostitution ring.

In addition to Flanagan's protection of the performance, with his unusual no-talking policy, he maintains a special rapport with his performers, often cultivated through humor. On the podcast *You Made It Weird* with Pete Holmes, Holmes, in 2015, calls Flanagan "very, very funny." Flanagan, for his part, tends to program people he likes. That connection paves the way for a unique creative experience, with good humor going a long way in making Largo a place of collaboration and experimentation.[6]

Musical comedians on the Largo playlist, with Flanagan their affable host, have included Bo Burnham, Demitri Martin, Margaret Cho, Chelsea Peretti, Zach Galifianakis, Garfunkel and Oates, and Flight of the Conchords, among many others. Many of these comedians and Largo itself are linked to the elusive category "alternative comedy," or alt-comedy. In 2016, Jake Kroeger, writing about Largo for *Vulture*, explained, "Over the last few years it's become the home away from home for the top tier of alternative comedians." The term itself, however, is so broad and varied in definition that it's effectively useless. In 2012, comedy writer River Clegg hilariously played on that clarity problem in a *McSweeney*'s "FAQ": "The regular comedian says something clever. The alt comedian also says something clever, but only a certain type of person will enjoy it." In practice, the term is generally linked to hipster cool, pop culture references, and a certain niche or nerd sensibility. According to English professor Adam Stott in his book *Comedy: The New Critical Idiom* (2014), the alternative comedian may also reject patterns from the past, including "easy racism and fast delivery of the gag comic." Generally, then, alt-comedy is unconventional, offbeat, and sometimes musical.

Flight of the Conchords, who performed one of their first shows in the United States at Largo, is a special favorite of mine. From New Zealand, the duo, Bret McKenzie and Jemaine Clement, are often remembered for their HBO show, *Flight of the Conchords*, which ran from 2007 to 2009—a rough approximation of their own struggles as musicians, with related fantastical breaks in song. The show is chock-full of musical jokes, as in episode six, which addresses Bret's mock concern that he doesn't live up to the image of the novelty musician, as if this oft-dismissed musician could ever be the ultimate sign of musical success. In the episode, Bret browses through the fictitious magazine *Novelty Music Scene*, with a picture of Weird Al on the cover, and later, thanks to a visit from Jemaine as David Bowie, decides to wear an eye patch. Bret and Jemaine met at Victoria University Wellington in 1996 and formed their band several years later. According to their website, they named themselves after a toilet called the Concorde, the spelling switch—Conchords—apparently a nod to the musical term *chord*. In concert, they are known for dry, self-deprecating patter inserted between comical songs like "Business Time" and "A Gender Reversal"—highlighting often clumsy approaches to sex and romance: "You've been learning sex moves."

Garfunkel and Oates, guitarist Riki "Garfunkel" Lindhome and ukulele player Kate "Oates" Micucci, are often compared to Flight of the Conchords, even called the "female Flight of the Conchords" (fine, if you need to measure talent based on a male standard). With their funny songs about sports ("Sports Go Sports") and blow jobs ("The BJ Song") as well as their own self-titled musical show (see chap. 10), they have been regulars at Largo for years. In an interview, the two ladies described to me the beginnings of their association with Largo: "Flanagan has been so great to us. When he first saw us perform, he suggested we do our hour-long shows at the theater so Largo became a home for us."

Bo Burnham models a different take on the connection between comedy and music, with music the topic of his stand-up routine. In his Netflix special *Make Happy* (2016), a set he also performed at Largo in May 2016, he takes on rap and country music, poking fun at various conventions of musical genre. In one bit, he offers up a sick beat, coupled with a nursery rhyme. The song still seems cool despite the words; the takeaway is that lyrics don't always matter much in popular music.

Fred Armisen has also made music the focus of his comedy. He is known for his offbeat show *Portlandia,* with punk comedian and member of the band Sleater-Kinney Carrie Brownstein, as well as his stint on *Saturday Night Live,* which ties him to other talented *SNL* musician-comedians like Adam Sandler, Maya Rudolph, and Andy Samberg. In 2018, Armisen debuted his Netflix special *Stand Up for Drummers*. He then expanded the concept in the show "Stand Up for Musicians but Everyone Is Welcome," which he performed at Largo on June 15, 2019. As he directs many of his jokes at musicians themselves, part of the fun can be a joke gone bust, nonmusicians missing the punchline. In a sampling of this sort of humor, on *Conan* on TBS, September 19, 2018, Armisen performed his impression of a guitar player having to stop strumming during a singer's political rant. It's a very specific joke for a very specific audience, involving very little: Armisen standing awkwardly, staring at the audience with his big eyes wide. In

2014, Armisen became band leader for the show *Late Night with Seth Meyers*, highlighting the comedic corner of music occupied by late-night band leaders, including Paul Shaffer, David Letterman's longtime collaborator; and absurdist musical comedian Reggie Watts, currently on *The Late Late Show with James Corden*.

Unlike the multitalented Armisen, Galifianakis is often thought of as a comedic actor first, associated with his role in the movie *The Hangover* (2009) and its sequels. But he too is musical. In fact, he first incorporated piano playing during a stand-up routine at Largo, making use of the piano already on its stage. The combo, which he duplicated at other venues, is a comedy of contrasts—his telling of funny dick jokes as he noodles on the piano, creating a vaguely impressionistic, contemplative sound. With Apple often at Largo, Galifianakis invited her to sing some of his punchlines, another layer of expectation and its subversion. Their collaboration went both ways.

Apple and Galifianakis aren't the only comedy-musical team forged at Largo. In fact, Kanye West, who has also performed at Largo, saw Galifianakis at the club and, evidently impressed, asked him to make a music video for him. Left to his own devices, Galifianakis created the video "Can't Tell Me Nothing" (2015) on his farm, with Galifianakis lip-synching West's track from a tractor.

Singer-songwriter Aimee Mann, formerly of the new-wave group 'Til Tuesday, found her comic collaborator there as well, the comedian Patton Oswalt, who is not necessarily musical, though he has ranted about Creed and Nickelback during his stand-up sets. In 2004, he also performed at rock clubs during his tour and in the movie *The Comedians of Comedy*. In the film, he explains the idea as a musical crossover, a way to encourage fans to follow comedians the way they follow musicians. Mann herself has had a few breakout comedic roles, a cameo on Armisen's *Portlandia* (she met Armisen at Largo) and in the cult comedy *The Big Lebowski* (1998), but she does not consider herself a comedian. For that reason, she asked Oswalt to perform funny, between-song patter for her during a performance at Largo. Oswalt then joined her on tour along with Mann's musician husband Michael Penn. In 2000, on stage, Mann explained Oswalt's role in the show: "I've never been too comfortable with the whole between-song-banter thing. So tonight's he's going to do it for me." "Hi, I'm Aimee 'Golden Globe' Mann," Oswalt said.[7] In 2011, Mann described the tour in an interview with *La Weekly*:

> One of the difficulties Michael and I both had with playing live is, if you're in the headspace to play music, it's not the same headspace as talking to an audience. So it's very hard to finish a song and then go into a sort of a banter-y thing with the audience. So we started playing these shows, and the idea was like in baseball, when they have a pinch hitter, and they get the expert batter to come in and sub for them. So why don't we get the expert, the guy who's good at bantering with the audience—a comedian—let's get him to come in and do our banter for us.

They called the tour "Acoustic Vaudeville," a great title recalling past traditions of comedy and music combined in performance.

On *The Robcast*, Bell calls Largo a "magical club," with Flanagan a "curator of a community." In our interview, Lindhome and Micucci expanded on the metaphor: "There is always something special going on there. And Flanagan (the owner) is the best at mixing comedians and musicians. It is a full experience there ... walking into this theater that has so much history, you can feel it in the walls. The backstage always feels magical." That atmosphere helps solidify real relationships—collaboration and friendship. In the 2008 article "Largo Nights," Mann told the *New Yorker*'s Dana Goodyear, "Almost all of my friendships are a direct result of going to Largo, meeting these people, and trying to mix comedy and music." In the same article, Apple similarly said, "I've never been to Flanny's actual place of residence, but in my head when I go to Largo I feel that I'm going to a different party at his house. All my friends are there." One friend is Flanagan (or Flanny) himself. In 2013, Patton Oswalt told Elina Shatkin, in *Los Angeles Magazine*, "When it was on Fairfax I really, really liked it. I became friends with Flanny and it became a crucial venue for me." Of Largo, Margaret Cho sums up, "It's an integral part of a lot of really amazing artists' lives."[8] With all of that in play, Largo has hosted some truly innovative performances, and not just in musical comedy. Comedian Tig Notaro, who had been hosting a regular show at Largo, famously turned inward on the Largo stage on August 3, 2012. Replacing her regular set with a deeply personal rumination on her current struggles, she began, "Good evening. Hello. I have cancer. How are you?" In the audience that night, Louis CK was blown away and, after the show, helped convince her to release the audio of that original "workout set" as a for-purchase album.[9] It's hard to imagine that series of events taking place anywhere else.

In the 2008 film *Largo*, Flanagan (with filmmaker Andrew van Baal) attempted to capture that magic in an evening at Largo, with performances by Galifianakis, Mann, Apple, indie musician and extreme whistler Andrew Bird, Flight of the Conchords, the musical group Nickel Creek, comedian Paul F. Thompkins, comedian Sarah Silverman, author and comedian Greg Behrendt, and many others. In his set, Galifianakis makes an especially musical joke: "I call my balls Belle and Sebastian," riffing on the name of the indie band Belle and Sebastian. Behrendt does too, pointing out the ills of the phrase and lullaby-turned-Queen-song "we will rock you." "May I rock you," he makes clear, is the more polite wording.

The live innovation, cooperation, and unique blending of melody and laughter at Largo have spilled over into thoughtful musings on craft as well as the combination of music and comedy, often across various media platforms, including television, podcasts, and YouTube. (These conversations, like many musician-comedians associated with Largo, perform and operate in a transmedia space—different performances and performance platforms today linked in promotion and broadcast.) In these varied conversations often involving Largo artists, the word *weird* surfaces several times, highlighting an assumption that this mixing of music and humor is somehow unnatural. While it's true that comedians and musicians can carve out very different performance experiences, music and comedy of course have much in common, in attitude and structure. That combination, with these similarities, can create new depths in comedy and music—art that deserves top billing rather than "alternative" sidelining.

For one, both humor and music are ephemeral, here in performance and then gone. The two are also part of play—we play music, and we play through humor as well, often signaled by laughter. With laughter, both music and comedy are physical. We feel music in our bodies, vibrating in our bones. As Nietzsche claimed, "We listen to music with our muscles." Likewise, when we laugh, it's a physical response—a sound, like music. Aimee Mann, for her part, believes there's a similar honesty in music and comedy, "a dynamic of emotional honesty": "Comics are best at layering," she tells *Uproxx*, "with jokes having this layer of honesty." In that honesty, words matter. Referencing her friend Oswalt, Mann explains, "The words he chooses are perfectly chosen, carefully chosen for a reason"; "like in songwriting, there's deliberation."[10]

Garfunkel and Oates identify rhythm as another link. In an interview with Mike Hilleary for *Under the Radar* magazine (September 25, 2014), Lindhome explains, "I feel like comedy is all a rhythm. A stand-up comedian *is* doing music in my mind. There's beats and there's timing. It's sort of the same thing." She adds, of her act with Micucci, "We're just putting some chords over top of a set in some way." To me, they clarified, "Stand-up comedy is totally musical. It's the timing of every sentence, every breath, every pause." With a common focus on rhythm and words, comedian Chelsea Peretti finds that she shapes hilarious turnarounds in both stand-up comedy and funny music. To do so, she establishes a premise or musical mood, which sets up that surprising twist. Promoting her 2020 album *Foam and Flotsam*, devoted mostly to comedic songs about coffee, she illustrates this switch-up in her song "Late." In it, she complains about people with their "big dumb face," showing up late with coffee in hand. In the end, however, we realize she's complaining about herself. Unable to forego the latte and scone, she's late, and—here's the kink—that "big dumb face" is her own.[11]

This turnaround spotlights structural overlap in music and humor, including the connection between the comedic callback and the musical refrain. In a musical piece, the repetition of a musical idea, a chorus or refrain, unifies a composition. And there's something satisfying in the resurfacing of a familiar sound. Likewise, in comedy, a line can reoccur, sometimes in a new way, and that line offers both closure and the pleasure of getting an inside joke. In the show *Flight of the Conchords*, that callback can stretch across multiple episodes, as in the ongoing comedic rift between the musical duo and Australia. Or it can be visual—for example, Bret's singular hair-helmet. For some comedians, the callback itself is a musical reference—like the many mentions of Steely Dan in Nick Kroll and John Mulaney's Broadway show *Oh, Hello*: "It's a billion percent Steely Dan."

But there is also a connection in the distinctions between comedy and music, especially at Largo. Sometimes it's the differences between comedy and music that make them complementary, both enriched in combination. In one episode of his YouTube series *Live from the Great Room*, Andrew Bird talks with Galifianakis about Largo and the ties between music and comedy, noting the oft-cited attraction between musicians and comedians: musicians supposedly want to be comics, and comedians want to be musicians. He says, "Comedians want to be musicians really badly." It's a "grass is greener" situation, Galifianakis muses. But Galifianakis himself says he wishes he had never quit piano lessons. The revelation seems to remind Bird of an encounter he had at Largo with comedian and filmmaker Kevin Smith. Smith, who was watching Bird with his instrument, commented wistfully, "If I could do that." The implication is that if Smith were a musical prodigy, he would have been chasing music rather than Amy, Silent Bob no more. In an interview with Kelly McCartney of the *Bluegrass Situation* (March 29, 2017), Mann admits that same longing in reverse: "My comedian friends are the ones I envy the most." This envy along with the backstage interaction, Bird notes, is part of the "interesting dynamic" at Largo, with comedians and musicians mixing freely. It's a "weird mix," Galifianakis agrees.

Galifianakis and Bird also highlight a switch in energy at Largo, when a comedian appears on stage and then a musician. There's almost something comedic in it, a play with expectations. And Galifianakis wonders if that setup ever hurts the musician—an audience primed to laugh at a serious performer. But Bird counters, claiming that the combination is inspiring. A preceding comedian can even influence his performance—he picks up "an accent," he says, the rhythm of the comedian. Like "hanging out with Madonna," Galifianakis jokes.

Mann, in an interview with the *Wisconsin State Journal* (2011), also describes the dynamic as helpful for her and the audience. While performing with comedians may help her feel more "at ease on stage," as she told LA *Weekly* in 2011, comedy can help listeners engage more generally with a performance. On her Acoustic Vaudeville tour, she noticed, "when people are laughing, they kind of listen more attentively when you're playing. The two really do go together, in a weird way." As many public speakers know, a good way to get an audience's attention up front is with a good joke. In a musical performance, that laugh pulls them into the show; their sound is part of the performance. Oswalt, in his interview with Shatkin, gives the comedian's perspective on that shift: "Sometimes if the transition is clumsy, it's even better because you get a laugh out of that." The musician is comedic fodder—and sometimes quite directly. In his appearance on *The Robcast*, Flanagan describes an organic interplay at Largo between the serious singer and the comedian, with comedians "making fun of songwriters." And the singers often like it, he insists.

In these ways, performers associated with Largo consider the ways in which comedy and music complement each other, even in their difference. At Largo, audiences experience the connections between comedy and music—in rhythm, phrasing, and deliberate word choice—as well as an inspired live cross-pollination between the two. In 2008, in the "Christmas Trilogy," for the website Funny or Die, Aimee Mann and many of her friends from Largo played up that overlap, making a joke seemingly tailor-made for this chapter. Sitting with Thompkins in the sketch, Mann explains the premise: she needs some big guest stars for her Christmas variety show. In her requests, Thompkins advises her to play to the celebrity ego: go big. The visual cuts to actor John Krasinski walking into Largo. Mann is on stage and begins playing a song for her audience of one, Krasinski, who appears uncomfortable. With a melancholy piano accompaniment, Mann croons, "Unless you hate baby Jesus, then I'll know the answer is no." After the serenade, Krasinski assumes Mann is in love with him and leaves. Mann's first attempt to secure a celebrity guest is evidently a bust. Back to the drawing board, Thompkins advises Mann to ask actress Emily Proctor, from the show *CSI: Miami*. At her door, Proctor appears in the same style of clothing as Mann; inside the house, it just gets stranger when Proctor plays Mann's hit "Save Me" badly, with a newly bought electric guitar, tag still attached. Thankfully, Mann can rely on her pal Oswalt, whom she calls next. We see Oswalt answer the phone in bed, but he is hesitant to commit to Mann's plan. Sure, he has enjoyed touring with her in the past, he says, "But I think I'm just at an age now that I just know that comedy and music do not mix." The camera pans to his side, revealing Weird Al in bed next to Oswalt. Mock offended, Yankovic exclaims, "What? I'm out of here," before he storms out of the room. To many, comedy and music are very different. But at Largo, the commonality comes into focus in surprising ways. And Mann and Oswalt, Largo regulars, know that better than most.

—⚂—

During the pandemic, in early July 2020, Conan O'Brien announced in a statement that he would begin filming his late-night show from Largo, then empty: "I got started doing improv at the Coronet in 1986 and I'm glad we've figured out a way to safely keep that theater going during this lockdown." The late-show format makes some sense at Largo—with its own long tradition of music and comedy in combination—as does the medium, with Largo and its artists connected to various platforms of song and humor, whether on television or online. Of course, the move was also important in a basic way for Flanagan, who added, in his own statement (quoted on My News LA, among other sites), "We can breathe a little easier, and keep this boat afloat until we can see you all again." Performing in the first broadcast from Largo to a lone audience member, his longtime assistant Sona Movsesian, Conan further explained the move: "Why am I here? Well a lot of theaters across the country are struggling right now and we really wanted to help one of the local empty theaters here in LA so we chose Largo. Largo's a very special place to everyone." He also made clear his own ties to the space, its burgundy exterior visible in the opening shot: "I started here doing improv." "I got my first laughs here in 1985 and got my last laughs here in 1991," he continued. "No laughs since. Bit of a drought."

The powerful experience at Largo is a credit to the quality, depth, and cleverness created by the combination of music and comedy. In the next chapters in part 1, I spotlight what's remarkable in that blending. But how do I evaluate humor in music? Whom do I choose as representatives of funny music in order to make its case?

Conan's first show from Largo, *Conan* on TBS, screenshot from YouTube.

At Largo, Flanagan has responded to his own performance favorites while supporting something inherent in the combination of music and comedy, especially in live performance. Music, like laughter, is universal—something found in all cultures.[12] But like music, humor is not a universal language. What people find funny will differ based on culture, education, and general background and personality. Flanagan admits, to Rob Bell, he had "no comedy background" before Largo. His approach to programming has been ultimately subjective. But is there an alternative? Should this book, exploring the natural link between comedy and music, follow a similarly subjective path, driven by the tastes of this author, a perhaps unreliable narrator? While I've studied music, I have no professional experience in comedy. And my kids would certainly say that is for good reason, given my love of puns and corny word play. On the other hand, perhaps I'm being deceptively self-deprecating, a favorite move in comedy. After all, I have written about comedy before, and I have benefited from interviews with several comedic legends (as I detailed in the introduction). I have also recently made an effort to understand humor from a different perspective by writing comedy, submitting various attempts for publication on humor sites. Successful efforts include "A Rich White Guy Explains the Utopian Aspects of Cryptocurrency," "I'm Your Kid's Saxophone and, Frankly, Enough Is Enough," and "Hi, I'm Reader #2, and I Wouldn't Be Doing My Job If I Didn't Tell You Your Writing Is Garbage." Still, I have a lot to learn. So, I have to ask, in comedic music, is there a respected model?

If there ever was one, a specialist in comedic music, it's Barry Hansen, aka Dr. Demento, another Los Angeles institution. But "respected," for some, is up for debate. Even with serious credentials (a master's degree in music from UCLA), he's dealt with dismissal of funny music and his own work by extension. Nevertheless, in the next chapter, he helps us move from connections between music and comedy to the evaluation of funny music, a demented enterprise to be sure.

NOTES

1. Natalie Nichols, "Largo Gets New Lease on Life at the Old Coronet," *Los Angeles Times*, May 18, 2008.
2. Interview in Jim Sullivan, "What Will the Future of Concerts Look Like after the Pandemic?," WBUR.org, May 4, 2020, https://www.wbur.org/news/2020/05/04/coronavirus-pandemic-music-industry-concerts.
3. See also Michele Hilmes, "The Evolution of Saturday Night," in *Saturday Night Live and American TV*, ed. Nick Marx, Matt Sienkiewicz, and Ron Becker (Bloomington: Indiana University Press, 2013), 36.
4. Quoted in Jesse Hamlin, "His hungry i Helped Put S.F. on the Map as Rebel Artists' Haven," *SF Gate*, April 4, 2007.
5. Quoted in Neal Weiss, "The Artist Rules at Largo, the Most Vital Performance Space in Los Angeles," *Los Angeles Times*, February 22, 1998, 7.
6. A shared comedic sensibility has been pivotal in collaboration in other settings. A case in point is the famous first meeting between the Beatles and their producer George Martin. Martin had been known for comedy albums, recordings of stars like English comedian and singer Peter Sellers (part of *The Goon Show*), but he wanted to sign a pop act.

When the Beatles played for him, he delivered a litany of criticism, finally asking, "Is there anything you don't like?" "Well, for a start," George Harrison said, "I don't like your tie." Martin laughed, and the meeting's tone shifted. See Kieran McGovern, "Why Did George Martin Almost Not Sign the Beatles?," *Medium*, March 28, 2019.

7. Quoted in Jenny Slater, "Aimee Mann, Michael Penn Open Tour with Romance, Cynicism, and Comedy," *MTV News*, January 26, 2000.

8. Quoted in Weiss, "Artist Rules at Largo," 7.

9. See Andrew Marantz, "Good Evening. Hello. I Have Cancer," *New Yorker*, October 5, 2012.

10. Quoted in Katie Hasty, "Hit Fix Interview: Aimee Mann on New Album, Patton Oswalt and Bummer Songs," *Uproxx*, September 28, 2012.

11. Jesse David Fox, "Chelsea Peretti Interview," *Good One: A Podcast about Jokes*, April 21, 2020.

12. Matthew Gervais and David Sloan Wilson, "The Evolution and Functions of Laughter and Humor: A Synthetic Approach," *Quarterly Review of Biology* 80, no. 4 (2005): 397.

TWO

STAYING DEMENTED

WITH A VAST RECORD COLLECTION, circa fifty years in the radio industry, and a special focus on mad music, Barry Hansen is perhaps the only bona fide authority on funny music. His mother thought he might become a professor. For a 1991 article in the *Los Angeles Times*, he told Claudia Puig, "My mother wanted me to become a writer or a college professor. And I kind of took it for granted that I would become a professor." Though he never took up residence in that ivory tower, despite his years of higher education, he has indeed become a "doctor" of funny music, and not just by way of his Dr. Demento handle: "First and foremost, I'm an entertainer. But I'm an educator, too." As such, he has impacted music and musicians with a reach far beyond that of any conventional academic authority in music. Indeed, he has educated generation after generation of funny musicians with his long-running radio show, what Larry King called in 1985 "one of the most popular shows on the radio." In 2009, he was inducted into the Radio Hall of Fame, and the show was officially celebrated for its contribution to the medium of radio. He is also associated with the Funny Music Project (FuMP) and its sponsorship of the Logan Whitehurst Memorial Awards for Excellence in Comedy, an annual honoring of funny music. In this chapter, Hansen's

Dr. Demento on *Larry King Live* (1985), screenshot from YouTube.

career and unique standing in the world of funny music offer us introductory instruction in the history and evaluation of comedic music, a potential map for the chapters to come. His course also highlights what's at stake—the prejudices against funny music and the serious work that goes into that music, countering its dismissal and encouraging its general promotion.

Born in 1941 in Minneapolis, Barry Hansen came by his love for novelty records and comedic music honestly. His father's own collection proved influential. In 1991, Hansen showed Richard Harrington of the *Washington Post* a pick from his father's stash, *Cocktails for Two* by the great Spike Jones (1911–1965), a musician and bandleader known for humorous arrangements of popular and classical music. "It was one of the first funny records I heard," he said, "but also the best known and most successful by Spike Jones, who was really the first person to make novelty records into—and I hate to use this word—a serious art form." In a 1985 interview on *Larry King Live*, Hansen again named this record when he responded to King dismissively asking about his collection of funny records: "When did this problem begin?" Hansen's father brought home the Jones record when Hansen was four. Though Hansen played the piano as a child, the perfection of the phonograph was far more attractive. And the perfection of that record's humor was too. Before Jones, Hansen clarified, funny music fell into "two categories: either somebody taking a funny song and doing it pretty straight or somebody doing a more or less straightforward song and making funny noises."[1] Growing up, the two, father and son, would together hunt for other "weird" recordings, the beginnings of what would become, even by high school, an impressive personal collection of little-known musical wonders and oddities. His growing stockpile of sound made him the DJ of choice for high school dances and even after, at Reed College in Portland, Oregon.

In 1963, Hansen graduated Reed with a major in music and went on to graduate school at UCLA, where he joined the new folk music studies program, one of three founding students alongside guitarist John Fahey, who himself employed at times a rather surreal humor in his work. In fact, Fahey adopted a distinct persona, "Blind Joe Death," much like Hansen would as Dr. Demento. Recording under that name, Fahey would fool some listeners into believing he was a real-life old blues singer, with authentic roots deep within that tradition.[2] For Hansen, that tradition would be the focus of his master's thesis, a study of the evolution of the blues, making Hansen an official musicologist—a term, Hansen told James Brown in a 1974 interview in the *Los Angeles Times*, he finds "a trifle pompous" (as a musicologist, agreed).

While still a student at UCLA, Hansen got a job as usher and light-man at famed folk and blues club Ash Grove, which had a major influence on the music scene during its fifteen years in existence, 1958–1973. Bob Dylan once said, "I'd seen posters of folk shows at the Ash Grove and used to dream about playing there." That job encouraged Hansen's move away from academia. In 1993, he told Jim Washburn in the *Los Angeles Times*, "I got to meet these creators and hear this great music [and] all the while I was studying more theoretically over at UCLA. And when I was working there, the whole folk-rock and blues-rock phenomenon started coming into being, and that distracted my attention away from the ancient ballads, the narrative folk songs of the 18th Century and all that." He recalled, "I began to think maybe it would be more exciting to be involved in the pop music business than to be a professor."

His nonacademic path was set when he accepted his first professional DJ gig at KPPC-FM in Pasadena. Another DJ, Steven Segal, known as the Obscene Steven Clean, had heard of Hansen's ever-growing collection of music (now in six figures) and invited him to be a guest on his show. He was working at the time at Specialty Records, but, in 1970, several additional guest spots led to his own program on the station. On air, he made space for his taste in the unusual. In the Puig interview, Hansen explained, "I always loved Spike Jones and funny stuff of all kinds. But it was only part of everything I liked. I was always very eclectic." For a time, he showcased that range. But novelty recordings were soon the main offering. To Weird Al superfans Dave Rossi and Ethan Ullman on their *Dave and Ethan's 2000" Weird Al Podcast*, Hansen outlined his show's quick evolution—first it had a few bizarre recordings; six months later, novelty songs made up about half the show; soon after, they were almost the whole program. In his book *The Golden Age of Novelty Songs* (2000), Steve Otfinoski defined *novelty* with three words: "funny, timely, and weird." When Larry King asked Hansen to describe novelty music, Hansen was careful to avoid traditional disparagement of the category, often seen as trivial with little staying power. Instead, Hansen cited the music's newness as well as a certain humor. Elsewhere, he has made it clear that novelty music also has resilience, with a lifespan hard to predict.[3] King followed up (judgment again implied), "Is the novelty tune important?" Hansen insisted, "Of course." After all, it "makes people laugh." In the foreword to Otfinoski's book, Hansen went further: "There's a little insanity in all of us, and what better way to let it out than by singing or enjoying a silly song. Just think—this might be your guide to lifelong mental health!"

It was this silly bent that earned Hansen his on-air name, Dr. Demento. On one of his first guest appearances, he played "Transfusion," by Nervous Norvus, released in 1956, about terrible driving. Someone in the room said, "You've got to be demented to play that!" He said to Puig, "It hurt my feelings very momentarily." The next time he was on-air, one of the other on-air personalities introduced him as Dr. Demento: "I started calling my show 'The Dr. Demento Show' about a week after that." His signature look, a top hat and a tux, was part of the character. As King pointed out, always the contrarian, no one can see the ensemble on the radio. His implication: What's the point? Hansen insisted that it helped him "get in the spirit of it." In this elevated opera-house look, Hansen sounded on air with horns and honks, his voice good-natured with lively changes in pitch, especially in the delivery of his regular lines: "Wind up your radio"; "the Doctor is in."

Hansen's playlist as Dr. Demento (the complete listing is available at dmdb.org) prized "weird" music, a "very subjective" criterion.[4] But that criterion, Hansen explained, excluded "boring songs (hopefully)." In this way, his selection process was based on the negative, cutting songs that were "too serious or too conventional," music that was "poorly performed and/or recorded," or songs that were so offensive the affront outweighed "the humor or other positive things about the song." He also of course responded to humor. In 1991, he told Richard Harrington of the *Washington Post*, "I've never been a connoisseur of written humor. I came to humor through music."

This formula hit a nerve, and, in 1972, Hansen moved to a bigger station, KMET, with syndication in 1974. That year, Brown observed, "Locally, he has dominated the ratings to such an extent that they would often double those of the nearest rival." His program was in fact the most popular Sunday-evening radio show in Los Angeles. And the program had a surprisingly wide audience. Brown wrote, "College professors, students, World War I pilots, garbage collectors in Beverly Hills and Little League shortstops listen to it. Perhaps it's on the sly, but they listen." Many musicians and music enthusiasts cite Dr. Demento's show as an inspiration, including late-night talk show host Jimmy Fallon as well as Jack Black of Tenacious D. Even those who couldn't listen to his show name it as an influence. NPR music editor and founder of the *A.V. Club* Stephen Thomson explained to writer Sam Adams, "As a budding nerd, I was always really glad to know that show was out there, even if it wasn't broadcast in an area where I could listen to it."[5]

No one else was programming similarly irreverent fare. And Hansen had a special sense of the absurd at its best. To Mark Dago, he clarified, "Over forty-plus years I've developed a feeling for what my listeners will probably like.... It helps if the lyrics are funny, of course, and it's best if they establish themselves as being funny rather quickly. It helps if the music is listenable, especially if the performer has feeling and what one might call charisma. Of course, now and then there's something that's so bad that it's funny on account of that." One of his all-time favorites? A truly mad tune called "They're Coming to Take Me Away, Ha-Haaa!" by Napoleon XIV, actually recording engineer Jerry Samuels.[6] In the wildly popular song of 1966, Napoleon maniacally makes a threat turned real, that he would go crazy if his girlfriend leaves him. And away he goes: "To the funny farm where life is beautiful all the time."

But, to stay relevant, Hansen has had to stay abreast of changes in comic sensibilities and related funny music. Hansen recalled, "People in the past were more easily amused; they didn't need or even want to be shocked into laughter. On the other hand they were not at all shocked by things that outrage and shock people today, especially the racial and ethnic jokes."[7] Music genres have transformed as well, further impacting changes in funny music. Early on, Hansen found folk music an especially rich site of comedy: "The popular folk music of the late 1950s and 1960s lent itself very well to funny songs, and some of my best material still comes from 'folk singers.'" In 1991, to Harrington, Hansen highlighted folk singer Christine Lavin, who also records with the group Four Bitchin' Babes. Humor in country music and rap, in contrast, have swapped centrality: "Funny songs were always a part of country music, though not as much lately." "When I started," Hansen observed, "rap music did not exist, but now there are plenty of novelty raps to play."[8] He singled out as especially funny Darrell Hammond and Christopher Snell's "Wappin'," with rap in the spirit of Bugs Bunny.

Hansen's funny song collection could have sustained his show. But decade after decade, Hansen received piles of unsolicited tapes with homemade songs—many released annually to fans on Hansen's famous Basement Tapes. Demento is credited with discovering some of the best in funny music in this way, including the song "Fish Heads" (1978), sent in by the duo Barnes and Barnes, Bill Mumy and Robert Haimer masquerading as brothers. The song, the "most requested" in the show's history, was inspired by a bad meal at a Chinese restaurant.[9] It's a catchy Chipmunk-esque rumination on eating fish heads but also interacting with them: "Eat them up, yum," but they're "not good dancers, they don't play drums."

Demento is also cited as the mentor of "Weird Al" Yankovic, whom Hansen has called "the Beatles of my little genre."[10] In the 1970s, Hansen spoke at high schools about music, educating audiences in person about unusual songs of the past. After Dr. Demento spoke at Yankovic's high school in 1973, Yankovic approached him for an autograph. In the extensive liner notes accompanying Yankovic's compilation *Permanent Record: Al in the Box*, Hansen remembers Yankovic as one of the few students to do so—though "he was too shy to say much." Soon after, Yankovic sent Dr. Demento a tape with the song "School Cafeteria" and, shortly thereafter, "Belvedere Cruising." In 1976, Dr. Demento played "Belvedere Cruising" on air, and it was voted into his show's top ten. The song, a comedic original, celebrated the Yankovic family's big black car, a 1964 Plymouth Belvedere with red upholstery. In it, Yankovic compares his ride to all its failing rivals. Hansen remembers thinking, as he listened to the song, "This kid has some talent." The accordion was a draw, but Hansen also responded to one line in particular: "There's something about a Comet / That makes me want to vomit."[11] To date, Yankovic is one of the most successful comedic artists in music history, with fourteen studio albums and a career spanning forty years and counting. His *Mandatory Fun* (2014) was the first comedy album to debut at number one on the *Billboard* Top 200 chart and won him a Grammy Award for Best Comedy Album, another Grammy for the pile that began in 1984 with his "Eat It" victory for Best Comedy Recording.[12]

Hansen had significant relationships with other legends of funny music as well, including Frank Zappa, whom he interviewed several times. In a 1981 interview, Hansen sits with his customary top hat beside the colorfully attired avant-garde musician, who is wearing purple pants and a steely expression. Asked to describe his music, Zappa calls it "specialized entertainment" for those tired of the other stuff. Hansen, with good humor, asks tough questions, bringing up the controversy around Zappa's song "Jewish Princess" (1979), which earned Zappa rebuke from the Anti-Defamation League. As Hansen lightly laughs in the background, Zappa defends himself, addressing the "Jewish princess" directly: "I care. I wrote a song about you." In an interview for Southern California Public Radio, Hansen recalled of Zappa, "I think we had a whole lot of respect for each other. I certainly had for him, still do."

Many of Hansen's favorite artists eventually recorded with the Los Angeles–based independent record label Rhino Records, which began as a record store in 1973. Even Weird Al came to Rhino, with his song "My Bologna," which would become his first big hit with Capitol Records. Rhino label cofounder Harold Bronson described the meaty record that could have been in his book, *The Rhino Records Story* (2013): "I told Al I was interested, and suggested issuing the record to look like a package of bologna, with the record a lunchmeat picture disc." Rhino began recording in 1975, under the leadership of Rhino Records store founder Richard Foos and Bronson, the store's onetime manager. In 1975, local street performer Larry "Wild Man" Fischer helped Rhino transition from store to label when Bronson recorded Fischer's song "Go to Rhino Records," which inexplicably became a hit in the UK. The duo subsequently focused on novelty songs, local bands, and reissues of out-of-print songs, sometimes packaged in imaginative ways. In 1982, Bronson told the *Los Angeles Times*, "The records we're most passionate about are our reissues from the mid and late 60s. There's a positive, joyous quality to the music that you can't find anymore." And that joy existed at Rhino Records itself. Musicologist Daniel Goldmark remembers his time working at Rhino fondly, explaining that "Foos and Bronson treated their employees like family."[13] In addition to artists featured on Dr. Demento's show, the label issued compilations of music handpicked by Dr. Demento, like early release *Dementia Royale* (1980), with liner notes by the Doctor himself, and, in 2000, the forty-two-track *Dementia 2000!* In 1988, the City of Los Angeles honored the label, proclaiming February 29 "Rhino Records Day," with Dr. Demento in attendance.

In his career, Hansen looked backward, bringing funny songs of the past to current audiences. At the same time, he inspired new music, which was sometimes released on the Rhino label. In 1993, Washburn pronounced, "For nearly a quarter-century on his weekly radio show, Hansen's alter ego has been the last defender of the novelty song, playing quirky tunes about fish heads, dead puppies and monster eggplants that ate Chicago. These songs have all but disappeared from the slick radio formats of today, but they still thrive on his show, which is syndicated in 150 cities." Today, Hansen continues to support funny music with his online show. And the online format makes some sense given the prevalence today of amateur funny songs on the internet more generally. In *Memes in Digital Culture* (2013), Limor Shifman points out how quickly such songs spread online since people are more likely to share positive or funny content. Since 2005, just as Hansen's Basement Tapes once did, YouTube has provided an assumed democratic platform for amateur and aspiring artists participating in funny music, and parody songs are a favorite on the site. In 2007, musician and comic artist Rob Balder launched a website dedicated specifically to these musicians, the FuMP, in which Hansen is also involved. The FuMP's team posts new funny music, offering musicians a promotional platform, but the group also puts out compilation CDs of its artists' music every other month, to date a total of seventy-nine volumes. Since 2014, the FuMP has also hosted an annual festival of funny music. Hansen has called the FuMP "the best thing to happen to funny music since Al went weird." And he listens to the songs the site posts every week.

Insane Ian, or Ian Bonds, has been one of the core members running the FuMP since 2012. He told me, "Barry (or Dr D if you prefer) is probably the biggest influence on the comedy music world. He resurrected 'novelty' songs on his radio show for the general populace, brought new, unheard songs to the world, and 'discovered' Weird Al. If we didn't have Dr D, we wouldn't have comedy music as we know it today. I can't think of any comedy musician who doesn't know of or owe thanks to what Barry has done (and STILL does) for 50 years." Bonds himself is a second-generation funny musician—his parents are part of a filking (or music based in fandom) group called the Omicron Ceti III. Still, he modestly told me, "Anyone who has listened to my work can guess I've never taken any music lessons." Bonds first came to Hansen's attention around 2009, when his song "Guitar Hero," a parody of Foreigner's "Juke Box Hero," became the number-eleven song on Hansen's show that year. It was great validation for Bonds, who shared his thought with me: "that #11 is just the #1, twice." Today he is in charge of the official Dr. Demento Show group on Facebook—keeping in touch with Hansen regarding group-related news. He also has contact with Hansen as the chairperson of the Logan Whitehurst Memorial Awards for Excellence in Comedy.

The Logan Awards started in 2010 when founders of the FuMP decided to find a way to honor specific contributions to comedic music. As it states on the awards webpage, "Comedy music has long lacked recognition." The awards honor musicians annually in three different categories—"Outstanding Comedy Music Video," "Outstanding Original Comedy Song," and "Outstanding Parody Song." It also pays tribute to musician Logan Whitehurst, drummer for the indie-rock band the Velvet Teen, comedic creator of Logan Whitehurst and the Junior Science Club, and a favorite on the Dr. Demento show before his untimely death in 2006 at the age of twenty-nine. When he was asked about the possibility of another Weird Al on Dave and Ethan's podcast, Hansen named Whitehurst, comparing him to funny songwriter Randy Newman, known for songs like the satirical "Short People" (1977) and the warm-hearted "You've Got a Friend in Me" (1995). He would always have a "soft spot" for Whitehurst, Hansen said. On Whitehurst's beautifully illustrated record *Goodbye, My 4-Track*, a reissue of the 2003 album of the same name, by Needlejuice Records, it states, "Please be aware that any attempt to 'pirate' this album will result in your losing one or more of your extremities, which will then be replaced by a peg, hook, or patch, depending upon the area of affectation." In the liner notes, Dr. Demento writes, "I'll get right to it—this album is a total masterpiece, the

Sgt. Pepper of comedy music." Hansen also describes listening to the album on CD in 2003, with my personal favorite, "Monkeys Are Bad People," which makes bananas a teaching moment between a monkey-hating father and his frustrated son. The lesson: "Monkeys can't be trusted." By the song "Robot Cat," writes Hansen, "I was hugging the CD case." Along with chairperson Bonds, Hansen serves as the awards' permanent juror.

I had to ask Bonds, "Comedic music is often judged harshly—dismissed—how do you pick out a winner in a supposedly losing genre? What are the criteria?" He answered, "Comedy is one of the most subjective forms of entertainment." And he realizes that there can be no set criteria. He stated the standard simply: "What makes you laugh?" In 1983, on *Late Night with David Letterman*, Hansen said something similar. Asked for his "taste guidelines," his playlist criteria, he said, it's "very subjective." He brought up a song then popular on his show, "Dead Puppies Aren't Much Fun," by Ogden Edsl. "Dead Puppies Aren't Much Fun" works, he told Letterman, but "Dead Puppies Are Fun" doesn't. That's the line.

Dr. Demento is a true icon in funny music and a Los Angeles institution. And he offers us a certain model for assessing humorous songs: look for charisma, musical skill, and funny lyrics. Nothing boring, nothing conventional. At the same time, as Bonds and Hansen make clear, humor is indeed highly personal. What makes you laugh? How I respond to musical comedians and comedic music might differ from how you, the reader, react. And the funny music included in the chapters to come may not line up with the songs another author would choose. But, like Dr. D, I spotlight the unconventional, a trait made more likely by the coming together of music and humor, opening up new possibilities of inventiveness, wit, and technical innovation.

Though sometimes disparaged as demented, this music attracted the highly intelligent and inquisitive Dr. Demento, who ultimately made funny music his life's work, supporting and inspiring new generations of musicians and comedians similarly intrigued by the radical potential in humorous music. In so doing, he forged his own path, with no one like him before or since, promoting funny music with the help of Rhino Records and groups like the FuMP. As Dan Pasternack wrote for *McSweeney's* (2015), "While somber-voiced DJs were exploring the far reaches of contemporary music, Dr. Demento was an island unto himself." His career, like Largo, is a lesson in innovation, experimentation, and boundary transgression. And perhaps that's the real criteria of musical comedy—criteria that ultimately make funny music inherently unfixed and, yes, subjective. In fact, while humor itself is admittedly subjective, the addition of music might make it even more difficult to assess without overt bias. After all, a listener's response to music varies widely, conditioned by a person's individual experiences with music and knowledge of it. As we will see in the next chapter, listeners will get musical jokes, or not, to different degrees. And that's not the fault of musical humor; that's part of its depth, adding to the fun. But when audiences do understand the humor, they are often treated to something quite new and often profound. And it's definitely not boring, especially when it turns out, as in the following chapter, that a famous pop singer is masquerading as an out-of-tune lounge act. With a sound both hilarious and unbearably sharp, funny music can apparently succeed by failing.

NOTES

1. Interview in Richard Harrington, "Dr. Demento's Slipped Discs," *Washington Post*, September 11, 1991.
2. See George Henderson, *Blind Joe Death's America: John Fahey, the Blues, and Writing White Discontent* (Chapel Hill: University of North Carolina Press, 2021).
3. Quoted in Jim Bessman, "Dr Demento Marks 30 Years of Funny Music with Rhino Set," *Billboard*, February 26, 2000, 11.
4. Julie Simmons, "Dr. Demento: Talking Turkey about Comedy and Novelty Music," *Music Makes You Think*, November 25, 2015.

5. Sam Adams, "Farewell, Dr. Demento—and the Novelty Song?," *Salon*, June 13, 2010.
6. Harrington, "Dr. Demento's Slipped Discs."
7. J. Simmons, "Dr. Demento."
8. Simmons.
9. David Buck, "Eat Them Up. Yum!," *Tedium*, July 18, 2019.
10. Quoted in David Segal, "'Weird Al': Confessions of a Parody Animal," *Washington Post*, August 17, 2003.
11. Quoted in Randy Lewis, "Parody Master Yankovic Stays a Step Ahead with New, Seriously Silly Moves," *Star Advertiser*, February 28, 2017.
12. For more information, please see Lily E. Hirsch, *Weird Al: Seriously* (Lanham, MD: Rowman and Littlefield, 2020; expanded ed., 2022).
13. Daniel Goldmark, "Anthologizing Rock and Roll: Rhino Records and the Repackaging of Rock History" (unpublished manuscript), Microsoft Word file.

THREE

BAD SINGING

THE AMAZON TELEVISION SERIES *The Marvelous Mrs. Maisel*, which premiered in 2017, focuses on a woman breaking gender norms as a female comic in the late 1950s. The featured music is period perfect, including "You Belong to Me," covered by Jo Stafford in 1952, at the time a wildly popular song of separation and bittersweet longing. But the choice of the Stafford song, I realized as I watched the first season, was more perfect than even the show's producers might have known. Stafford, after all, was funny herself. Alongside her fame as a serious crooner, she won acclaim for a challenging type of musical humor—bad singing. And she did so in an unusual way, under the alias Darlene Edwards. Darlene was not a simple nom de plume—a George Eliot or Mark Twain. No, Darlene lived and breathed beyond the pen as a fully fleshed-out persona, a rather upright lady trying to do her very best despite her obvious and obnoxious musical shortcomings. As Dr. Demento knew, sometimes music is so bad it's good. And by good, I mean funny.

Darlene performed in this way with her pianist husband Jonathan Edwards—Stafford's real-life husband, music arranger Paul Weston. Many of the biggest fans of the Edwards act were musical themselves: Sid Caesar, Groucho Marx, and Jack Benny, comedians who all trained as musicians, as well as the pianist George Shearling. But why would musicians respond to poor musicianship? I reached out to Stafford's son, Tim Weston, hoping to find out more about Stafford and the Edwards act, and he kindly agreed to meet me for lunch. For this opportunity, I happily braved the infernal Grapevine, driving from Bakersfield to Weston's favorite lunch spot, the Country Deli in Topanga, California. There, Weston made a big claim, telling me that the Edwards act had a specific appeal to musicians: "It's kind of inside. It's kind of musicians' humor."

It seems, in some ways, the Edwardses were a musician joke made real:

Q: What's the difference between a world war and a singer?

A: The singer's performance causes more suffering.

As inspiration, there have always been singer stereotypes, jokes directed in particular at the soprano. And those jokes can be harsh and unfairly gendered. But the Edwards act was also a send-up of other musicians, including failing lounge acts and, far more specific, the producer and sing-along innovator Mitch Miller, who was responsible for the 1960s family-television hit *Sing Along with Mitch*. More recently, Miller's music, accompanied by superimposed words for ease of group participation, has been used to chase away teenagers, a means to reduce loitering through broadcast music in public spaces. The strategy plays on Miller's corny rep—a rep he gained even at the height of his fame. But, before this breakout role, he was apparently offending singers rather than hipsters. As one of the men in charge at Columbia Records in the 1950s, often responsible for the repertory of Columbia artists, he helped push Stafford toward an unprecedented joke in music's history. That joke spotlights another aspect of the seriousness in comedic music: humor in music can be seriously hard to execute and seriously hard to recognize, the joke building

Jo Stafford and the Pied Pipers, "It Started All Over Again," screenshot from YouTube.

on knowledge of music and musicians. That can make the punchline all the more rewarding and exhilarating in the end, whether a listener gets it immediately or recognizes the humor only with time or explanation. Bad singing may then be better in some ways than good singing—in terms of difficulty and reward in recognition. Of course, a punching down, in this case, may cloud the humor to some extent, at least for some—a moral consideration hardly unique in comedy.

Born in cow-town Coalinga, California, in 1917, Stafford started out singing with her sisters as the Stafford Sisters. She had a buttery tone and unusually accurate intonation. She explained her pitch trick: "I can't tell you physically how you do it. It's a mental thing. You know the song, you know the note you're going for. And a split second before you sing it, you hear it in your mind. And it gives you a real edge on hitting that note."[1] Breaking with her siblings, she sang next in a group of seven male singers called the Pied Pipers. This group attracted the attention of Paul Weston and Axel Stordahl, who worked as arrangers for the Tommy Dorsey Band. The Pipers' sound stood out, Weston recalled, but he also remembered as remarkable the group's appetite. In his autobiography (written with Stafford), *Song of the Open Road* (2016), he described their first meeting, at a house he had rented with Stordahl, Dorsey vocalist Jack Leonard, and producer Herb Sanford: "We sat around the house in pleasant anticipation when all of a sudden the Pipers pushed their way through the front door, eight strong, and made a beeline for the kitchen before the introductions were even completed. They hit the refrigerator and ate everything in sight. I remember that they cleaned out our meager supply of catsup and quickly drank all the cooking wine."[2] The rather large group didn't last long, and the fridge was soon restocked, but Stafford found a new gig when she received a call from Tommy Dorsey himself: "I can't use eight voices, but I would like a quartette with you in it to join the band and be a regular part of the Dorsey organization. What do you say?" Stafford agreed, often backing up Ol' Blue Eyes himself, Frank Sinatra. Their recording of the song "I'll Never Smile Again," in 1940, became the first number-one single issued by *Billboard* magazine. Two years later, in 1942, Stafford recorded her first hit with Dorsey, "Little Man with a Candy Cigar."

With this success, in 1944, she signed as a stand-alone act with Capitol Records, the label newly established by songwriter Johnny Mercer, and she quickly became a favorite voice among American servicemen during World War II and the Korean War. With this popularity, she earned the nickname G. I. Jo. Gene Lees, in *Singers and the Song II* (1998), writes, "She was a very pretty girl, as seen in pictures that were hung up in the barracks of soldiers and over the swaying bunks of sailors, but she seemed more like, well, the girl next door than like the sweatered catch-me-if-you-can girls." She recorded forty-eight hits for Capitol before her move, by 1950, to Columbia Records, along with her music director Paul Weston, whom she would marry in 1952. At Columbia, she recorded "You Belong to Me," which sold two million copies. But she was remarkably versatile, bringing her smooth sound to genres beyond pop, including spirituals, folk songs, and, yes, comedy.

Stafford's first foray into recorded comedy was under the alias Cinderella G. Stump. In 1947, Capitol recording artist Red Ingle, who recorded with Spike Jones as a funny country singer, was creating a silly version of the sleek hit "Temptation," popularized in a version sung by Bing Crosby. Ingle intended to find humor in a clash between country music and the original's pop sound, dubbing the new cover "Tim-Tay-Shun." But the female singer he had hired for the track never showed up, leaving him a voice short. Someone suggested fellow Capitol recording artist Stafford as a last-minute replacement. Stafford's son Tim Weston told me, "She was actually out in the hall at Capitol Records when he was making his record. And somebody pointed to her and said, 'Oh, there's somebody that could do it.'" Stafford's management wasn't thrilled she had participated in the musical joke, but everyone else was. With a convincing hillbilly accent and her Cinderella cover, she helped the spoof reach number one on the charts—no glass slipper required.

A more lasting comedic effort began some ten years later, a collaboration between Stafford and her husband, Weston. But the act had roots in their earlier musical play as well as their dissatisfaction with existing music industry norms. At the end of recording sessions, Stafford had a habit of "musically crucifying" songs she and the musicians found lacking. It was a way for them to release a certain frustration, forced as they were to record music without a say in song selection—the repertoire instead being subject to the desires of Columbia music director Mitch Miller. In her autobiography, she recalled, "Since the record company paid for everything I had to be cooperative and a lot more cooperative than the artists who pay for their own sessions have to be these days. I was literally cornered and there was no escape from the fearful choices of songs handed me." If they finished up early, Stafford and the musicians would give certain songs the treatment they felt the songs deserved, performing them "book style," with no emotional attachment or necessary interpretation, just "square and corny." Stafford might also sing these loathsome songs sharp, slightly higher than the intended pitch, even more offensive than flat, just below the pitch. In her autobiography, she insisted, "Sharp is worse than flat, much worse—sharp makes your teeth hurt."

While Stafford put her musical chops to work making fun of objectionable song choices, Weston took on musicians themselves, specifically the unprofessional pianists he encountered again and again playing clubs and restaurants. At Hollywood parties, he would even assume the character himself, becoming, in his own words, "the most horrible cocktail pianist . . . wrong chords, wrong rhythm, wrong melody." Some listeners found the character especially funny—one was Dean Martin's wife, Jeannie, who would often implore Weston to "do that silly thing you do." But the act became something more in Key West, Florida, at a Columbia Records convention in 1956. In the hotel dining room, a pianist was earnestly performing badly: "Pouring out pathetic chords, twisting melodies into private traumas, courageously pounding away at his very personal and bewildering versions of popular songs." When the fellow was finished, Weston at his table felt a familiar pull. In his autobiography, he wrote, "It was an irresistible temptation." Without preamble, he quietly began playing a mangled version of "Stardust," by Hoagy Carmichael. It was all in good fun for Weston, though at the expense of that initial piano player. But this time, Weston was surrounded by recording professionals. Laughing, Columbia higher-ups George Avakian and Irving Townsend insisted, "Hey! You've got to make an album of that." These two executives were amused and absolutely serious.

Message received, Weston got to work as a character named Jonathan Edwards. In his autobiography, Weston explained, "The name came from Columbia Records executive, George Avakian, who was a Yale graduate. George remembered that Jonathan Edwards had been a fundamentalist preacher and, at one time, the president of Yale University. To George's keen mind there was an analogy in that Roger Williams, who was then a famous pianist on the American pop music scene, was named after or had the same name as another Roger Williams, once a fundamentalist preacher in Rhode Island . . . To me, the melding of the two preachers and pianists was a brilliant stroke." He had the name, but he still wasn't sure he alone could fill a whole album in character. Aware of Stafford's comedic gifts, he asked her to join him, and she did so as "darling Darlene Edwards." Like so many comedic musicians, the ruse involved and even necessitated an alter ego.

In the recordings, against Edwards's mangled playing, Darlene sings in earnest, often just sharp or flat, at her own pace (despite the score markings), and with occasional ad-lib. Though he gave the Edwardses high marks (forty-eight stars), music critic Leonard Feather observed, referencing famous jazz standard "Take the 'A' Train," that Darlene was the "only singer to get off the A train between A and B-flat." The out-of-tune singing was tremendously precise and difficult to render—it was a horrible sound that takes real talent and technique to produce. And to sustain that sound across multiple songs was remarkable and remarkably hard to listen to, at least for me. On their first album, *The Piano Artistry of Jonathan Edwards* (1957), Stafford sang "You're Blasé," "Autumn in New York," "It's Magic," and "Cocktails for Two." The album cover features a woman (not Stafford) and a pianist, with a focus on his two right hands. In an early Edwards premiere, LA radio personality Dick Whittinghill played "It's Magic" on the air, declaring in introduction that he had discovered a new singing sensation. But it certainly was not magic, as the final note on the word *you* slowly and inexplicably moves higher, up, up, and away from the correct note. Listeners were outraged, calling in, "We have trusted you all these years, all our lives. This woman is terrible, how can we ever believe in you again?" The true identity of the Edwardses was subject to immediate speculation, even with a few radio contests bent on discovering their true identities. But only months into the ruse, the jig was up (a great expression here, by the way, that combines joking and a musical dance). A *Times* article outed Weston and Stafford, to their relief.

Despite the big reveal, the act more than continued. In 1961, the Edwardses' second album, *Jonathan and Darlene Edwards in Paris* (1960), won a Grammy for Best Comedy Performance (Musical), beating out Tom Lehrer, who revealed to me, "I was nominated and was happy to be beaten by Jonathan and Darlene Edwards." Between 1957 and 1982, the Edwardses put out five albums, including a single in 1979 featuring "Stayin' Alive" and "I Am Woman." Stafford and Weston, as the Edwardses, also had several television appearances—one on *The Garry Moore Show* and another on *The Jack Benny Show*. Moore introduced the two: "Jonathan is the epitome of all the bad cocktail pianists in the world, but he feels—and vehemently so—that slavish adherence to the chord patterns of the composer are not for him. He is much more of an artist than that and Darlene feels a few notes out of tune here and there are her prerogative and her skill demands such liberties." Though listeners didn't always catch the joke and were sometimes concerned that the mistakes were inadvertent, Moore had properly prepared his audience, and the applause was intense. In short, the explanation worked.

Their appearance on *The Jack Benny Show*, however, was far less successful, at least according to their son, then a young child and in the audience. In his autobiography, Weston described his son's reaction: "Timothy... was then about four-years-old and a great fan and truly devoted admirer of Jack Benny. We took him to the show and sat him with his Aunt Tina in the audience, thinking it would be a special treat for him. After the show, when it came time to go home, we fetched him, but he adamantly refused to get into the car with us. His aunt had to take him home and for the next twenty-four hours he refused to speak to us because he felt we had played a joke on Mr. Benny." Today, Tim himself can't remember the show, but, responding to his father's version of events, he told me, "It sounds like something I would feel about the situation."

Besides the television appearances, the Edwards act was not live. Nonetheless, the Edwardses, for Stafford and Weston, existed beyond recorded sound, with a life all their own. Stafford recalled, "I found myself referring to Darlene as being real, substantial, an alter ego." And she knew this alter ego well: "When discussing wardrobe, for instance, I'd say, 'No, no she wouldn't wear that. Not on your life!' Darlene may not be a terrific singer, but she's certainly not a clown." In a 1975 interview for the *Los Angeles Times*, "The Westons' Gag That Got out of Hand," Weston insisted, with a smile, that he resented the Edwardses: "They won a Grammy. Jo and I never did" (though, in his autobiography, he claimed the Edwardses were "a little confused at receiving the award in the category Best Comedy Album"). Still, he maintained, Darlene was the real problem: "She's a drag," Weston said. "Jonathan's all right, but I don't think Darlene is a nice person. She's just going along for the ride, taking advantage of his talent." Stafford countered, "I don't know. I think perhaps she's the power behind his career." But, according to the fictional Jonathan Edwards, in a letter to the editor of *High Fidelity* magazine, Weston and Stafford had their own issues: "Because of temporary financial embarrassment, Darlene and I have been forced to live with the Westons, and it's no picnic, believe me. They keep mentioning things they did in the 'big band' days that Darlene and I don't think ever really happened."

The Edwardses recorded popular songs, but the selections were often sentimental, even overly mawkish. In Tim's words, they were "lame." But the guiding mantra in repertoire choice was perhaps more varied—songs that would be funny performed by these two specific characters, Darlene and Jonathan. Some of the standouts, as I listened to an album of the Edwardses' greatest hits, include "I Am Woman," "Take the 'A' Train," and "Stayin' Alive." "Take the 'A' Train," written by Billy Strayhorn for Duke Ellington in 1939, is defined by a series of leaps that require true control of tone as well as vocal range. The element of technical difficulty proved perfect fodder—there was plenty of material for Darlene to mangle. And mangle she did, with little attention to the song's rhythm or swing. The incongruity between the original version's style and the Edwardses' performance is a basic part of the fun—a left turn turned laugh.

The powerful anthem "I Am Woman," written by Australian Helen Reddy and Ray Burton and first released in 1971, was also ripe for Darlene's mistreatment. The song, part of the women's liberation movement, loses its transformative conviction in Darlene's pitchy rendition. The song's bravado simply deflates. At first, I couldn't even listen to the song. It's terrible. But, aware of the joke, knowing the great Stafford was purposely making so many overt and egregious errors, I started to smile. And during this particular song, I also thought about Darlene as a purported person, trying to celebrate her strength as a woman while failing musically. As she sang, "If I have to, I can do anything," I had my doubts. The mismatch—declared potency and audible inability—became ridiculously funny, in concept and execution. At the same time, in this particular example, there is something almost tragic. When women needed to effect change through power, as they still do today, Darlene undermined the song's promise with a toothless roar.

"Stayin' Alive," performed by the Edwardses, didn't have the same issue. But it too undercut something about the song, specifically its coolness. With that effect, the Edwardses' version was quite popular but not with the Bee Gees themselves. The 1977 disco smash, by the brothers Gibb, was featured in the movie *Saturday Night Fever*. It had swagger—until, that is, it didn't. Stafford, as Darlene, sings the song in a straight tone, stiff, no feeling, and off pitch as usual. She seems to be trying to keep up with the song's fast pace, spitting out the words in a game of chase she was sure to lose. After the fact (and typical of the Edwards character), Darlene would admit no wrong. In a playful interview for the *Los Angeles Times*, Weston as Edwards discussed their version of "Stayin' Alive," similarly evading reality by explaining his rhythmic mistakes as an intended "disco rest": "I invented this thing called the 'disco rest,' where halfway through the selection I can play some of my own piano stylings unencumbered by the rhythm of disco. Some carping critics have said that I invented this only so I have free rein for my remarkable artistic abilities." Stafford, in character, joined the ruse: "Some of the 7/4 bars tend to be constricting, and they weren't suited to my particular talents as a vocalist. I was just trying to get through that song. I didn't really have enough time to let my vocal talents come through because there were an awful lot of words." In a discussion of funny cover songs, the staff at covermesongs.com put it perfectly: "The Bee Gees disliked this version intensely, it seems. I can't think why."

While in part release for Stafford and Weston, the Edwards act in practice spoofed any clueless musician, those who displayed a sense of import they had not earned musically. To some, there's a cruelty in that sort of humor, but it was also a release of understandable frustration for Stafford and Weston. And Tim confirmed that his parents, during their careers, certainly had to work with various musicians of that type, Miller for them being the epitome. To be fair, Miller, a talented oboist himself, had earned his position at Columbia. He had a sense for commercial appeal and is credited as both a hit maker and a star maker. He pushed Tony Bennett to record "Because of You," which turned out to be a big success and the start of Bennett's next-level fame. He did something similar for Rosemary Clooney, with the song

"Come On-a My House." But Miller's control was bound to rub certain musicians the wrong way. And Stafford and Weston were certainly not alone in their negative reaction to Miller and related industry practice. Sinatra famously complained about Miller, who compelled him to record "Bim Bam Baby," "Tennessee Newsboy," and "Mama Will Bark." The latter was a duet between Sinatra and a then-popular television celebrity named Dagmar, with actual dog barking by "dog impressionist" Donald Bain (not Sinatra himself, as some people suspected). Aware of the accusations, Miller would mount his own defense: "A lot of people tried to paint me as a tyrant, but how can you be a tyrant in the recording business? If the artist doesn't want to sing the song, they're not going to sing it."[3] In a telegram to a congressional subcommittee, Sinatra nonetheless complained that Miller had denied him "freedom of selection," assigning him instead "many, many inferior songs." When, years later, Sinatra and a friend saw Miller at a Las Vegas casino, Sinatra responded to his pal's idea of a reconciliation: "F*** you, keep walking."[4] Stafford never took Sinatra's route, campaigning against Miller in political circles. Instead, she got her revenge in the Edwards act. And Weston was happy to take on Miller as well. Tim told me, "My dad and Mitch Miller did not get along or see eye to eye." In 1962, their takedown extended to Miller's sing-along gimmick, with the Edwards sing-along album, *Sing Along with Jonathan and Darlene Edwards*. Tim summed up the effort: "The entire record was devoted to spoofing the whole Mitch Miller concept." With Miller as its overt target, the album was a bit different from previous Edwards albums. "So if there was even an ounce of maliciousness, it would have been in that record," Tim said, with a laugh. Citing that album, Miller would blame the couple for effectively ending his successful sing-along run.

Of course, the intent, for Stafford and Weston, wasn't all criticism or contempt. In their other Edwards albums, in particular, there was cathartic play. Their comedic work together was also a means of bonding and a reflection of Weston's and Stafford's personalities and relationship. The two were an unusually equal match, at least at the time, with a deep love and an obvious respect for each other's musical talents. In an early letter to Weston, dated May 11, 1945, Stafford wrote, "I still have an awful acute crush on you and hope you are the same." Two days later, after hearing a new Stafford performance, Weston wrote, "You really sound better than I've ever heard you before. I got quite knocked out today and that is a rare experience for me in my old age. Naturally I pine for you continually—probably in vain. But time will tell as the poets never say." They were also both quite funny. Their son remembers their "very good sense of humor." Growing up, he told me, comedy was a big part of life, but not jokes—more "a sense of the absurd." Even Stafford? I had to confirm. After all, she was pretty, I said, with a half smile. Tim admitted that, yes, she was. And she was "totally preoccupied with her looks." She had been overweight as a child, and when she became a solo act, there was "a tremendous makeover that occurred," with pressure to be thin and beautiful, and she "sort of became glamorous." But, as is true of female comedians generally, being conventionally pretty didn't cancel out her ability to be funny. In Tim's words, "She wasn't just one thing." And, while Darlene took herself very seriously, Stafford never did. In fact, in many ways she was a "reluctant star"—according to Tim, "the most reluctant star you'll ever meet." She didn't enjoy performing in front of an audience, but she was proud of her singing and enjoyed recording music. She was a beautiful woman who was down-to-earth enough to clown around, having fun while doing what she loved to do in the studio.

—⚜—

The Edwards act was then personal, part of the story of Jo Stafford and Paul Weston. But it also has a special place in the history of comically bad singing. Comic actor and singer Danny Kaye famously ruined the Cole Porter song "Begin the Beguine," but this ruse was just one of many gimmicks in Kaye's comic repertoire. Before the Edwardses, during the 1940s socialite Florence Foster Jenkins displayed a more consistent sonic floundering. It was funny, but there is no confirmation that she was in on the joke, as Weston and Stafford were. On October 25, 1944, Jenkins rented Carnegie Hall for a public recital. Critic Earl Wilson called the performance "one of the weirdest mass jokes New York has ever seen."[5] In the 2016 movie *Florence Foster Jenkins*, Meryl Streep plays the title role. Auditioning pianists to provide her accompaniment, she reveals a refined ear. After a particularly powerful audition, Jenkins comments, he's "raping my ears." But when she herself sings, she shows nothing of this sensitivity, much like her closest allies. She ridiculously swoops on and around the pitch and eventually, mercifully, stops. Only the pianist, Mr. McMoon, reacts, mirroring the response of the audience. Upon his return the next day, McMoon giggles uncontrollably, lost in the memory of Jenkins's unexpected vocal pyrotechnics.

In 1957, with the Edwards act just underway, a silent-film actress, Leona Anderson, similarly made herself heard with the release of *Music to Suffer By*. Unlike Jenkins, Anderson clearly intended to suck. She in fact billed herself as "the world's most horrible singer." Almost a decade later, another bad singer, Mrs. Miller, made her debut. Born Elva Connes in 1907, the then-married Mrs. Miller aspired to be a singer. As a woman of some means, she spent her own money recording an album. Fred Bock, a conductor and arranger, heard Mrs. Miller's recording and encouraged her to sing pop standards instead of her preferred repertoire of religious hymns. He recognized the comedic mismatch between her style—semioperatic with an unruly vibrato—and popular song. When Bock brought a recording of her singing "Downtown" to Capitol Records, they signed her. And Lex De Azevedo, at Capitol, upped the gag, having her sing rock as well. In 1966, her first album, *Mrs. Miller's Greatest Hits*, sold over

250,000 copies. It wasn't just her talent—or lack thereof—that listeners responded to. Listeners found it amusing that a fifty-nine-year-old woman was enthusiastically singing out of tune and off beat, missing words and whole lines. Though Mrs. Miller may not have been in on the joke—a moral issue, to be sure—her production team certainly was. Bock's wife would later insist that she and Bock had been honest with Mrs. Miller: "We told her it would be funny. And the audience loved it. The more they laughed, the more she would, you know, work it. I don't know if she knew more than she let on because she was always quite a character. But she loved audiences."[6]

A new play, *Mrs. Miller Does Her Thing*, will help keep the memory of Miller's short-lived fame alive. But she and other bad singers echo in the shenanigans of shows like *American Idol* and *Canadian Idol*, as would-be stars audition confident in a singing ability they do not have. Sue Brophey, who worked for *Canadian Idol*, described the appeal of those auditions: "We got huge numbers for those audition shows, because people like to see a train wreck."[7] William Hung, who auditioned for *American Idol* in 2004, is consummate proof. After he sang Ricky Martin's "She Bangs," judge Simon Cowell pronounced, "You can't sing, you can't dance, so what do you want me to say?"[8] Hung became a viral sensation and even earned a record deal. Though many listeners were laughing at him rather than with him, he remains grateful for his *Idol* opportunity. "Regardless of how they portrayed me," Hung has said, "showing me on TV is like opening doors."[9]

None of these bad singers had concurrent success as good singers, at least at Stafford's level. And none of them performed under an alias, as the Edwardses did. Stafford and Weston's use of an alternate name served to distance the Edwards act from the couple's more sincere musical efforts. I asked Tim, Was that by design? Was there any anxiety that the Edwards act might threaten Weston and Stafford's established reputation as artists? "No," he said, "I don't think there was ever any concern about that at all." More significant, the alias, as an alter ego, enhanced the act's humor. The Edwardses' pretention was at odds with the couple's many musical mistakes. It's one more humorous clash. Once Stafford and Weston were outed, which happened quite quickly, the alias also marked the joke as a joke. While "Magic" on the radio tricked early listeners who were unaware of the humor, Moore on his show effectively set up the joke for the Edwardses. Knowledge of the name change did so as well. Larry Etue, a Stafford fan and my coffee-shop pal, remembers the Edwards recordings. I asked him, "Were they funny?" "I knew it was an act so it was funny," he said. I followed up: "What if you hadn't known?" He acted out his imagined reaction: "What are they putting this on for?"

While the alias had a comedic purpose for listeners, the Edwards act, simply put, was also fun for Stafford and Weston. As Shawn Amos claimed in 2009, writing for the *Huffington Post*, an alias can give performers a revelatory sense of freedom. In reference to groups like the Blues Brothers or Spinal Tap (see the next chapter), he wrote, "When you're just faking it, you have nothing to lose. And with pretending comes a sense of abandon that most real bands can't bring themselves to summon." Stafford's and Weston's recurring references to the Edwardses in interviews, even into the 1980s, seem proof that the two didn't want the merriment to end. The Edwards act was their decades-long joke, a pleasure for them and those in the know, often those musically inclined.

In general, the Edwardses' humor was both more nuanced and better defined than a simple laugh at the expense of a bad singer—a punching down—though it certainly was that too. With purpose, Stafford and Weston committed specific offenses musicians are expected to avoid. Tim explained, "So with Jonathan and Darlene records, if you can get through them more than once, you're going to enjoy certain passages again and again, like, 'Oh, wait till he plays this,' and 'Remember when she sings this.'" Not everyone was going to notice each offense. Tim Weston remembers his dad telling a story of a golf outing. With no idea that Weston was Edwards, his golf partner commented on the Edwards act: "You know, she's not so bad, but the piano player, I don't like." He had not only missed the joke; he had heard Darlene in an entirely unexpected way, as a good singer. Thankfully, Weston and Stafford weren't trying to appeal to everyone. They didn't need all listeners to get every aspect of their intended humor. They had a thriving career, and the Edwards ploy was something they did for amusement. Other than a few television appearances, they also didn't perform live. Tim insisted, "This was just for fun. So they never even tried to market it and capitalize on it." They didn't really have to compromise, then, I responded: "They did exactly what they wanted to do here." And they did it for *their* people, often other musicians.

Tim shared an anecdote—a story his mom would tell. On tour with the Tommy Dorsey Orchestra, she and the other musicians would travel at night on the bus. One morning, she was sitting next to one of the other guys, looking out the bus window. There were people out on the streets below. She said, "You see those people? Those are day people." The night people, the musicians, those were her people. There was a divide then between Stafford's world, the musicians, and the world of day, the nonmusicians—a truth for Stafford played up in an absurd skit on the show *Comedy Bang! Bang!* In the episode "Schoolboy Q Wears a Patterned Bucket Hat and Glasses," musicians aren't just marked by their sleep patterns; in a riff on X-Men, they're basically mutants.

Musicians are expected to perform well. With so many aspiring musicians, the spectacle of truly terrible singing can come as a humorous surprise for those aware of the joke. The digital age, with the technical means to achieve audio perfection, only makes that subversion a more pronounced punch. For Stafford, the persona of Darlene Edwards helped define the joke. Darlene too expects a flawlessness she will not achieve. And we hear the radical turnaround in sound: the popular and beautiful Jo Stafford falling flat in a variety of ways on purpose, performing certain songs as they were arguably meant to be, Miller be damned. In this way, the humor of the Edwards act is in the upending of many different assumptions about music and how to approach music: the assumed perfect performance, one true to the specific style of each song—its rhythm and interpretation—and the expectation that a self-serious star has the goods to back up that self-seriousness. It took knowledge of music and true talent to perform as badly as Stafford and Weston did under the Edwards guise. Their humor built on music as art, taking established patterns and breaking them down. Does everyone know the patterns? Does everyone laugh? No. But the more you know about music, the greater the likelihood that you will laugh. The Edwards act can come off as ridiculous singing or something more particular. That divide certainly could be part of comedic music's poor standing. Musical humor will inevitably play differently for different listeners, based on their prior experience with music. And it's easy to dismiss what a person doesn't fully get. But, with knowledge of music and its history, we can all be in on the joke to a certain extent.

In the next chapter, a similar problem exists in humorous film music. This time, however, it's even easier to miss the joke and thus dismiss the music. After all, in this context, a person isn't even supposed to notice the music—funny or not. But what if we did? Again, there is much to gain if a person digs into film music, comedy in film music, as well as the humor in other musical genres—each with their own histories, musicianship, and traditions of humor. Hopefully, you the reader, can then forgive me for being *that* guy, killing that frog and, in effect, giving humorous music the same attention so-called serious music gets in written form. If it helps, I promise to go big, all the way "up to 11."

NOTES

1. Quoted in Gene Lees, *Singers and the Song II* (New York: Oxford University Press, 1998), 108.
2. Paul Weston and Jo Stafford, *Song of the Open Road: An Autobiography and Other Writings* (Albany, GA: BearManor Media, 2012), 13.
3. Mitch Miller, quoted in Howard Reich, "Mitch's New Pitch," *Chicago Tribune*, November 15, 1987.
4. Quoted in Bruce Klauber, "Mitch Miller: The Kitsch of Mitch," Jazzlegends, www.jazzlegends.com, http://www.jazzlegends.com/mitch-miller-the-kitch-of-mitch/.
5. Tom Huizenga, "Killing Me Sharply with Her Song: The Improbable Story of Florence Foster Jenkins," NPR, August 10, 2016.
6. Quoted in Bill Caldwell, "Joplin Singer Achieved Flash-in-the-Pan Fame, Devoted Following," *Joplin Globe*, March 2, 2019, https://www.joplinglobe.com/news/local_news/bill-caldwell-joplin-singer-achieved-flash-in-the-pan-fame-devoted-following/article_961c61ab-91a8-5aad-b56c-e118084e5045.html.
7. Quoted in Tim Falconer, *Bad Singer: The Surprising Science of Tone Deafness and How We Hear Music* (Toronto: Anansi, 2016), 44.
8. Falconer, 51–52.
9. Katherine Meizel, *Idolized: Music, Media, and Identity in American Idol* (Bloomington: Indiana University Press, 2011), 99.

PART II

JESTING BY GENRE

FOUR

TAPPING INTO MOVIE MUSIC

AS THE STAFFORD RUSE SUGGESTS, it's easy to miss the hype of comedic music because it's easy to miss a musical joke. Mark Flanagan, at Largo, helps the comedian as well as the singer-songwriter by enforcing a strict no-talking policy. In 2002, he told the *Los Angeles Times*, "With serious singer-songwriters, or even comedy, you can't have a rowdy crowd." Understanding humor requires attention. But, left to our own devices, we rarely listen to music, *really* listen, without doing something else at the same time. Most often, music is preselected ambient noise—the soundtrack of our daily lives, from our morning jolt at the local coffee shop to time spent waiting at the dentist. The music we select ourselves fades into the background as we hit play and then begin work, conversation, or dinner. The way we consume music is then yet another blow to funny music. How can we appreciate the humor if we are not paying attention? And, to be clear, we are not paying attention.

Even with a bit more sustained attention, watching a movie, audiences can overlook a film's musical joke. As we have seen, with musical knowledge at the heart of much of the humor in music, not everyone will get the joke or understand it in the same way. A standout funny film, with music as a central topic, is the legendary *This Is Spinal Tap*. Though it is now a cult hit, upon release it made far from an impressive showing. The same is true of "Weird Al" Yankovic's film *UHF*. Frankly, based on how we listen (and don't listen) to music, I'm not surprised.

Funny film music similarly suffers, backed up by dismissal of film music and comedies in particular based on worn-out attitudes toward commercial success. If it's commercially viable, it must be somehow lacking critically.[1] While film music has a rich comedic tradition, that musical art is also especially easy to miss—partly by design. The movie scores of talented funny film composers, like Danny Elfman, Randy Newman, or Elmer Bernstein, often seamlessly work with the film as a whole—to such an extent that we just don't notice the specifics of the music or get the jokes in full. As Claudia Gorbman underscores in her book *Unheard Melodies* (1987), we are supposedly meant to hear a film score without really listening to it. That's a mark of its success.

Today, Theodore Shapiro is a go-to guy for comedy film music. In the last twenty years, he has produced the scores for nearly fifty comedy films. With serious composition credentials, including a graduate degree in composition from Julliard, his status in the world of comedy may come as a surprise to some. But it really shouldn't, given what it takes to produce effective funny music—funny music so good that audiences may not be consciously aware of it.

When I reached out to Shapiro, I was lucky to discover that he has thought a lot about how music can contribute to comedy in film, his own course in music, as well as the subtleties of music's work in funny films. In fact, in one of his most revealing moments, he explained to me, "In many cases the film composer's role is to manipulate the viewer without the viewer feeling manipulated. So transparency is often the film composer's goal. I think it gets additionally complicated in many comedies." At the movies, musical humor is not only readily overlooked—in intention and execution, you are supposed to ignore the specifics. With Shapiro's help, in this chapter, I pull back the curtain disguising music's significance in comedic movies—both funny films with a musical focus and funny film music—while exposing the curtain itself, the many reasons and ways in which we dismiss what music does in funny films. I also once again underscore the necessary musical ability and the vast synthesis of musical technique and labor that make comedic music successful and successfully overlooked.

—⋘—

Born in 1971 in Washington, DC, Shapiro began studying classical piano at the age of five or six, but he did not decide to pursue a career in music until college, at Brown University. There, he was involved in theater, wrote a musical, and became interested in film scoring. While a graduate student at Julliard, however, he considered devoting himself to classical concert music. With faculty member and composer John Corigliano—who was known for classical works, like his *Clarinet Concerto* (1977) and symphonies, as well as scores for several films, like *The Red Violin* (1998)—there was some sympathy for film music at Julliard. Still, Shapiro recalls receiving mixed messages about film music during graduate study: "I once had a professor tell me film scoring was fine only if you were able to write what you wanted to write and could express yourself freely—which of course is not the way film composition usually works." In an interview with *All Access* (2016), Shapiro describes the film composition process, the collaboration it requires, and his attraction to that necessary cooperation. "I like and value the process," he says—a dynamic free of the old "Western genius composer" model. Rather than composing tortured and alone in the mythic mold of Beethoven, film composition needs and values group work.

Today, Shapiro believes there is greater appreciation for film music—"a more general openness to the fact that good music is good music." But in his own career, he had to make a choice: "When I graduated from Julliard I spent a number of years writing for both film and TV and concert music. It ultimately came to a head when I received an opera commission at the same time that I was getting opportunities to work on bigger studio films. It felt like a fork in the road where I had to make a choice, and ultimately, film was really the medium I wanted to work in most." He became involved in comedy in part thanks to friends. In the *All Access* interview, he explained his work and subsequent reputation in comedic films as somewhat circumstantial: "I have good friends who work in comedy." He developed these connections in part through work on the television show *The State* (1993–1995), which he scored early in his career, and those relationships brought him work in funny films as well as an established reputation in comedy. One comedy led to another, in his recollection, though he does credit his scoring of the thriller *Heist* (2001) as the reason for his job composing music for *Old School* (2003).

Still, he admitted to me that his comedic rep wasn't entirely accidental. Plenty of comedy scores made big impressions on him, influencing his approach to film composition: "Although I don't think of myself as being particularly attracted to music for comedy, there are a lot of comedies that have played a huge role in my life. And music from those films is deeply embedded in me." He cites the music of Elmer Bernstein, specifically his score to *Animal House* (1978); the 1974 spoof Western *Blazing Saddles*, including its opening song by John Morris and Mel Brooks; and the music of Danny Elfman: "Elmer Bernstein's score to 'Animal House' is fantastic. The main title song to 'Blazing Saddles' is brilliant. I just rewatched 'Midnight Run' for the first time in around thirty years and was amazed by the degree to which Danny Elfman's score had stayed with me. I guess I'm the same as everyone else: I don't think of music for comedy as being important to me, but it really is."

—⚜—

Elmer Bernstein (1922–2004), like Shapiro, was trained at Julliard and studied with composers Roger Sessions and Stefan

Wolpe. He was often confused with another composing Bernstein, Leonard, whom some distinguished as Bernstein East. Bernstein West (Elmer) earned his nickname due to his close association with composition in Hollywood rather than Leonard's classical world. He composed the music for over two hundred films, including *To Kill a Mockingbird* (1963), *Animal House* (1978), and *Ghostbusters* (1984), a movie Shapiro would score in its 2016 remake.

Unlike Bernstein and Shapiro, Elfman (1953) was self-taught. Born in Los Angeles, he traveled abroad after high school graduation, eventually meeting up with his brother, Richard, who was part of a musical-comedy troupe called Le Grand Magic Circus. Danny became the group's conga drum player. When Richard returned to Los Angeles, he founded a similar group, Mystic Knights of the Oingo Boingo, eventually just Oingo Boingo, and Danny joined as the troupe's composer. As a part of the group, Danny came to the attention of director Tim Burton and actor Paul Reubens, who asked him to score the movie *Pee-wee's Big Adventure* (1985). In a 2015 interview, Elfman told *Vulture*, referencing Italian film composer Nino Rota, "I really went heavily into a Nino Rota inspiration for *Pee-wee's Big Adventure*, so if you heard something circuslike, I can only imagine that it came from that place." Generally, his approach involved a manipulation of tradition, as he explained elsewhere: the customary means of composition "goes through some funny circus mirrors in my head."[2] This first collaboration was the start of a significant partnership between Elfman and Burton, resulting in an extensive list of quirky-comedic scores: *Beetlejuice* (1988), *Edward Scissorhands* (1990), *Mars Attacks* (1996), and many, many others. He also wrote the scores for more serious movies, though he remembers some resistance when he was hired to score one of his first, *Batman* (1989). In a *Rolling Stone* interview (2015), he said, "I'd never scored action. I was the quirky comedy guy. I'm sure they would have been much happier if they could get a more experienced composer, John Williams or somebody."

—⚏—

In addition to the work of these great film composers, Shapiro has responded to funny movies with a focus on music. At the top of his list are the films of Christopher Guest: "I don't know if anything can beat the three amazing Christopher Guest films, 'This Is Spinal Tap,' 'Waiting For Guffman' (which is a music film of sorts), and 'A Mighty Wind.' They are treasures." He had a slew of candidates from which to choose: The movie *The Wedding Singer* features funny original songs by Adam Sandler and a surprise A Flock of Seagulls hair joke; *Pitch Perfect* is another option, a comedy set in the hilarious world of a cappella singing, much like the television show *Glee*; *School of Rock* spotlights a different musical world, centering on a selfish would-be rocker, bent on "liberating people" with his music, played by the especially comedic-musical actor Jack Black; and *Popstar: Never Stop Never Stopping* (2016) takes on the pop industry, with the mock pop star Conner4Real, played by Andy Samberg.[3] There are also classics like *The Blues Brothers* (1980), starring John Belushi and Dan Aykroyd; Ethan Coen and Joel Coen's *O Brother, Where Art Thou?* (2000), heavy with folk music; and *Wayne's World* (1992), set in the hilarious world of hard rock. But Shapiro is not alone in singling out Guest and his movie *This Is Spinal Tap*, though there are many reasons audiences might not have recognized the humor upon first viewing.

In *Spinal Tap*, Guest, who in real life plays the clarinet, mandolin, and guitar, stars as Nigel Tufnel, the lead singer of the fictional band Spinal Tap. Along with Rob Reiner, Michael McKean, and Harry Shearer, Guest wrote the script and music, following the trials and tribulations of the made-up band in a parody of a musical documentary. Guest describes the movie as a "comedy that's done in a documentary style," distinguishing it from a "mockumentary," a term often applied to the movie, which Guest believes inaccurately suggests that there is a certain mean-spirited mockery in the film. Actor Fred Willard, who often appeared in Guest's films, clarified, "I don't think he's ever cruel with people." Instead, the characters appear "very human."[4]

Released on March 2, 1984, the movie bombed at the box office. It cost $10 million dollars to make but brought in only $4.5 million. Initially, the movie confused some viewers who assumed it was real. These unsmiling filmgoers wondered why the film didn't chronicle a famous group like Led Zeppelin. Part of the problem then was parody—the creation of a new work through the repurposing of an older work or model—a popular device in funny music and American popular music more generally. As John Thomerson maintains in his study of the device, parody is "the compositional technique most familiar in the musical experiences of Americans."[5] Though it is often ignored as less creative than so-called original art, parody is remarkably dynamic. It can denigrate, criticize, and mock. It can be funny and playful. It can also offer up tribute or homage. Still, the joke does require some recognition that the work is in fact a parody. With so many potential effects, even those who get the basic premise won't necessarily respond to the parody in the same way.

Aerosmith guitarist Joe Perry recalled, "When we watched *Spinal Tap*, my wife and I saw it, and we fell on the floor. It was great. Every bit is brilliant as it was supposed to be." Though he understood the joke, lead singer Steven Tyler wasn't as pleased: "That movie bummed me out," Tyler said, "because I thought, 'How dare they? That's all real, and they're mocking it.'"[6] In "This Is Spinal Tap Mocks Metal and More, a Lot More" (2019), metal writer Deena Weinstein recalls her similar reaction upon the film's release: "Why should I enjoy a movie that made cheap jibes at my favorite genre?"

These reactions can change over time, conditioned by new circumstances or just repeated viewing and reconsideration.

More recently, Weinstein rewatched the film: "Instead of my original focus on the movie's scathing satire of heavy metal, I was delighted by its really insightful take on social relations within heavy metal." That appreciation can depend on knowledge of past documentaries as well as heavy metal itself. A scene featuring Guest's character Nigel Tufnel proudly presenting his many guitars, for example, is an homage to a similar scene with Jimmy Page in the Led Zeppelin rockumentary *The Song Remains the Same*. There's also the Zeppelin reference in Tufnel's solo involving a violin rubbed against his guitar strings, a parody of Jimmy Page's famous use of a violin bow in his own guitar playing. A bit with the band getting lost on the way to the stage was based in reality as well. In *Newsweek* (2009), Jennie Yabroff outlined Rob Reiner's real-life inspiration: "Some of the stuff in the movie was inspired by actual events, such as when the band gets lost on the way to the stage, which happened to Tom Petty and the Heartbreakers." The oft-cited "up to eleven" moment in the film is another joke based in familiarity with metal, in this case metal's loudness. Rather than the traditional ten, Tufnel's amplifier goes all the way to eleven. Only recently did I notice another joke: a gag centered on the guitarists' choice to play bass guitars during the movie's song "Big Bottom." It's a great pun. The song is ostensibly about big butts, but it also has a big musical bottom, with the string switch-up. As Weinstein concluded, "The more people know about metal, about rock bands, about the rock industry or about documentaries, the potentially funnier they find *Spinal Tap*."

This slow burn, appreciation of the film over time, is hardly unusual in funny films about music. Despite its initial failure in theaters, *Spinal Tap* was a hugely popular rental on VHS, and it has been rereleased several times in theaters since, with a special twenty-fifth-anniversary Blu-ray disc edition in 2009. Today, it is considered a cult classic, the ultimate among music-centric films and comedies of all types. The movie *UHF*, starring "Weird Al"

Nigel Tufnel showing off his gear in *This Is Spinal Tap*, screenshot from YouTube.

Yankovic, followed a similar trajectory, from initial disappointment upon release in 1989 to radical fan veneration. In the film's oral history, for *AV Film* (2015), Yankovic described the early letdown: "It was a pretty dramatic rise and fall. I won't say that I spiraled into depression, but I was pretty bummed."

In the film, Weird Al plays dreamer George Newman, determined to make his uncle's failing television station a success. The movie also boasts a cast of colorful supporting characters, including a pre-*Seinfeld* Michael Richards and comedienne Fran Drescher, also in *Spinal Tap*. In the oral history, Yankovic recalled the casting of Drescher, with her distinctive nasal voice: "I thought, particularly for a broadcaster, for Fran Drescher's character, it was funny, because that's not the kind of voice you normally hear as a news anchor." The premise supported a string of parodies, musical ones and references to other movies, television shows, and even commercials, with the famous "Spatula City" spot: "We make spatulas and that's all!" In the film, Newman, a "guy with a good imagination," watches a clip of the show *Beverly Hillbillies*, which segues to a parody of Dire Straits' "Money for Nothing." These jokes were easy to miss in full. Often, there is something funny in the parody itself, but the humor can also depend on awareness of the target. Would audiences recognize the reference to the Dire Straits original? A few years after its premiere, when the film was released on DVD, there were signs that *UHF* would find its audience. Yankovic's longtime manager, Jay Levey, remembered, "When it came out on DVD, of all the DVDs being released that week—including recent films, recent blockbusters—we were in the top 10, several years after the movie came out." Yankovic said, "Somehow, it's really found its audience." I'm still waiting for *Popstar*, which tanked at the box office in 2016, to find its own redemption. And I'm fascinated by the current reception of Weird Al's latest film, *Weird: The Al Yankovic Story* (2022), a parody of Yankovic's real life, which is driving the confused Google search: Did Weird Al really date Madonna?

As a musician, Shapiro can appreciate funny films about music, with their buried musical references. But he is aware of the distinct challenges, especially in funny film music. In comedy film scoring, however, he explained to me that the reception issue is different. It's not necessarily inside knowledge hiding the depth of funny film music but instead the compositional process itself—the way composers actively work to conceal the effect of their music to some extent. And it's not just the composers participating in this subterfuge. Values around film music are part of the issue—long-standing notions that film composition is less important than concert fare, somehow more commercial or unoriginal. In concert halls, programmers mark that difference in surprising ways, including the food on offer. When the featured repertoire is film music, symphony audiences are allowed to munch on popcorn. Suddenly, the regular no-food rules no longer apply, as if the distraction of snacking is not an issue when it's *just* film music. Though I'm all for popcorn, the messaging is of course off. After all, there is a lot to notice in film music, and

Average Joes versus Purple Cobras in *Dodgeball*, screenshot from YouTube.

perhaps even more so when the music is composed for funny films.

Film music is meant to be organic, connected to the visual story in a harmonious whole, despite the serious work behind and in film composition. In an interview with Alberto E. Rodriguez in *Pop Disciple*, Shapiro highlighted that work: "When I was in graduate school, they didn't offer anything related to writing for film at the time, but I did get a very strong grounding in compositional skill. It's funny because you put all these tools in your toolbox, and you don't know when you're going to use them, but you can pull them out at will." As an example, he referenced his scoring of the film *Dodgeball*, starring Vince Vaughn as underdog Peter and Ben Stiller as his rival, the two forced to work out their frustrations in a high-stakes dodgeball tournament. The film is a broad comedy, and yet he found himself "pulling out the tool of writing a fugue," a learned compositional technique associated with J. S. Bach and the ornate world of the Baroque. In a game pegging opponents with a fast-moving ball, the only thing Baroque is normally a person's nose.

Various approaches to film scoring in comedy further affect appreciation of the musical joke, including the regular use of allusion. In his score of the animated movie *Captain Underpants: The*

First Epic Movie (2017) (a film to which Yankovic also contributed with a song), Shapiro highlights the two main characters' torturous relationship to school, as they sadly walk through its halls accompanied by a mournful musical reference to the "Battle Hymn of the Republic," complete with harmonica. School is prison and war, playfully made clear in the dramatic musical citation. Not every viewer will recognize the specific tune, but the score sets the mood, communicating so much about school for these boys. The same is true in Shapiro's score for *Trolls 2* (2020), an especially musical comedy pitting various genres of music against each other. When the pop heroes happen upon the world of classical music, Symphonyville, recently destroyed by the hard-rock trolls, a sad arrangement sounds of the most recognizable theme from Mozart's G Minor Symphony no. 40. It's another moment that doesn't require detailed recognition of the music to be effective but can nonetheless change with that recognition.

Sometimes, composers choose certain allusions hoping an audience will not only respond to the hoped-for mood but also know the piece itself. The recognition can be a second layer of fun. But at other times, film composers seem to enjoy a joke meant only for a few or even just themselves. In early silent film, musicians used "cue sheets," with a list of appropriate compositions—a collection of existing pieces to be called on section by section. After 1915, composers and arrangers began to create original film scores. Animated films excelled early in the use of music toward comic ends. Carl Stalling, working for Disney and Warner Bros., was one of the best. He used music to highlight the visual gag. In animation, a basic means of such highlighting was "mickey-mousing," a term associated with animated features and a sound synchronized with the action—an ascending scale accompanying a character as they climb steps, for example. Certain signs and symbols of musical humor could similarly underscore a joke, including a light or lively tune or some sort of cue designed to draw attention to the comedic moment.[7]

This semiology of funny music was not cordoned off in cartoons. More overt symbols originated in other genres, like jazz, with the rimshot—ba-dum-pum sting—a drum pattern credited to big-band percussionist Gene Krupa; or, in comedy, the invention by Jordan Brady of "bow-chicka-bow-wow" to signal music in pornographic film. But comedic symbolism was not always so overt in film. Some people created hilarity by adding music that did not match the action. Stalling also created layers of hilarity not everyone would or could get. In one cartoon featuring a bee, he inserted an instrumental rendition of the song "I'm a Busy Little Bumble Bee." But who would recognize the tune, composed in 1906? Who would recognize Stalling's humor? The same goes for his inclusion of Felix Mendelssohn's *Hebrides Overture*, inspired by Scotland's Fingal's Cave, in a scene with a cave. In *Tunes for 'Toons* (2005), musicologist Daniel Goldmark reveals the many levels of humor in Stalling's work—the music providing a lively supporting sound for the bee and, if audiences identified the tune itself, a second punchline. Obviously, familiar tunes would work best in the creation of this double humor. But Goldmark wonders if Stalling might have enjoyed obscure melodies too: "I cannot help wondering if Stalling employed such songs to create yet another level of humor in the cartoons, to be understood and appreciated by the connoisseur of obscure music."

I asked Shapiro if he ever did something similar, using music to create an inside joke. He told me, "I do sometimes entertain myself with musical jokes that no one else, or only my music editor, will probably ever get. In 'Spies in Disguise,' the villain has an army of killer drones at his disposal. The drones' theme is a fast pattern of synthesizer notes which use all 12 pitches." Referencing a complicated system of atonal music defined by an initial tone row, an arrangement of the twelve different notes in a distinct pattern, he explained, "We referred to this theme as the 'drone row.'"

Viewers don't notice the full joke in some musical allusions, but they aren't always meant to. The deception is only supported by attitudes toward animation, often meant for children. We wouldn't necessarily look for a complicated musical joke in music for kids, which is rarely treated in any serious way. Ethnomusicologist Patricia Shehan Campbell connects the dismissal of children's music to the idea that children have no culture of their own. Instead, they're "waiting to become something more than themselves."[8] In the 2013 *Slate* article "Kids' Music is Not so Bad," Rob Harvilla put it more bluntly: "People hate children's music. Viscerally." Barney, the purple dinosaur, comes immediately to mind, his theme song literally used as torture. Sure, there are better-received examples: original songs in NPR's *Story Pirates* podcast, the music of the Okie Dokie Brothers, or songs in John Mulaney's Netflix special "John Mulaney and the Sack Lunch Bunch" (which builds on Mulaney's hilarious *SNL* Lobster Diner trilogy), with a standout performance by actor Jake Gyllenhaal as Mr. Music. But, in general, we don't expect much from kids' stuff.

I asked Shapiro if his approach to animated features differs from his scores for adult films. Referencing *Captain Underpants*, he maintained, "It called for larger, sillier gestures to help tell the story. But the approach to comedy is no different." In his animated movies as well as comedies for adults, Shapiro adds to the general deception of film music by avoiding obvious musical gags—slapstick sounds, the equivalent of the percussionist's rimshot. Shapiro explained to me, "If someone is telling you a joke, but keeps interjecting how funny the punchline is going to be, they're going to kill the joke. The same principle is true with music for comedy. If the score is telling you that the material is funny, it's going to hurt the comedy." This general philosophy leaves little room for mickey-mousing—a technique still funny in its sometimes "ironic" use.[9] In the *All Access* interview, Shapiro confirmed, "I don't see how funny music really ever works." Rather, Shapiro prefers to play it straight. The music as straight man can up the humor through incongruity—serious music alongside a silly setup. But the music can also help the audience invest in comedic characters and plot; the laugh is bigger thanks to this enhanced engagement with the movie. Shapiro again takes his music for *Dodgeball* (2004) as an example:

> The score treats the dodgeball competition as any serious dramatic sports story. It plays to the grand stakes and emotions of the story. The audience laughs their way through the film, but what I think ultimately makes "Dodgeball" successful is that the movie succeeds in making the audience really feel something for the characters and feel genuine exhilaration at the outcome. I think the music contributes a lot to that—but that's a complicated thing to understand as an audience member—"I'm laughing at this movie, but I'm also more emotionally invested in it than I have any right to be." I think that cognitive dissonance makes it harder to acknowledge what the music is doing.

In a 2016 NPR interview, "What Makes a Comedy Funnier? Music with a Straight Face," Shapiro credits Bernstein (West) with a similar approach. Bernstein explained of his score for *Ghostbusters*, "Part of it is comedy, and yet you have to take the ghost business quite seriously. You have to believe, along with these guys, that the ghosts really do exist. Therefore the score also has to walk a very fine line. What I did with the guys was to get a kind of 'antic' theme—it's kind of cute without being really way out. . . . The other element was the last part of the film, all the stuff with the possession and climax on top of the building. I treated that in an awesome and mystical way."[10] Other funny film composers have also looked to serious music to support funny films. Randy Newman, who began recording his original songs in 1968, also successfully scored funny movies and animated films, including the *Toy Story* franchise, *A Bug's Life*, *Monsters University*, *Cars*, and *Meet the Fockers*. In 2009, he told *Animated Views*, referencing the animated movies created by Pixar, "In each of these Pixar pictures, I've taken the emotions of the characters seriously." Legendary funny film director and comedian Mel Brooks, responsible for the songs in his comedy *Blazing Saddles*

(1974), would support the approach: "You never do funny music for a comedy. The humor must come from the truth of the situation, the juxtaposition of serious music and bizarre behavior."[11]

Still, Shapiro allows himself some flexibility: "I would never make a statement about one approach to film scoring always being the correct one. You never know—maybe someday I'll find a film where violating all my previously-held principles is an interesting approach. But the principle that does hold true throughout all films is that the score is there to help the filmmaker tell the story." With that, Shapiro never wants to undermine the joke by highlighting it in an overly silly way. He strives to support the story and its emotional force, though, in doing so, he does include allusions meant for only a few. His approach builds on the work of other compositional greats in funny films. But, with his straight-man strategy, he has carved out his own prominent place in the world of film.

With that place defined by comedy, I had to ask Shapiro, "Are you concerned that you've been pigeonholed?" "A thousand times," he said. "I think my resume probably prevents me from being considered viable for some films. Because I hold myself in high esteem as a composer, that's a tough pill to swallow, even though I also know I'm incredibly fortunate to have the career I have." As Dr. Demento recognizes, funny music can box in an artist. Hansen told the *Washington Post*, "After doing the City Slickers, Spike Jones tried serious music again and wasn't successful." That cordoning off of the funny musician is related to the general dismissal of comedic music. If they work in funny music, so the thinking goes, they can't possibly create serious art. But part of that rejection relates to how we consume entertainment, which often prevents us from getting every musical joke in full. Film music, by design, works to conceal some of that depth. As a unified whole, audiences aren't supposed to be aware of the specifics of the film's score, and some composers, like Shapiro, actively avoid attention-getting movies that might overshadow and thereby kill a comedic scene. Playing the straight man, the score subtly pushes us toward the on-screen action and the emotional force of the story. In that way, we don't register certain allusions or complicated compositional devices, like Shapiro's fugue in *Dodgeball*. The work of music is effortlessly overlooked, as is its composer.

Movies then spotlight another consideration in the assessment of funny music. Its poor standing may be additional default rejection. With so many ways to miss the joke—the music being subtly embedded in the action, the viewers' lack of attention, and the many references buried in parody—audiences can avoid confronting their own misunderstanding by dismissing or dissing humor: it's not me, it's you. The humor is the problem, they reason, not my lack of preparation. But with repeated viewing, the jokes can come into focus. With a little bit of effort, we get the joke. And in this way, an apparent weakness is a potential strength. In an interview in 2000, with Stephen Thompson of the *A.V. Club*, Tom Lehrer commented on the longevity of his funny songs from the 1950s and '60s: "The reason some of my songs have lasted longer is there's a lot of stuff packed in there. You want to hear them more than once." There's a similar motivation in funny films about music and funny film music: we may revisit these movies because there's more to discover. The music is dense with meaning, allusion, and discovery, especially in the capable hands of composers like Shapiro, who uses his vast wealth of compositional tools to make us laugh.

In the next chapter, our main focus, Peter Schickele, also depends on skill in composition. Like Shapiro, Schickele is a serious composer who uses his musical chops to create and serve complex jokes. If we dig a little deeper, we'll earn a musical punchline. And the story of Schickele's ruse alone is worth the extra effort. So grab a snack—this isn't your typical concert-hall fare; it's classical music with a twist, composed by a real composer impersonating a fake one!

NOTES

1. See John Mundy and Glyn White, introduction to *Laughing Matters: Understanding Film, Television and Radio Comedy*, ed. John Mundy and Glyn White (Manchester: Manchester University Press, 2012), 12.

2. Quoted in Neil Lerner, "Danny Elfman: 'Funny Circus Mirrors,'" in *Sound and Music in Film and Visual Media: A Critical Overview*, ed. Graeme Harper (London: Continuum, 2009), 524.

3. Honorary mention goes to *Walk Hard: The Dewey Cox Story*, with an absurd send-up of a Bob Dylan song.

4. See John Kenneth Muir, *Best in Show: The Films of Christopher Guest and Company* (New York: Applause Theatre and Cinema Books, 2004), 4.

5. John Thomerson, "Parody as a Borrowing Practice in American Music, 1965–2015" (PhD diss., University of Cincinnati, 2017), 1.

6. Quoted in Coleman Gray, "35 Years Later, *This Is Spinal Tap* Still Rocks Harder Than Ever," Rotten Tomatoes, March 2, 2019.

7. See Daniel Goldmark, *Toons for 'Toons: Music and the Hollywood Cartoons* (Berkeley: University of California Press, 2005), 13–14.

8. Patricia Shehan Campbell, *Songs in Their Heads: Music and Its Meaning in Children's Lives* (Oxford: Oxford University Press, 2010), 6.

9. See Daniel Goldmark, "Sounds Funny / Funny Sounds: Theorizing Cartoon Music," in *Animation and Comedy in Studio-Era Hollywood*, ed. Daniel Goldmark and Charlie Keil (Berkeley: University of California Press, 2011), 269.

10. Quoted in Jon Fitzgerald and Philip Hayward, "Paranormal Product: The Music and Promotion of Ghostbusters," in *Sounding Funny: Sound and Comedy Cinema*, ed. Mark Evans and Philip Hayward (Sheffield, UK: Equinox, 2016), 97.

11. Quoted in Maurice Yacowar, *Method in Madness: The Comic Art of Mel Brooks* (New York, St. Martin's, 1981).

FIVE

CLASSICAL MUSIC IS COMEDIC (AGAIN)

CLASSICAL MUSIC, THOUGH SEEN AS supposedly sublime or transcendent, has been a great field of play for comedic music. British singer Anna Russell, born in 1911, trained as an opera singer at the Royal College of Music before she realized, quite by accident, that she had comedic talent. In a 1976 interview with John Rosack (rebroadcast by *Weekend Edition*'s Liane Hansen), she recalled, "When I sang everybody would fall about laughing. My feelings would get hurt." But she took the hint and turned a negative into a positive. She eventually found promoter Jack Petrill, who helped guide her unique course as a comedian in classical music, including her New York City debut in 1948. It helped, Russell believed, that she came on the scene shortly after socialite-singer Florence Foster Jenkins, who combined classical music and comedy, whether or not that was Jenkins's intent. One of Russell's most popular bits was her twenty-two-minute explanation of Richard Wagner's music, "The Ring of the Nibelungs (an Analysis)," based on careful and extensive research. The comedy was all in the delivery—her blunt reading of the excessively complicated operatic tale, with legend, incest, and one incredible ring. "I'm not making this up, you know," she would say, encouraging the audience's laughter.

The Danish-born pianist Victor Borge also made a name for himself carousing in classical music. Borge, like Russell, studied as a serious music student. A piano prodigy born in Denmark in 1909, he was awarded a full scholarship to attend the Royal Danish Academy of Music. He performed for a time as a classical concert pianist but soon settled on a combination of piano music and jest. For a time, his tour in Europe in 1933 included anti-Nazi jokes. With a Jewish background and political material, he was forced to emigrate in 1940 and quickly adapted his comedic act to American audiences. He had many gags—famous one-liners ("I don't usually do request numbers—unless, of course, I am asked to do so") and staged falls (the punchline, a seatbelt attached to his piano bench). But he could also execute classical compositions brilliantly, as he did at the Kennedy Center in 1987 during a performance of Leonard Bernstein's *Candide* overture. Of course, that was part of his humor. On the edge of their seats, listeners waited for the music to break, revealing the gag. But he just kept playing. That *was* the joke.

P. D. Q. Bach, like Borge and Russell, is legendary in this realm of musical humor. But unlike the other two, P. D. Q. Bach never actually existed. He was the invention of composer Peter Schickele, born in Iowa in 1935, who told me Borge was for him "an inspiration," both "smart and friendly." Schickele supported his act as P. D. Q. Bach with compositions he wrote himself and ascribed to this lesser-known Bach, in-character performances as PDQ, and a fully invented PDQ biography, which he wrote and published in 1976. In the mock tome, Schickele writes, "At the age of five, the boy still had not been given a name, and it was only after repeated exhortations by his eldest brother, Wilhelm Friedemann, that his father bestowed upon him, not a name, but—at least—three initials: PDQ. When Wilhelm Friedemann asked what the initials stood for, his father said they stood for nothing, which indeed could be said of PDQ himself later in his life."

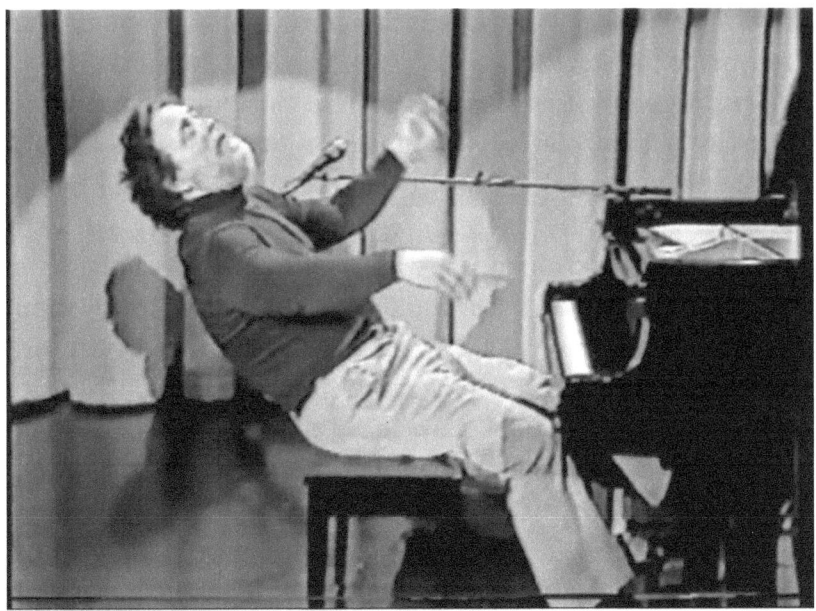

Peter Schickele performs as Schickele and P. D. Q. Bach on *Johnny Carson* (May 28, 1987), screenshot from YouTube.

Despite the differences, much of the humor in the work of Russell, Borge, and Schickele stems from the clash of classical music, perceived as serious, and the variously silly shenanigans of these comedian-musicians. As with the Edwards example, it took knowledge to make and get these jokes. Focusing on Schickele, thanks to an interview with the man himself, this chapter shows the remarkable depth behind this humor. Schickele created a realistic world of funny classical music based on conventions in classical music and its history. His work subtly and smartly upended that history as well as his own career in classical music. But when I asked Schickele about his history as P. D. Q. Bach, he made an important distinction: "When I started out, there were aspects of how classical music was presented that made the 'classical music concert' ripe for decorum-deflating parody." It wasn't the music per se that he targeted but how the music was typically performed. After all, classical music itself was actually pretty darn funny from the start.

A History of Western Music, a standard music history textbook, begins its musical journey with consideration of the aulos, a Greek wind instrument typically ascribed to women, wine, fertility, and unreason, apparently played by prostitutes at drinking parties. If we can get over the obvious gender divide here, we can begin to appreciate the potential for humor. We don't know much about the aulos, but we know that it was not played at stuffy, overly serious affairs and was instead meant for pleasure and fun (though maybe not for the ladies). Skip ahead to the Middle Ages—an era associated with religious persecution and plague (see Monty Python)—and you discover one of the funniest musical forms out there: the motet. It's a vocal piece with more than one line, each with a different text, sometimes in different languages, sacred and secular—all sung together. To modern listeners, it can sound like a nonsensical mash-up with craft well above clarity. And some composers, even then, took advantage of the confusion to bury musical jokes. In the motet "Musicalis Sciencia/Sciencie Luadbili" (hilarious title, I know), the Latin text warns of breaking specific musical rules—rules governing composition at the time—while the musical notes themselves go ahead and break all of those rules. Musicologist Zachary Wallmark, writing about this particular motet on his blog, astutely notes, "What we have here is an early case of irony in notated music. Perhaps if the composer of this motet was alive today he would frequent hipster bars and sport a mullet, gas station attendant jacket, and mustache." No doubt.

There was also the satirical *Roman de Fauvel*, an epic narrative that inspired well over a hundred musical pieces. On Twitter, professor of musicology Douglas Shadle called it the Randy Rainbow of the fourteenth century, referencing political parodist Rainbow, a viral phenomenon, who found fame after uploading his early hit, "Randy Rainbow Is Dating Mel Gibson." And, in medieval France, a specific traveling performer, the jongleur, blended singing with playful storytelling as well as other means of court entertainment, including juggling and acrobatics. He was a one-person cabaret or variety show, a vaudeville act before there was vaudeville, and early evidence of the close tie between music and comedy.

During the Renaissance, the madrigal emerged as a favorite form, with musical notes depicting words—text painting—with much lyrical innuendo. Death wasn't death but a euphemism for orgasm. And in Italian composer Jacques Arcadelt's "Il bianco e dolce cigno" (1539), a performer sings, "With a thousand deaths a day I would be content," highlighted in the music with the line's over-the-top repetition.

The Baroque, in contemporary retellings, was dominated by J. S. Bach (PDQ's would-be father) and his well-designed, many-voiced compositions. But there were also comical vocal forms, like the musical comedies chronicled by Ross Duffin in his exhaustive book *Some Other Note: The Lost Songs of English Renaissance Comedy*. One exceedingly silly example is G. P. Telemann's *Don Quixote*, based on the original source material featuring the hapless Sancho Pansa and the delusional hero himself, Don Quixote.

During the Classical era, humor in music depended on the setup—some comedic giveaway that prepared audiences to laugh. One popular method of signaling that joke was in the work's titling. *Scherzo* was a rather nebulous musical heading that literally means "joke" but often translated in practice into a fast or light musical section or movement of a quartet, symphony, or sonata. *Divertimento* was also imprecise in meaning: an instrumental piece during the period with this title suggested an intention to entertain or amuse, to divert. Haydn wrote 162 divertimenti, Boccherini nearly 100, and Mozart circa 35, including his witty *Musikalischer Spass* (*A Musical Joke*), which amuses by breaking musical rules, much like that medieval hipster's motet.[1] Of the Classical composers, Mozart is often portrayed as the prankster in chief. And he certainly was clever and witty in his music and personal letters, including texts filled with puns and sexual suggestion, even in correspondence with his female cousin. But his humor could also be quite mean and abusive, as comedy and comedic music can be. Take his famous and still much-performed 1787 opera, technically a *drama giocoso* (drama with jokes), *Don Giovanni*, about Don Giovanni, a serial seducer or rapist, depending on who you ask. His servant sings a would-be hilarious aria outlining the Don's many conquests—one that, in the age of #MeToo, is more disgusting and disturbing than funny, though his librettist must of course share some of the blame. Perhaps the work's categorization as a *drama giocoso* partly disguises the problem—*It's just a giocoso*—along with the assumption that the titular character is somehow a hero.[2]

Honestly, for my money, I'll take Haydn and his abrupt, loud chords any day. And he created plenty of other funny musical moments too—all based around the unexpected, including sudden rests or pauses "and his extended repetitions of the same soft chord, or note."[3] With so many expected patterns and musical conventions, especially during the Classical period, Haydn clearly had a lot of comedic material with which to work. The second of his quartet collection op. 33 is nicknamed "The Joke." In its final movement, in the highly patterned form of the rondo, Haydn includes a number of pauses that trick the listener into believing the quartet is over, again and again. This "eccentricity" earned him criticism similar to that of more recent funny musicians. In a letter of March 9, 1814, German composer Carl Friedrich Zelter explained to writer Johann Wolfgang Goethe that Haydn's music was subject to dismissal early in his career because "it immediately made a burlesque of the deadly seriousness of his predecessors."

But comedy continued in music, even during the Romantic era and after. The French composer Erik Satie, for one, is an obvious candidate for inclusion here based on wardrobe alone, a constant rotation of velvet suits. Another French composer, Claude Debussy, is also widely cited as funny, with his famous quotation of the imposing Wagner in the context of a piano piece for children, "Golliwog's Cakewalk." During the Romantic period, Gioachino Rossini's comic operas earned him a special backhanded compliment from his hero Ludwig van Beethoven: "I love your comedies. They suit you. Don't trouble your soul with serious music." Beethoven's burn may be evidence of jealousy—Rossini was wildly popular as an opera composer (in comical and serious composition), while Beethoven's major opera *Fidelio* bombed when it premiered in Vienna in 1805. But the dig also had a foundation in changing perceptions at the time, the Romantic turn toward valuation of the sublime and serious in music. Those perceptions worked to hide the history of comedy in classical music while providing an endless list of potential comedic subjects.

―᭣―

In the nineteenth century, to make a living wage, composers wisely settled on a strategy of self-promotion, lauding themselves and their music as somehow extraordinary, even transcendent, despite the utility of music throughout time and a related lowly early status. It was a smart marketing tool, really, with the patronage system at an end. Performance practice fell in line, with an evolving set of rules around concertizing—all meant to frame music in the most hallowed of light. Gone were the gossip and food that attended the rowdy performances of Mozart's work in the eighteenth century. The concert hall became like a church, with the same rules of respect and reverent silence. Audiences were happy to oblige, with the bourgeoisie increasingly in charge of music, standing in for aristocratic musical patrons of the past and anxious to signal their comparable status and breeding. Their deep attention to music was a barely concealed cry for help: Please don't send us back down the societal ladder.[4] Music then had a big job. It was meant to confirm the greatness of its composers and its audiences. And that could happen only if music too was elevated in serious performance—no clapping between movements, no talking, and certainly no snacking. And with the advent of recording technology in the twentieth century, many of those rules became practical too: a way to guarantee a good take.

With this treatment, classical music—funny or not—became serious. Romantic theories about music and related performance practice in some ways erased classical music's comical past, a past all but forgotten. Thankfully, Schickele has worked to remedy that wrong. Right off the bat, he brought back the play in playing classical music. In the *New York Times* (2015), James R. Oestreich paints the scene of a Schickele (as PDQ) show:

> The stage was set, the orchestra was ready, the announced time for the concert had arrived. But the star of the evening—its perpetrator and host, Peter Schickele—was nowhere to be found.
> Bill Walters, the droll stage manager audiences loved to hiss, would saunter out, upbraid latecomers, peer at his watch, shrug his shoulders and slouch back to the wings. Time dragged.
> Then a shout rang out, and Mr. Schickele would materialize in a box or balcony, hopelessly disheveled in formal dress and work boots. He would clamber over the rail, shimmy down a rope to orchestra level and mount the stage, and the show was on.

These concerts showcasing Schickele's fictitious alter ego were an annual affair, starting in New York in 1965. Sometimes Schickele varied his unusual entrance—swinging onto the stage by rope, for example. In a more recent appearance in New York in 2015, Schickele at eighty had to limit the physical humor, performing instead in a wheelchair. But even that entrance would draw laughs. William Walters, or Bill Walters, an actor and "backstage jack-of-all-trades," played the grouchy stage manager in Schickele's performances. But his bad temper was all part of the show; he was a Schickele collaborator and coconspirator. In an interview, Walters explained, "What we've learned over the years is that no matter what happens at the beginning of a show, people think it's a joke."⁵

During the performance, there were other breaks with tradition, including "New Horizons in Music Appreciation," a presentation of the first movement of Beethoven's *Fifth Symphony*, a composition originally a part of the initial Romantic push toward solemn musical reception. Rather than the prescribed hush, Schickele and his stage manager Walters treated the piece as if it were a game, the two men sportscaster and referee, offering a play-by-play and doling out occasional penalties. In the piece *Echo Sonata for Two Unfriendly Groups of Instruments*, the instrumental players themselves acted out the comedic scenario. Rather than the gallant collaboration central to group music-making, these musicians clearly didn't get along, with the brass players musically mocking the woodwind players.

Many of the other punchlines were "visual," part of the performance. In a *New York Times* article of 1977, Schickele told writer Allan Kozinn, "There are the exaggerated mannerisms of the concert pianist. Or, I may get my finger caught in a mousetrap on the keyboard. At the end of a piece, the piano bench may blow up." I asked Schickele about any specific models, and he cited the physical comedy of the Marx Brothers and Buster Keaton as well as the musical humor of Victor Borge. Still, in practice, that physicality wasn't always easy: "Swinging in on a rope is a great way to start a show," he said, "but it sure is scary to do."

Of course, Schickele's humor was also in the music itself. The ruse began in 1953 when Schickele was Swarthmore's only music major. But on break, he was home hanging out with his brother David and a friend named Ernie. The group was experimenting with home tape recording, specifically overdubbing using two recorders. Schickele came up with a take on J. S. Bach's *Coffee Cantata*, which he called the *Sanka Cantata*, and the three recorded it using their new technological know-how. They settled on a name for the piece's fictitious composer, P. D. Q. Bach, a play on the many Bach children known by initials alone as well as a 1920s expression meaning "pretty damn quick." "It was the 1920s equivalent of ASAP," Schickele explained to Frank J. Oteri in 2004 (the interview available on the New Music USA site). In 1959, while a composition major at Julliard (where he studied with composers Roy Harris and Vincent Persichetti), PDQ made his first public appearance in a humorous concert with conductor Jorge Mester. The two performed the funny music again in Aspen, a Julliard/Aspen event that became an annual concert. The repertoire expanded with each performance, and in 1965, Schickele had enough material to seek out and secure a contract with Vanguard for his first recording as P. D. Q. Bach.

In Schickele's pieces as P. D. Q. Bach, the titles set up the joke, "keying" the context for humor; the comical intention was well established. In 1976, Schickele fleshed out the jest in book form: his fictitious but full biography of PDQ ascribed to another character of sorts, named Peter Schickele, a supposed "very full professor" of musicology and "musical pathology" at the University of Southern North Dakota at Hoople. This third character, a great dig here at academic pretention, created some confusion—real Schickele or not? Schickele once said, "The only thing I would do differently if I had it to do over (and certainly *would* do PDQ), would be *not* to use my real name for the professor . . . I'd use Glutzenhopf or something."[6]

In the book, Schickele includes a preface to the English-language edition, though the book itself has always been in English, before he outlines a life that never was: "P.D.Q. Bach was the last, and by all means the least, of Johann Sebastian Bach's twenty-odd children, and he was certainly the oddest of the lot." And the kazoo didn't help: "After Big Daddy Bach (as he was never called) died, his family gradually dispersed. . . . P.D.Q., characteristically enough, was left with virtually nothing: his share of Bach's legacy was one kazoo." As a young man, PDQ apparently worked as an apprentice carpenter, his first project "an attempt to fashion a set of locks for all the major and minor keys, an endeavor as hopeless as it was pointless." Pun fun!

After a short stint studying to be a castrato, without the "requisite anatomical modification," PDQ set off to visit the Dublin Bach, another invented Bach, before eventually settling in Vienna, where he accepted his fate, writing music for the first time at age thirty-five, the same age at which Mozart died. And what of the musical style? Schickele enigmatically asks, poking fun again at academics, with their sometimes overly complicated writing, "Was the mind that formed the musical style itself formed by the formative years herein described, or was the nature of those formative years formed by the mind that formed the musical style?"

The compositions' titles often support the comical foundation in name and biography: *Fanfare for the Common Cold* (1962), an ode to Aaron Copland's *Fanfare for the Common Man*, and the *Pervertimento* (for bagpipes, bicycle, and balloon), a variation on the divertimento. Schickele, as musical pathologist, writes, "Since the discovery of the *Pervertimento*, even his detractors have had to admit that P.D.Q. Bach must be considered history's greatest late-eighteenth-century Southern German composer of multi-movement works for bagpipes and chamber orchestra." It was a very specific designation and a reminder that I too can be the greatest writer if the category only includes writers who look like me and live in my house.

In *The Short-Tempered Clavier*, a funny play on father Bach's *The Well-Tempered Clavier*, Schickele also includes an unexpected musical quote, "Shave and a Haircut," a comedic call-and-response that Schickele builds into a complicated fugue—an unexpected mash-up of genre and time, a popular ditty and a Baroque technique. That clash of genre in Schickele's output as PDQ is not unusual. In another piece, the *1712 Overture*, he includes allusions to the Beatles' "Day Tripper," "Pop Goes the Weasel," and "Yankee Doodle." I asked him about the mix of genres, and Schickele said, "I see continuity in great music across genres, and

I enjoy sharing great music with other people. As for PDQ Bach, I work with whatever inspires me, I don't worry too much about divides in music." This clash of genres can seem like a statement, but it is also funny in its incongruity, with popular songs clashing with each other and the classical context. Other funny musicians have used a similar formula, including Weird Al, with his polka medleys—a rearrangement of popular songs for accordion—as well as Luther Wright and the Wrongs, a bluegrass group who in 2001 recreated Pink Floyd's rock album *The Wall*.

Schickele plays with other musical expectations much like Haydn. But he takes any Haydnesque surprise to the extreme— with unexpected key changes and wild dissonances or clashing notes. PDQ also seemed to enjoy invented instruments. His 1959 *Sinfonia Concertante* builds on the common mix of instruments in the Classical form. But PDQ upped the stakes with lute, balalaika, double-reed slide music stand, ocarina, left-handed sewer flute, bagpipes, and strings—both the double-reed slide music stand and left-handed sewer flute homemade. In his invented biography of PDQ, Schickele describes the *Sinfonia Concertante*, from the composer's "Soused Period": "The left-handed sewer flute and the double-reed slide music stand were not uncommon in the eighteenth century—both Bach and Handel were quite familiar with them, which is why the repertoire for these instruments does not include anything by Bach and Handel—but P.D.Q. Bach was, as far as we know, the only composer with enough daring and ignorance to write for both simultaneously, using their incompatibility as a structural element in the composition."

In *Sonata for Viola Four Hands and Harpsichords* (1966), Schickele uses traditional instruments but has them played in new ways. While four-hand compositions abound for keyboard, Schickele extends the idea to the viola, with two players meant to play a single viola. In the score, he dictates, "the two viola players sit almost facing each other: Player I holds the instrument and plays in a normal fashion, while player II, who is sitting at the other end of the viola (just beyond the scroll) and facing player I, plays the instrument like a cello." As Tammy Ravas observes, taking Schickele's ruse quite seriously (in the 2005 article "'The Initial Plunge,' 'The Soused Period,' and 'Contrition'? Moving Towards a Style of Peter Schickele's Funny Music in His P.D.Q. Bach Works"), Schickele is incredibly inventive and varied in his approach to composition as PDQ.

While Schickele's humor often plays with a perceived incongruity between humor and classical music, undermining the rigid performance practice that took shape during the Romantic era, he at the same time supports the seeming divide between comedy and classical music by playing up the clash for laughs. And yet, his work as PDQ is in many ways true to the humor and fun already in the classical music tradition. To get all the jokes, some knowledge of classical music comes in handy. To laugh at the title *Gross Concerto*, it helps if you know there was such a thing as the concerto grosso. So too with the *Schleptet*, an homage to Beethoven's *Septet*. Some awareness of operatic history likewise informs the joke in PDQ's *The Stoned Guest*, which features the titular guest, Il Commendatoreador. In Schickele's words, the character's "inebriated state limits his singing role to a mere six notes, after which he stands around staring at everyone." It's a contemporary and comical take on the stone guest in *Don Giovanni*, by Mozart, a composer Schickele much admires. Mozart's "Musical Joke," he told me, was "a lifelong favorite," and the connection is cemented further by a citation of an especially silly and sexual letter from Mozart to his cousin Maria at the start of the PDQ biography.

With knowledge a plus, conductor Leon Botstein, in "Laughing with and at Classical Music, in Public" (2017), wonders if Schickele's type of musical humor may soon disappear. He writes that P.D.Q. Bach "may be the last successful foray into making comedy based on concert life and classical music." Since audiences are less and less familiar with classical music, he assumes listeners will be less and less likely to get the joke. Schickele himself admits that his humor relates to an earlier era. To Oestreich, he explained in 2015, "The mid-60s were the heyday of the L.P. The Baroque boom had set in, and the time was ripe for a Baroque backlash. It would be very difficult to start doing this now." But even then, not everyone understood the joke or the joke in its entirety. And some even walked out midshow: "That's what we call a walking ovation," he explained in 1982.[7] Still, Schickele told Kozinn, "I don't think people have to be deeply into classical music to enjoy the show, but it is true that the more you know the more there is to get." He has had many fans in the world of classical music, like pianist Emanuel Ax—fans who would fully get the gag—but, he told me, "I've always tried to make the humor accessible to people who don't have knowledge of classical music." I asked him, "Has the audience reaction to PDQ Bach noticeably changed over time, based on audiences' musical education?" "Not that I've noticed," he maintained.

Schickele has, however, experienced the flip side, some backlash from within the classical world. Schickele relayed to Oteri a conversation between Mester and, in Schickele's words, "a composer/educator who was a head of a musical education." The composer/educator had asked Mester, "Are you still doing this P.D.Q. Bach thing with Peter Schickele?" Mester responded *yes*, "Isn't it great?" The man replied, "No, I can't agree with you. Peter Schickele makes fun of things that some of us hold sacred." "I've always wished that he said that in public because I would have used it on my posters if I could," revealed Schickele. Anna Russell experienced similar rebuke. In her autobiography, she recalls certain negative responses in the United States to her Wagner *Ring* routine: "Some people were shocked that I would send up this august piece of music, but I don't consider it a sendup. I merely tell the story as accurately as possible and play the bits of music exactly as written. I can't help it if the story is absurd."

—☙—

Another interesting side effect unique to Schickele concerns his parallel efforts as a composer under his own name, including his popular works and regular commissions for film, orchestra, and chamber groups. In 1977, Schickele told Kozinn, "I have some friends who like my serious music very much and who tell me that I ought to stop doing P.D.Q. Bach. They say that it's a big mistake and that nobody will take me seriously until I put that in the past. In a way, I think they may be right." Indeed, Schickele's strong association with PDQ has in some ways overshadowed his work as a so-called serious composer, a situation Stafford evidently never experienced (perhaps because her pop sound was never invested with the same level of seriousness that classical composers both expect and arguably need to be successful). When he is presenting his own music, audiences are often ready to laugh, missing the point of his other works. To me, Schickele admitted, "I do sometimes wish that I had done more to distinguish my comedy persona from my public side as a serious composer, but in the end, it's all worked out."

Others have had related reception issues, like comedian Tim Heidecker, who released the somber album *Fear of Death*. In an interview with Grayson Haver Currin, writing for the *Washington Post* (2020), he described navigating audience expectations, comments like "I liked you better when you were funny." Classical music comedians Anna Russell and Victor Borge didn't have the same problem. They never tried to work as two different people, in two seemingly different realms. In fact, Russell apparently knew the pitfalls of attempting to do so. In her autobiography, she observed, "When anyone is seen purely as a comedian for any length of time, people are apt to laugh even before anything is said—it's a simple reflex action." Despite the differences, all three—Schickele, Borge, and Russell—have a similar standing in the world of comedy, one slightly elevated. Though to some the comedy was insulting to classical music, the association with classical music at the same time lent their comedy a certain respectability. Charles Garrett claims, of Russell, "Ironically, it appears she was marketed as the best in the world at her craft of musical parody in part because of her engagement with high culture."[8]

Thomas M. Kitts and Nick Baxter-Moore responded similarly, in their book on popular music and humor, distinguishing "low-comedy" and the "more cerebral" comedy of Borge.

—⁂—

Comedy in classical music occupies a conflicted position in music and comedy. It plays on perceptions of classical music that were invented in the Romantic era—notions of music that confuse the history of humor in classical music. Given those perceptions, some have reacted negatively to comedy in classical music—a comedy that can be seen as threatening to the supposed solemnity of classical music. At the same time, the association with classical music, for others, elevates the humor. That elevation is not enough to support Schickele's efforts as a "serious" composer, a parallel career neither Borge nor Russell attempted. Schickele was then caught in a web of competing values around comedy and classical music. But when he swung onto the stage, that web, for a time, dropped away. He was the lost Bach, the least of the Bach children, and audiences could laugh at the absurdity of an invented composer backed by a real one, writing his own character's biography as another version of himself, a pseudo-professor. It's a remarkable three-for-one deal in the comedic history of classical music—one that exposes so much about humor in classical music and the parallel effort to hide it, those who would like to keep that least Bach lost. It is also, best of all, an amazing example of the ingenuity, expertise, and talent involved in funny music. That impressive humor, in the hands of Schickele, involved a complicated ruse spanning composition, performance, the writing of musical history, and a fully fabricated Bach, dismissed in his origin story, like comedic music itself. Frankly, it's hard to think of a more complex or creative example of "serious" composition, unless of course J. S. Bach was actually a humorous invention too.

NOTES

1. Rossana Dalmonte, "Towards a Semiology of Humour in Music," *International Review of the Aesthetics and Sociology of Music* 26, no. 2 (1995): 178.
2. See Kristi Brown-Montesano, *Understanding the Women of Mozart's Operas* (Berkeley: University of California Press, 2007), xxii–xxiii.
3. Alfred Brendel, *Alfred Brendel on Music: Collected Essays* (Chicago: A Cappella Books, 2001), 102.
4. Alex Ross, "Why So Serious? How the Classical Concert Took Shape," *New Yorker*, September 1, 2008.
5. Quoted in James Oestreich, "Peter Schickele Brings P.D.Q. Bach Back to the Stage," *New York Times*, December 16, 2015.
6. Quoted in Dennis Davis, "Humor, Structure, and Methodology in Selected Works by Peter Schickele" (PhD diss., University of Kentucky, 2010), 251.
7. Quoted in Davis, 251.
8. Charles Hiroshi Garrett, "'Shooting the Keys': Musical Horseplay and High Culture," in *The Oxford Handbook of the New Cultural History of Music*, ed. Jane F. Fulcher (Oxford: Oxford University Press, 2011), 253.

SIX

HIP-HOP MEOW

WHILE INVENTED CHARACTERS IN FILM roles and alter egos, like the Edwardses and PDQ, are part of the fun in comedic music, musicians also play themselves in funny music, trading on the potential laugh in other musical genres, including rap. Take Michael Render, aka Killer Mike, as case study. He has found distinct ways to build on the comedic tradition in rap, often making significant cultural and political points in the process. In episode 5 of Netflix's *Trigger Warning* (2019), we find him rapping over a barbershop quartet in order to reach out to an elderly audience. His hope is that, with a little creative thinking, he might expand his audience, attracting new fans from circles assumed anti-rap. With the quartet already on stage, a man introduces Killer Mike: "Here's a man you're sure to like." But some do not—one man leaves midperformance (Schickele's "walking ovation"). The show, in Killer Mike's mind, is still generally successful, and he decides his idea could be more. If he brings musicians from various backgrounds with various ideas—a feminist, a white nationalist, a Black Christian, a Juggalo, a Jewish Renaissance enthusiast—together in a single group, performing a political anthem for all, maybe he can reach out to everyone, healing rifts old and new. This plan won't necessarily diversify his music's market but will instead work toward a greater good—bridging society's widening gaps and combatting hate. The song's chorus is on message: "I don't want to be boxed in."

The line could easily apply to Killer Mike himself. Defying singular definition, he's most often cited as a rapper, one half of the lauded duo Run the Jewels, with Jaime Meline, stage name El-P. But he's also an activist, advocating against injustice, including police brutality and prejudicial profiling, as well as the use of rap lyrics as evidence at court.[1] At the end of May 2020, he famously delivered an impassioned plea alongside Atlanta's mayor in the wake of the mass protests following a police officer's murder of George Floyd (quoted in the *New York Times* and elsewhere): "I'm mad as hell. I woke up wanting to see the world burn yesterday, because I'm tired of seeing black men die." He spoke with passion, expressing the frustrations of so many people in the ongoing high-stakes fight for equality.

But Killer Mike is funny too, and sometimes funny for a cause. He and El-P remixed their second album, *Run the Jewels 2*, with cat sounds—and donated the money generated to the families of Eric Garner and Mike Brown, two other Black men brutally killed by the police. The result, *Meow the Jewels*, boasts the same lyrics, replacing the original instrumental tracks with highly manipulated, sci-fi cat-tronica. One song, "Close Your Eyes (and Count to Fuck)," becomes "Close Your Eyes and Meow to Fluff." Another, "Lie, Cheat, Steal," turns into "Lie, Cheat, Meow." The latter could describe every cat I've ever known, and the whole concept makes me laugh. But the sound isn't just funny; it's surprisingly impressive musically, a dystopian soundscape with a furry political edge. Like Stafford's bad singing, this is another musical moment in the history of comedic music without immediate rival. It, alongside Killer Mike, also brings to the fore the conflicted role of comedy in rap—in this case, comedy with weighty significance. In so doing, it draws attention to the ways musicians are funny in and around rap, often in clever and

Killer Mike with a barbershop quartet on *Trigger Warning with Killer Mike*, screenshot from YouTube.

complex ways, sometimes working toward an overtly political end and sometimes playing on racial associations. The latter aim is tied to certain expectations of rap—that rap is not funny or, if it is, that that particular rap or associated rapper is somehow white. But rap has a long history of comedy. And that history can be serious too.

In reception, rap is indeed generally considered at odds with comedy. Comedy doesn't always fit its serious facade. In "This Ain't Funny So Don't You Dare Laugh" (2011), a lyric from the song "Just Another Case" turned article title, culture writer Chris Vognar writes, "Love it or hate it, rap was supposed to be serious business." After all, rap is viewed and promoted as authentic—a reflection of real life. And that life is often depicted as hard—a masculine throw-down with violence and sexual domination the norm. To be fair, there is honesty in rap, but a certain roughness in rap is also part of the performance and product of rap. Rap propels and is propelled by these aggressive expectations of the genre—rough, tough, and real. And that seriousness is important given a history of rap's dismissal.[2]

Some musicians have created humor by playing with and exploiting that serious perception as well as other notions of rap and who a rapper is supposed to be. At the same time, these rappers may use humor to negotiate difference. Charles Hiroshi Garrett, in "'Pranksta Rap': Humor as Difference in Hip Hop" (2015), notes the value of comedy in this way for rap's outsiders—especially white rappers like Eminem and the Beastie Boys, who may be seen as inauthentic, interlopers in Black-only culture. In the '80s, the Beastie Boys maintained an easy, ironic attitude toward rap, which kept critics at bay. How can you seriously attack rappers when you're not entirely sure they're taking their own music seriously? In *Beastie Boys Book* (2018), member Michael Diamond reveals that playful posture in the group's very name: "BEASTIE was an acronym for Boys Entering Anarchistic States Toward Internal Excellence." He clarified, "While the acronym alone made no sense, it made even less sense when combined with 'Boys.'" "Now the name was ridiculous *and* redundant," he added. With the song "(You Gotta) Fight for Your Right (to Party)," the Beastie Boys in 1986 offered up a mock party song. Though not everyone recognized the humor, accepting the song as a sincere asshat anthem, the song was meant to make fun of dirtbag boy-culture as well as cheesy music videos of the era. Their song "Cookie Puss" (1983) was another joke—prank calls loosely set to a beat. It was a send-up in part of Malcolm McLaren's song "Buffalo Gals" but also an ode to Carvel, the self-proclaimed "original neighborhood ice cream shoppe," which made a cake called Cookie Puss. Their last album, *Hot Sauce Committee Part Two*, was a more elaborate prank—every song was based on fake samples. Member Adam Horovitz wrote, in *Beastie Boys Book*, "It was meant to be a sort of record collector's unattainable nightmare. . . . We listed each fake sample in the liner notes and the artwork. Complete with fake song titles, band names, and fictitious record labels. Unfortunately, not only do people not study album art the way they used to, but big ideas are irrelevant in the pop music medium."

Much of Eminem's output has been earnest and sincere, but he similarly includes humor. He has said, "A lot of my rhymes are just to get chuckles out of people."[3] His revelatory "My Name Is," from *The Slim Shady LP* (1999), introduced Eminem and his race in a comedic take on rap norms. Musicologist Loren Kajikawa confirmed the effect: "Turning his racial identity into a humorous act, the single preempts possible criticism that he is white."[4]

And yet, this type of humor can also confirm stereotypes, especially when musicians and comedians play on assumptions around rap—its hardness but also its Blackness—assumptions that at the same time make the genre a particularly ripe comedic target. The Lonely Island, a comedy/rap group with former *SNL* player Andy Samberg as well as Akiva Schaffer and Jorma Taccone, is a great example. Responsible for YouTube's early hit "Lazy Sunday" (first an *SNL* short), the group takes on different aspects of rap's conventional practice for laughs. Yes, they are white, which already sets up a perceived humorous genre flip. But in the song "I'm on a Boat" (2009), they also riff on other trends, like bragging and the playing up of material wealth. In the accompanying video, they appear in formal wear and sunglasses, alongside T-Pain, earnestly rapping on repeat:

> I'm on a boat
> I'm on a boat
> Everybody look at me, 'cause I'm sailing on a boat

In another song ("Spell It Out"), they exaggerate the spelling of words in rap and, in "I Don't Give a Honk," the perceived repetitive, overuse of profanity. In another clip, they remix the rap battle as a compliment battle. After comparing his "cute" opponent to Garfield's cat-frenemy Nermal, Samberg drops the mic.

Other parody artists laid the groundwork for the Lonely Island—2 Live Jews (a play on 2 Live Crew) and, in particular,

"Weird Al" Yankovic, who famously upended Coolio's "Gangster's Paradise" ("Amish Paradise") as well as Chamillionaire's "Ridin'" ("White and Nerdy"). But the earliest may have been Mel Brooks, with his 1981 single "It's Good to Be the King," which made him the first white artist to land a rap song on the R&B charts. More recent acts—in nerdcore and on *SNL*—play on the same humorous incongruity, a mismatch between rap and white, rap and nerdy, even rap and Ruth Bader Ginsburg (the Notorious RBG). Wes Tank's rap rendering of Seuss classics over Dr. Dre beats belongs on this list as well. But this popular incongruity at the same time supports the expectation. The joke can become some sort of truth. Rap is supposed to be Black, and to many, a white rapper must be, well, funny. Writing for the *Stranger*, Sean Nelson in "Cock Mobster" (2002), confirms, "Few things are funnier on a basic level than white people rapping." He clarifies (kind of), "Not all white rappers are *just* funny, but all white rappers are funny sometimes."

White and Jewish, rapper Lil Dicky has struggled with this assumption. Kevin Hart produced his comedy series, *Dave* (which premiered in 2020), focused on Dave Burd, aka Lil Dicky, as he pursues rap as his destiny. The show's cocreator Jeff Schaffer, also an executive producer for *Curb Your Enthusiasm* and *Seinfeld*, in an interview for the *New York Times*, compared Burd to Larry David but also Don Quixote, "a rap Don Quixote tilting at the 'legitimacy' windmill." It's a basic comedic premise, playing on the supposed cultural roots of rap. But Lil Dicky himself also has real rap ambitions. At one point in his rap career, which first gained international attention in 2013 with the release of his single "Ex-Boyfriend," Lil Dicky admittedly viewed himself as a comedian first and foremost. And his music flips rap norms, much like the Lonely Island as well as Weird Al—for example, in his song "Save Dat Money," a song in praise of frugality. He has also complicated his whiteness by comically rapping about his Jewishness, much like 2 Live Jews in their "Jewish Flow," a rap battle featuring

Hitler. But now Lil Dicky views himself as a serious rapper as well. Of his music, he has said, "I wouldn't say it's comedy, I'd say it's rap music. I think it's misguided if you think it's comedy, I think I'm a rapper who's funny." Journalist Lucas Garrison isn't having it. In "I Have Some Serious Problems with Lil Dicky's Joke Raps, Seriously" (April 20, 2015), he writes, "He wants to be able to make people laugh, mock hip-hop and then be accepted and taken seriously by hip-hop . . . It doesn't work that way."

Lil Dicky's song "Freaky Friday" (2018) reflects the tension. Ordering at a Chinese restaurant in the song's video, Dicky sits with two friends, his hair a curly mop and, on his shirt, a picture of a polar bear. A fan recognizes him and excitedly explains to his girlfriend that Lil Dicky is a rapper. She responds, with obvious skepticism, "Oh, you're a rapper?" The fan helpfully clarifies, much to Dicky's chagrin, "Nah, he's not like a rapper rapper. He's a funny rapper." Lil Dicky sighs, but, thanks to the restaurant's ancient magic, he somehow finds a solution, a way to be cool and, though he doesn't say it, Black. He exchanges places with Chris Brown. Finally, he's Lil Dicky no more, if you know what I mean: "I woke up in Chris Brown's body." It was Freaky Friday. He raps, "I wonder if I can say the n-word," before gleefully running with the word to the discomfort and offense no doubt of scores of listeners.

The first episode of *Dave*, which debuted in March 2020, similarly skirts around the issue of race. Dave busts into Studio A but is promptly kicked out, along with his tuna sandwich, while Black rapper YG (Young Gangster) records. In the lobby, he considers how he might be taken seriously rather than dismissed as a "YouTube rapper." Instead of naming the issue of whiteness, he blames his YouTube stardom, though there is talk of his shirt's shade, peach, another color problem. The answer, Dave realizes, is to get a real rapper, like YG, to collaborate with him. Again, he doesn't explicitly acknowledge the value of YG's Blackness. His red-haired friend in the series comes closest to the issue when he calls Dave an "unemployed Jew who pretends to be a rapper." Lil Dicky's Jewishness makes his whiteness a bit messy, placing him in a conversation that includes other Jewish American comedian-musicians like Allan Sherman, musicians who had to negotiate their white and American identities.[5] But Dicky still plays on his white identity for laughs, calling attention to the issue while at the same time arguably confirming the stereotype.

The incongruity in the clash between serious perceptions of rap and race seems to work well in the creation of comedy—and it is obviously a popular strategy. But this tactic is certainly not rap's only connection to humor. Rappers also have become favorite targets for comedians, a stand-up link further cemented by Russell Simmons's *Def Comedy Jam*, a former favorite on HBO. Mike Birbiglia, for example, has some fun imagining Dr. Dre as a practicing doctor. Aziz Ansari has a great bit about rapper 50 Cent ordering grapefruit soda ("Why isn't this purple?" In the joke, 50 Cent has never seen a grapefruit and assumes he is requesting grape soda. You know, grape-fruit, apple-fruit, orange-fruit, Ansari explains.) And in his 2016 Netflix special *Make Happy*, Bo Burnham, a particularly musical comedian, takes on Kanye West and his grandiose autotuned ranting with a send-up of the gimmick. Burnham's own more mundane technologically enhanced complaining focuses on the size of the Pringles chip tube opening. A standout rap target in stand-up, however, is rapper Lil Wayne, a topic for Kat Williams, Chris Tucker, Jay Pharoah, and Dave Chappelle, among others, based at times on Lil Wayne's notorious musical references to the vagina. In 2018, Bianca Giuloione reported (in "How Often Does Lil Wayne Say the Word 'P*ssy' in His Entire Career?") that the rapper, across 1,009 songs, mentions the pussy 766 times. Chappelle ran with the lyrical truth, linking Lil Wayne's vaginal interest to the rapper's potential skill in identifying certain bodily secretions as a detective on the show *NCIS*. Then there's comedian and actor Donald Glover, who is a rapper himself, as Childish Gambino. He made waves in 2018 with his controversial song "This Is America," a disturbing rumination on violence and discrimination with a smile.

But the reality of rap is far more complicated than this discussion so far suggests. Humor is not just something that surrounds rap. Comedy has been an active element in rap throughout its history. In fact, rap has certain inherent connections to comedy—with a common focus on words and a simplicity in personnel (often just a performer and a mic). There's a history of cross-pollination between rap and comedy as well. Garrett highlights party rap, MC battles, and the role of tricksters and signifyin(g) in hip-hop culture more generally. As Elijah Wald makes clear in his book *The Dozens* (2012), there are also ties between rap and the dozens, a tradition of escalating insults, often directed at "your mama." The verbal duel can be funny but also vicious, a precursor to a physical fight. Like in rap, the verbal play is significant. But the humor is central as well—related to comedy skits, which were used to fill out early rap albums. In 1988, for example, King Tee included on his album a "bag-off seminar": "Your mother so fat she roll over a dollar and make four quarters." The dozens also plays out in rap's various modes of battle—the rap battle as well as diss songs in general. In both, there is insult. But with a laugh, handshake, or hug, even a particularly harsh jab can remain playful. Riffing on that humor, the YouTube channel Epic Rap Battles of History, written by Peter Shukoff and Lloyd Ahlquist, pits famous historical figures against each other in hilarious rap contests with educational value.[6]

In the 1980s, several rappers also helped define their music through humor. As Cheryl Keyes notes, this style was "softer (less street-edged)." She includes in this category Dana Dane, "The Comedian of Rap"; Doug E. Fresh, "The World's Greatest Entertainer"; and many rappers who followed, including Biz Markie, DJ Jazzy Jeff and the Fresh Prince, De La Soul, and Kid 'n Play.[7]

Slick Rick has claimed to be the first MC to integrate comedy, in his 1988 album *The Great Adventures of Slick Rick*. On the Power 106 morning show, Rick said, "I just ran with the humor stuff, like Eddie Murphy started rapping or something. So I went that route, and it caught on. People liked it; people loved it. It's like Redd Foxx, Richard Pryor-type [style] that turned into Hip-hop. Humor and rap mixed together [and] created its own lane" (as reported in 2019, by Jake Paine, at ambrosiaforheads.com). Vognar describes Rick as "among hip hop's first master storytellers," with comedy as part of the narrative. In "Children's Story," for example, Rick offers a lesson about avoiding crime with comic detail: "Dave the dopehead shooting dope / Who don't know the meaning of water nor soap."

Marcel "Biz Markie" Hall was also known for his comedic skill in music, video, and dress, including his colonial-style clothing and wig. Critics Havelock Nelson and Michael A. Gonzales defined him much as Rick defined himself: he's "more than a rapper, [he] can be placed in the context of black comedians from Red Foxx to Richard Pryor."[8] In "Remembering the 'Clown Prince of Hip-Hop' Biz Markie" (July 17, 2021), NPR host Andrew Limbong recalls his early reputation as "a goofball rapper" with the song "Pickin' Boogers": "So go up your nose with a finger or two and pull out one or a crusty crew." After he lost a court case for sampling without permission, he humorously titled his fourth album *All Samples Cleared!* (1993). And even his big hit "Just a Friend" (1989) was light and fun, with a self-deprecating edge as his quest for love ends in defeat.

Women in rap have deployed humor as well, with sex as a predominant theme, according to Gail Hilson Woldu in "'Don't I Look Like a Halle Berry Poster?' Humor and Irony in Women's Hip Hop."[9] Missy Elliott, voted class clown in high school, is a legend in this regard. In her 1997 video "The Rain," Elliott smiles at the camera, appearing at times in a huge, black plastic bag. She recalled, in an interview for *Elle* (2017), "I loved the idea of feeling like a hip-hop Michelin woman." In her song "Work It" (2002), she narrates her racy scene with routine beauty maintenance and a suggestive elephant noise covering for any explicit phallic mention:

> Not on the bed, lay me on your sofa
> Call before you come, I need to shave my chocha

In this way, she also flips rap's gender norms, replacing a focus on a man's sexual prowess with her own.

—⁂—

Killer Mike belongs to this history as well. And his comedic voice has a unique position in rap, one that involves cats and, in *Trigger Warning*, sleeping on a park bench for a good cause. Born Michael Render in Atlanta, Georgia, in 1975, he made his first high-profile appearances on "Trappin'" and "Snappin'" on OutKast's 2000 album *Stankonia* and on "The Whole World," a single from OutKast's album *Big Boi and Dr Dre Present . . . OutKast*. Following the success of his 2007 album *I Pledge Allegiance to the Grind*, Mike teamed up with El-P, who produced his 2012 album *R.A.P. Music*. A year later the two formed the supergroup Run the Jewels, known for powerful, relentless tracks, often devoted to political activism. Their second album, *Run the Jewels 2*, was released in November 2014. A month before, El-P and the group's producer were considering various preorder packages. Some were traditional (a signed poster), others just plain silly, like the promise of *Meow the Jewels* for $40,000—a remix made of "nothing but cat sounds for music." El-P told Eric Renner Brown, writing for *Entertainment Weekly* (2015), "It was a joke, 100 percent, which I thought was pretty funny at the time, being as stoned as I was at my kitchen table." A Kickstarter campaign followed, launched by music blogger Sly Jones. When *Vice* contacted Killer Mike at the time, he said, "I can't believe those crazy fucking bastards are doing it. If they actually pull it off, we're going to actually do it. I'm overwhelmed by it. On one front, it's wild and silly. On another front, it shows the power of independence." The campaign more than met its goal, and a joke would become reality. El-P, for one, was surprised: "As a guy who grew up with cats all his life . . . I'll put it this way, I underestimated the power of the cat on the Internet."[10] But the album would also have a charitable goal, with proceeds benefiting the families of Eric Garner and Mike Brown. El-P maintains, "Cats are infinitely amusing, don't get me wrong. The truth of the matter is that I wouldn't be wasting my time putting out a remix album with cat sounds if there wasn't money going to victims of police brutality." To Eric Renner Brown, he said, "We figured, hey, f***, let's fight injustice with pure, annoying stupidity."

The mechanics of turning an award-winning album into the world's first cat-rap album were nonetheless daunting, though El-P especially enjoyed explaining to Mike the cat-plan: "Mike is not a cat guy," El-P told Brown. Killer Mike clarified, "Being a black guy from the south, cats are kind of necessity only . . . You don't have a rat problem, you don't have a cat." But El-P and Killer Mike had allies. And many fans and artists reached out, including famous cat Lil BUB's owner, Mike Bridavsky. In fact, cat noises came from everywhere, with cat lovers submitting feline sounds to the duo for their album use. Some other less furry collaborators included talented producers, like Just Blaze and Alchemist. In an interview with Dee Lockett, Mike commented, "Well I prayed to God to one day work with Just Blaze; I didn't know God would deliver the prayer like this though. I say thank you God, but I also say you're a sneaky bastard, God." "He answered your meows," El-P supplied.

In a Mass Appeal clip, El-P playfully recruits cats for the album, playing some Run the Jewels music to kitties at Brooklyn's Bark animal shelter. A nearby dog growls, and El-P tells the canine that that's exactly why "this record is not called Bark the Jewels." But the cats are difficult too, showing him their feline backsides and ignoring his attempts to get their attention. With the melancholy theme from the movie *Love Story* playing in the background, El-P reflects on the challenges posed by working with cats. A joke he never expected to catch on is the cause of his new mock-somber reality.

But, really, El-P should have known. Of course the gimmick worked. Cats are not necessarily central to rap, though quite a few rappers use animal references in their stage names: Snoop Dog/Snoop Lion, Tyga, Nate Dogg, Bow Wow, and Pitbull, among others. There is also the phenomenon of Rap Cat—put simply, a cat who raps. But Rap Cat's popularity points to the main factor that made *Meow the Jewels* inevitable: not cats in rap but cats in cyberspace. Cats are an internet sensation. They are kings of the online jungle. As such, they were sure to up the success of any internet campaign, musical or otherwise.

Cats have a long history in art pre-internet. Cats were celebrated as divine and vilified as demons, associated with sorcery and witches in particular. Flemish and Dutch painters depicted the feline's predatory ways, often as a painting's humorous side story. Whether elegant or menacing, the cat was then a source of endless artistic fascination.[11] But cat sites surged alongside the debut of YouTube in 2006. According to "The Hilarious History of Cat Memes," "In 2007, LOLcats released the infamous site, I Can Has Cheezburger, and let's just say the rest is hiss-tory." In 2015, the Museum of the Moving Image in New York City dedicated an exhibit to the cat's place in online culture: "How Cats Took Over the Internet." Their online success, according to Amanda Petrusich in "Cats Meet Hip-Hop," may be a form of revenge, payback for a cat's indifference or, at best, fickle affection: "If you do not love us back, we will band together and humiliate you using our computers." But the internet may also be a safe space for celebration of the cat, kitty ownership being a point of shame for some, seen as a sign of a sad, solitary spinsterhood. And cats are uniquely internet-friendly, Abigail Tucker writes in an opinion piece for the *New York Times* (2017), with their quick moves perfect for short online clips.

Whether you like them or not, cats are undeniably funny as well. They can be unpredictable, suddenly pouncing from on high. They can be surprisingly aloof, even though they are dependent on people for food and housing, even a clean litter box. There is a humorous incongruity in their very way of life: I need you but hate you; I'm balloon-sized small but won't take your guff. I could go on. *Meow the Jewels* was the perfect storm of a popular rap group and the cat's hilarious star status in visual culture, online and not. In coming together, the album fulfilled philosopher Albert Schweitzer's oft-cited pronouncement: "There are two means of refuge from the miseries of life: music and cats." For Run the Jewels, there was also a greater message. El-P confirmed, "The bigger idea behind it is that we can all, with our own humor and our own community and our own culture, come up with weird and interesting ways to do good things for other people. If it takes some inside joke to make it happen, then I'm all for it."[12]

In *Meow the Jewels*, humor was comedy plus: comedy plus politics, comedy plus activism, but, still, comedy as art. Listening to "Close Your Eyes and Meow to Fluff," I'm struck by the power of certain passages: "run them fast," firing at high speed between digitized meows; "we out of order, you out of order," with a high-pitched meow. Rather than silly, the song is intense, moving, meowing. One cat cry descends in pitch, thanks to electronic manipulation, and the gravity of the lyrics comes into focus with the same fight for equality as in the original album. That fight is symbolized on the original album cover with two bandaged hands, one holding a necklace. The *Meow the Jewels* cover replaces the hands with paws, one holding a collar, but the bandages are still there. The album is undeniably ridiculous, musically and otherwise, but it is still affecting and impressive artistically, though El-P might not agree. To *Deadspin*, El-P said, "I would never even insult the world by saying [the album is] 'good.'" "But," he admitted, "it's certainly the high-water mark for cat-sound records, I think."

In interviews regarding *Meow the Jewels*, El-P emerges as funny. And, with assumptions around rap and comedy in rap, it might be easy to assume the white guy is the funny one, as Mark Beaumont did, writing in 2017 for the *Guardian*: "Mike is the old-school master, hyper-rapping boastful verses laced with jabs at societal ills; El-P is his comic foil, with hints of the Beastie Boys' puerile juvenilia." But Killer Mike is funny too. He's hugely likable in interviews, with a big grin and an easy laugh. As a guest on Stephen Colbert's show, he addressed his attire, formal sweats. This, he said, is my "PTA meeting outfit" (he has four kids). On Adult Swim, he offered advice on "things to avoid," including death, churches with air-conditioning, and clowns, unless they're riding the back of a bull. And in my favorite bit, also on Adult Swim, he appears on the *Eric Andre Show*, season 1, episode 5, with singer Lisa Stanley as she sings Gioachino Rossini's aria "Una voce poco fa" from *The Barber of Seville*. The "blewish" (Black and Jewish) Andre, who is funny and musical himself—a trained double bass player—introduces Killer Mike as Stanley's hype man, and as she sings, in Wagnerian garb, he rhythmically interjects with lines like, "We singing opera, ho."

Addressing his solo project *Trigger Warning*, the *Guardian* in 2019 calls Mike the "satirist for our time." Like *Meow the Jewels*, the show is a mix of humor and activism, art with a point of view. On the show, Mike puts into effect his most outlandish ideas—his "most absurd thoughts and arguments," as he tells Stephen Colbert, all meant to combat inequality and uplift the Black community. The results can be funny, involving a slew of interesting characters, but always with a poignant takeaway. In the first episode, he attempts to "live Black" for three days, buying goods that support only Black-owned businesses. Unfortunately, he experiences "white economy withdrawal," he explains, especially when he can't find a Black-made can opener to open his "black beans" or a Black-owned hotel, which forces him to sleep on a park bench for the night. When he meets up with El-P, he's beyond hungry, and El-P doesn't help when the two go out to a BBQ joint. With a pile of food in front of him, Mike finds out that the restaurant is Black-owned but the food source is not. He solemnly asks for a to-go box. El-P insists on detailing just how delicious the meal is as Mike looks on, the perfect deadpan. Poor Killer Mike can't even smoke weed. Though the dealers are Black, the suppliers are white, he tells El-P. El-P concludes, white people are "an unstoppable force." "That's what all the books say," Mike responds. The two have an easy rapport and obvious friendship, and both are hilarious while making a real point.

In the second episode, Mike hopes to find a way to help the Black community address its woeful rates of unemployment. First, he speaks to a group of first-grade students, hoping to facilitate future job market success by adjusting their expectations. His message, playfully delivered: forget your dreams and look for a vocation. But children, he decides with a principal's push, have some right to think big. He then sets his sights on adults, creating porn videos that teach vocational skills. In the third episode, Mike tries to help a gang monetize their brand with Crip-a-Cola. It's only fair, though, that he lets the rival Bloods in on the effort. The response, from one gang member: "Is it vegan?" In *Trigger Warning*, Killer Mike is an advocate for change while showcasing the individuality of people often singularly labeled. Yes, the Bloods member is in a gang, but he's also a unique person who avoids meat products. We are not one label. We are, all of us, more, Mike included—rapper, activist, and, for our purposes, funny.

—⁂—

Like rap itself, formed by voice upon voice, track upon track, there are different layers of comedy in rap—from Weird Al to Biz Markey. And rap's norms and verbal play offer more than enough comedic space for all. As Vognar argues, "Hip-hop is an art form with deep cultural lineage—an art form whose mastery and innovation of comic forms deserves to be taken seriously." Particular perceptions make rap an easy comedic mark. But comedic rap can harden those perceptions. They become rigid and unyielding, even in the face of contradictory evidence, evidence that has existed all along. Some may assume white rappers are funny, no matter their intention. And the idea that comedy in rap is white may mask rap's full comedic range and history. Some may then overlook the humor of Killer Mike, a serious and much-lauded rapper, who can be seriously funny too, like rap in general.

That misunderstanding can have practical fallout at court in the use of rap lyrics as supposed evidence of crime. The prosecution has in many cases introduced lyrics as a literal text or confession. In this way, courts sideline not only the music of rap and its commercial context but also the humor in rap. Rapper Snoop Dogg, for example, released the song "Murder Was the Case" on his 1993 album *Doggystyle*. When Snoop was charged with the murder of Philip Woldemariam, an attorney played off the song to make his case: "Murder is the crime they committed. Murder is the crime they committed." But *Doggystyle* itself had a comedic side, announced up front in the album art, a cartoon depicting stylized dogs involved in illegal and illicit activity. It was "grown-up comedy," as Russel Simmons calls much of gangsta rap. Admitting that truth and rap's history of humor should in no way function as a hit on rap's significance. Cat or no cat, it's part of the art form's versatility, power, and creative inventiveness. The courts may treat rap as a literal text, but rap is more complicated than that. Rap is more *comical* than that.

NOTES

1. The topic has also been a focus of mine. See Lily E. Hirsch, *Music in American Crime Prevention and Punishment* (Ann Arbor: University of Michigan Press, 2012).

2. See, for example, Cheryl L. Keyes, *Rap Music and Street Consciousness* (Urbana: University of Illinois Press, 2002), 2.

3. Quoted in David Caplan, "Hip Hop's Sophisticated Comedy," in *The Routledge Companion to Popular Music and Humor*, ed. Thomas M. Kitts and Nick Baxter-Moore (New York: Routledge, 2019), 92.

4. Loren Kajikawa, "Eminem's 'My Name Is': Signifying Whiteness, Rearticulating Race," *Journal of the Society for American Music* 3, no. 3 (2009): 348.

5. Zeke Levine, "*Lil Dicky Katz*: The Evolution of Jewish American Comedic Music" (paper presented at the National Meeting of the American Musicological Society, Boston, MA, November 2, 2019).

6. The nineteenth-century minstrel tradition, fundamentally racist, has its own echoes in rap. Though commonly remembered as white people donning blackface to get a laugh, reveling in a liberation from social norms at the cruel expense of an entire race, some Black performers joined in too—with verbal dexterity and improv as well as caricature and stereotype. Yuval Taylor and Jake Austen, *Darkest America: Black Minstrelsy from Slavery to Hip-Hop* (New York: W. W. Norton, 2012), 7.

7. Keyes, *Rap Music*, 81.

8. Quoted in Keyes, 82.

9. See Gail Hilson Woldu, "'Don't I Look Like a Halle Berry Poster?' Humor and Irony in Women's Hip Hop," in *The Routledge Companion to Popular Music and Humor*, ed. Thomas M. Kitts and Nick Baxter-Moore (New York: Routledge, 2019), 342.

10. Interview in Ted Simmons, "Run the Jewels' El-P Talks Making of Cat-Sampling 'Meow the Jewels' Charity Album and More," *Billboard*, September 26, 2015.

11. Caroline Bugler, *The Cat: 3,500 Years of the Cat in Art* (London: Merrell, 2011).

12. Interview in Phillip Mlynar, "We Chat with Cat Rapper El-P about 'Meow the Jewels,' a Crowd-Sourced Prank," *Catster*, February 17, 2016.

SEVEN

BANTER, BANJO, AND BUMPKINS

COUNTRY MUSIC DEFIES ITS OWN very different stereotypes in comedy—like the idea that country is the music of dimwitted rednecks. In the enduring country and comedy group Riders in the Sky, country music is anything but. The group, officially performing since 1977, boasts Douglas B. Green, or Ranger Doug, a singer and guitarist with a master's degree in literature from Vanderbilt; Paul Chrisman, or Woody Paul, "King of the Cowboy Fiddlers," with a PhD in theoretical plasma physics from MIT; Joseph Miskulin, or "Joey the CowPolka King," on accordion; and Fred LaBour, or Too Slim, the group's double bass player, with a degree in wildlife management from the University of Michigan. In a 2008 article for *True West*, LaBour explained, "In a terribly over-educated musical group, I'm the only one currently using his degree." After all, he clarified, "A Bachelors Degree in Wildlife Management has given me insight into the nocturnal behavior, migration patterns and mating rituals of the fiddle player."

Within the group, LaBour is a comedic star. And his wit garnered attention early. In fact, in 1969, as a student at the University of Michigan, LaBour published a satirical article in the student newspaper alleging that the Beatles' Paul McCartney was dead. The theory was that McCartney had died in a car crash but had been replaced in the group by a faux Paul, Billy Shears. LaBour offered purported proof under the headline "McCartney Dead: New Evidence Brought to Light," which highlighted a badge on McCartney's shoulder on the album cover of *Sgt. Pepper's Lonely Hearts Club Band*. "OPD," LaBour claimed it said, "officially pronounced dead." He also noted the word *walrus* in Beatles song titles and lyrics, which he claimed was Greek for "corpse." It didn't matter that the badge actually reads "OPP" and *walrus* isn't even Greek. The story caught on. McCartney himself responded to the rumors in 1969, telling *Life* magazine, "I'm not going to spoil their fantasy."

In 2015, Neal Rubin wrote about LaBour's prank in the *Detroit News*, with the title "Paul McCartney Still Isn't Dead. Neither Is the Story." In Rubin's piece, LaBour revealed that he has gotten asked about the story for years, even a phone call decades after his initial publication from a man claiming he had new evidence to support the tale. LaBour told the man, as gently as he could, "I wrote that story to make fun of people like you." In the *True West* article, he further explained that, with the article, he "wanted to poke fun at over-zealous critics who try to find endless meaning in every nuance of an art project." And with that, LaBour realizes, "I'm a footnote of a footnote of a footnote in Fab Four history."

In Riders in the Sky performances, LaBour's humor is a regular part of the show, especially in the group's hilarious on-stage banter. To find out more about the considerable history of comedy in country music, how comedy critically comments on country traditions, and the related practice of comedic stage banter, I reached out to Riders in the Sky and was lucky enough to interview LaBour himself. I was happy to learn that he had given comedy in country music "many hours of contemplation" and was willing to share his thoughts. On July 18, 2019, he responded to my many questions with wit and color, what I quickly learned was his typical style. I knew I was in for something remarkable as soon as he started: "Young men in hazmat suits are currently

Riders in the Sky on *Austin City Limits* (1987), screenshot from YouTube.

under my house spraying for fungus and mold, so, as the temperature climbs here in my office because the AC must remain off, it seems like the perfect time to consider the restorative gifts of comedy, music, and theater." I couldn't agree more.

Country music has a rich history of comedy—one that often plays with genre assumptions. Clever men, for example, perform as fools for laughs. Early hillbilly bands featured humorous skits, related in part to the minstrel show format, and blackface was a regular part of the performance. Examples abound in performances by the Skillet Lickers, an old-time string band that formed in 1926, with recordings like "A Corn Licker Still in Georgia." Don Cusic, in "Comedy and Humor in Country Music" (1993), also recognizes the influence of vaudeville on funny country song, especially the work of Uncle Dave Macon, one of the first big stars of the *Grand Ole Opry*, the Nashville-based radio program that began in 1925. The show's start was marked early by its distance from so-called serious music. When the announcer introduced Deford Bailey, a Black harmonica player, he said, "For the past hour we have listened to music largely from Grand Opera, but from now on, we will present the *Grand Ole Opry!*"[1]

LaBour told me, "Country music owes a huge debt to vaudeville and minstrel show traditions, and comedy has always been central to what folks think of as 'a good show.' Country entertainers who can tell a joke stay employed long after they're no longer being played on the radio." Early on, the humor was broad and sometimes racist, with performers playing up country stereotypes in portrayals of Black men or backcountry rubes—characters who still managed to get the better of city folk. As blackface thankfully fell out of favor, country music still cultivated controversial dress, with musicians (often bass players) cross-dressing or simply donning loud, colorful outfits of various types. In the mix, there were also successful women, like Minnie Pearl, a standout in appearance by virtue of her gender.

Born Sarah Ophelia Colley, she joined the Opry in 1940 with her impression of a mountain girl, Minnie Pearl. With her trademark greeting—"Howdee! I'm just so proud to be here!"—she won over audiences and quickly became one of the most beloved comedians in country music's history. Pearl had initially hoped to be a dramatic actress, but, in her opinion, her looks in part made her better suited to comedy. As quoted in Kristine Fredriksson's 2000 article "Minnie Pearl and Southern Humor in Country Entertainment," Pearl recalled, "I knew I could never be the beautiful lady leaning over the balcony tossing her scarf to the handsome knight passing below on his magnificent steed." As Minnie Pearl, she riffed on some of the challenges of being less than the accepted version of beautiful, reporting to her audiences the latest gossip in fictional Grinder's Switch, Tennessee, including her adventures "ketchin' a feller." To be clear, she was "single but willing."

Not everyone enjoyed the fun. From the beginning, there were critics of humorous country-music acts who spread the idea that country music was demeaning to the Opry's Nashville home. Nashville, after all, was the "Athens of the South," a nod in nickname to the city's early focus on education and eventually its replica of the Parthenon, built in 1897. In her book on country music, *The Selling Sound* (2007), Diana Pecknold points out that commerce too played a role in the snubbing of country music. Critics and businessmen involved in other areas of music, Tin Pan Alley and the like, criticized hillbilly music in part to safeguard their own earning power. Pecknold writes, "The publishers and labor leaders of the music industries enlisted a set of cultural meanings already circulating around the idea of the 'hillbilly' to bolster their economic prerogatives." Thankfully, the supposed import of music as art just wasn't important to most audiences. As Pearl writes in her autobiography, there was a saying at the Opry: "Nobody likes us but the people."

LaBour cites Pearl as an early inspiration, telling Cusic, "The first time I heard the *Grand Ole Opry* I was listening to WSM and heard Minnie Pearl say 'How-deee,' and the way the audience responded was just magic to me. It was a thrilling moment—the hair stood up on my neck. I heard her comic routine, and it just blew me away. She was certainly one of my earliest influences." He also brought up Pearl in our exchange, declaring, "Let us now praise Minnie Pearl, Queen of Country Comedy, and her foil Rod Brasfield." Brasfield formed a double act with Pearl in 1948, "double comedy" in Pearl's wording, defined by both players' doling out punchlines, no straight man. But Pearl did appear with the occasional straight man, like Roy Acuff, country musician and fellow Opry star. LaBour told me, "I was fortunate enough to know Minnie and work with her. A prized memory is when Riders and Minnie appeared at a local children's hospital. I jumped into her act and played the straight man—a la Roy Acuff—doing a bunch of her classic bits. It was heaven, especially when she smiled that knowing, saucy smile. A great, really funny lady."

By the 1960s, country comedy wasn't cordoned off in skits or specific characters. Some country artists included humorous songs in addition to their more "serious" fare. Gene Autry, for example, sang the novelty songs "Rudolph the Red-Nosed Reindeer" and "Peter Cottontail." And Roy Rogers made a splash with "The Ballad of Pecos Bill," chronicling the exploits of Bill, "the roughest, toughest critter, never known to be a quitter." But country music's comedic history of skits and costumes continued in the television variety show *Hee Haw*, the country version of *Laugh-In*, which featured funny sketches and country music and was created by Canadians John Aylesworth and Frank Peppiatt. In *The Corn Was Green: The Inside Story of Hee Haw* (2010), Aylesworth recalls the reaction among his show-biz pals to the show's premiere: "As our once admiring coterie gaped in shocked disbelief at our braying donkey, our chorus line of pigs prancing across the TV screen, and all those bucolic bumpkins uttering rustic wheezes from a cornfield, it became apparent that we were to become pariahs among our peers forevermore." Again, critics found the country comedy "degrading," but viewers tuned in, and the show hit its mark, with an impressive run from 1969 to 1992.

Today, some suspect that country music's comedic tradition is at a turning point. In his book *Country Music: Humorists and Comedians* (2008), Loyal Jones claims there is a contemporary decline in humor within country music. Audiences, the author maintains, now see a separation between funny or corny country music and serious or "authentic" country music, music to value. But there are still musicians and comedians having fun with country music in new ways, like country star Dierks Bentley with his '90s-inspired parody band Hot Country Knights. And sometimes these newer country comedy acts get a laugh while making an argument too.

Others find humor in riffing on country and perceptions of the genre. Just as he takes on rap in *Make Happy*, Bo Burnham manages to take a jab at country music in this way. He imitates a supposed famous country star as he pretends to know and love staples of the country genre, like dirt and ranching. As Burnham points out, such a wealthy star is surely pandering to his audience, aware of genre norms. Comedy duo Key and Peele, Keegan-Michael Key and Jordan Peele, have a different focus in the hilarious YouTube clip "Country Music," from 2012. In it, they play two new friends, both thankful to have another Black guy around. Key, in character, shares with his new friend his love of country music, explaining to the somewhat surprised Peele that he's from Texas. He then plays an obviously racist lick about a "good old American boy" who wants to keep his lady love safe from "the homies." When Peele insists the song is racist, Key says, "You hear the twang then you assume that it's racist." And Key has a partial case. The southern accent in and associated with country music certainly dredges up the Confederate past as well as current incidents of racism in good ol' Dixie. Maybe it's just that connection, not the music, Key seems to suggest. But then Key launches into the most racist example yet (composed for the sketch), singing about a hanging. Peele has had it and leaves. Left alone, it takes Key's character a moment to realize the song isn't about a tire swing. It's a funny moment that forces you to think about country music's real history of racism. Though country's whiteness is in fact somewhat complicated,[2] country music does wrestle with a racist past, including its connection to blackface and prejudice in past lyrics. In "I'm a White Boy" (1977), for example, Bakersfield's own Merle Haggard sang, "I ain't black and I ain't yella / Just a white boy lookin' for a place to do my thing." Like some comedy in rap, the perception of race, based in part on reality, can become the basis for humor in country music.

A similar humor is somewhat buried in Lil Nas X's 2019 hit "Old Town Road," which is both country and hip hop. But the song, like Key and Peele's sketch, also arguably plays on a perceived mismatch between country music and Black culture. To many, the mash-up is fun. But others have looked at the song in a different way, actively excluding it from country music. In a statement to *Rolling Stone*, *Billboard* explained its decision to remove the song from its country charts: "While 'Old Town Road' incorporates references to country and cowboy imagery, it does not embrace enough elements of today's country music to chart in its current version."[3]

In contrast, Cledus T. Judd, the comedic persona of radio personality Barry Pool, is apparently all country (racism included), at least until his retirement in 2015. In his humorous songs, he, as "country's court jester," takes on stereotypical assumptions around country music but also supports them, stretching country music's racist past into the present. In his song "Hip Hop and Honky Tonk," he claims to bring two genres together—country music and rap—singing about a couple from these two different musical backgrounds. The man is a country music fan, and the woman is from "da hood": "She sure looks good, and she thinks rap is great," he sings. Together, they attend "throwdowns" and "hoedowns." As John Thomerson argues in his writing on parody, Judd makes it clear in other songs that he, in contrast, does not think "rap is great." In "Martie, Emily and Natalie (The Continuing Saga Of)," a parody of Brad Paisley's "Celebrity," Judd paints rap as antithetical to the Americanness of country music. In the song, he attacks the Dixie Chicks (now the Chicks) as traitors, addressing member Natalie Maines's once controversial stand against the Iraq War. To make clear the depth of the group's treachery, he insists they will appear on *Soul Train* and tour with rapper Eminem.[4] Comedy does not always work toward useful or righteous ends, especially when it plays with racial perceptions of genre, as in this example.

—⚍—

Riders in the Sky, in contrast, belongs to the best examples of funny music—constructive, not destructive. The group seeks to keep the old, funny tradition in country music alive, minus the racism. They also promote a rich repertoire of cowboy songs, which depend on romanticized visions of the western cowboy, part of early film history. On their website, Riders in the Sky is billed as a classical cowboy quartet, "keepers of the flame passed on by the Sons of the Pioneers, Gene Autry and Roy Rogers"— the former a group that came together in the early 1930s with standout performer Roy Rogers. But some view the homage as parody.

To me, LaBour clarified, "There's certainly an element of parody, especially of the timeworn characterizations and tropes of what we think of as cowboy entertainment. We were described by one critic as 'Gene Autry meets Monty Python,' and there's some truth there. But I think we also hold a fundamental belief in the value of what we do . . . keeping alive this beautiful musical tradition and bringing it to new generations . . . showing by our very existence that you can, in fact, do what you want to do, and if you do it cleverly enough, and work hard enough, you can actually make a living at it."

Riders in the Sky first performed as a group on November 11, 1977, at Herr Harry's Phranks 'n' Steins in Nashville. While a musical tradition was the shared focus, comedy came naturally to the band. In a book about the group called *It's the Cowboy Way!* Don Cusic writes, "The evening was more than just music—there was a camaraderie on stage. . . . And the repartee . . . flew like sparks through the air, igniting snappy one-liners." Green recalls, "We were on stage just trying to crack each other up." In the book, LaBour adds, "We did a pretty good job of that. And the audience kept laughing too!" The night after that first performance, LaBour called Green, still laughing: "I don't know what happened back there, but America will pay to see it."

In *True West*, LaBour explained how he got his nickname, one he maintains in the group to this day: While on tour in the late 1970s, "the soup was extremely thin, and I got down to the 120s, weight-wise. People would say, 'You're slim. Too slim.' Since then, of course, the soup has thickened considerably, and I've evolved into 'Just Right.'"

During the early years of their act, the group attempted to showcase their musical humor at comedy clubs, but the venues didn't work as well as the musical stage. Green told Cusic, "The comedy clubs never really worked. I think we geared our act more towards comedy at those places, but our show sort of depends on that tension between a serious song setting up the comedy." Eventually, in 1988, they experimented with a new means of broadcasting their brand of comedy and music—radio, with *Riders Radio Theater* (1988–1996)—and, from 1991 to 1992, Riders in the Sky appeared on television as a replacement for *Pee-wee's Playhouse*. In *Singing in the Saddle*, Green describes the show as "a surrealistic half-hour filled with cliffhanger adventures and a broad cast of stock characters" as well as two songs per episode.

Though long successful, Riders in the Sky saw their star power intensify tremendously when they joined the *Toy Story* franchise. For the movie *Toy Story 2*, released in 1999, they recorded the songs "Woody's Roundup," "Jessie, the Yodeling Cowgirl," and "You've Got a Friend in Me," among others. Their tie-in album *Woody's Roundup Featuring Riders in the Sky* came out in August 2000 and led to their appearance at the Grammy Awards in February 2001. When they won for the album, Green told the audience, "As Gene Autry often said, 'I don't think I deserve this award, but I've got tendonitis and I don't feel like I deserve that either.'"

In an appearance shortly after attending the 2001 Grammys, Green described waiting backstage with big-name celebrities like Taylor Swift, Lady Gaga, and Eminem, who was one of the night's big winners. Paul interjected, "We were the only ones there I didn't know." LaBour jumped in, breaking into a rap he supposedly delivered to Eminem that night—one in which LaBour insists he is in fact "the real Too Slim Shady." It was the start of a new type of music for LaBour, he told the audience, a combination of cowboy music and rap. "What do you call it?" asked Green. LaBour's punchline: "Crap."

This sort of banter has been a hallmark of their shows. At performance number 6,316 (the group takes meticulous count), LaBour wore his signature tie, in the shape of a cactus—a "cac-tie," he jokes—and Green introduced him, maintaining that he was "aging like fine cheese." (Green, sometimes straight man and sometimes funny outright, claimed in his introduction that Paul was starring in the film *Oh Brother Where Am I*, a play on the movie title *O Brother, Where Art Thou?*)

In our interview, I asked LaBour about the creation of his group's banter, fundamental to their humor. He confirmed that the group's funny banter had honest origins: "It turned out we had a natural comedy chemistry—particularly between Ranger Doug and myself. Many of our onstage bits originated as improvised lines in response to something that someone else said, or something that happened in the audience, or something reflecting the news of the day. We've always been aware that when something off-the-cuff works, it stays in the act. Perhaps refined, edited, or recast, but I guarantee if it killed once, it's coming back. The reason is simple: it's hard to create original comedy, and the best way to do it is in collaboration with an audience of like-minded folks."

LaBour has especially enjoyed successful moments of on-stage improv. He told me, "The most satisfying moments onstage for me come when I improv an original line in response to an unexpected turn in the proceedings . . . a line timed perfectly, succinct, rich with left-field wisdom, and funny as all hell in an interesting way. It doesn't happen every night, but it happens enough to keep me in the game."

One of the group's best bits, oft-requested, is "And It's a . . . a . . . a . . . a Circus Train!" LaBour explained to me, "It's a bit I consciously crafted in the style of the Smothers Brothers, taking a simple situation and taking it in a surreal, hopelessly over-the-top direction, much to the displeasure of the stolid and straight Ranger Doug." Tom and Dick Smothers, two brothers who were known in the 1960s for their hilarious versions of folk songs as well as their popular show *The Smothers Brothers Comedy Hour*, colored their performance with such banter. As Dick attempted to introduce the tune with appropriate history or related information, Tom would often hijack the moment, interrupting his brother with irreverent and often absurdly meandering digressions. In a YouTube clip from a September 2013 concert in Seattle, we see Too Slim's own surreal detour, a circus train run amuck. During the group's performance of the song "Cattle Call," LaBour says, "No one sings that like you, Ranger Doug." Green responds, deadpan, "I know." Within a chorus of oohs, LaBour breaks out with a noise akin to a duck call. The sound roughly follows the oohs' pattern but is jarring in tone and volume. Green stops, admonishing LaBour: "We're trying to paint a portrait of the Old West in song over here." "I'm adding to the portrait," LaBour quips. Green insists, "You're destroying the portrait," "bawling like a sick cat." "There's a sick cat in the portrait," LaBour shoots back. LaBour then breaks into a mix of cat sounds, bringing to life a feline trying to find its mother as well as other animals, their noise provided by fiddler Paul. Much to Green's relief, LaBour eventually grows quiet, noting the "silent purple hills." "At last," Green says, attempting to resume his original portrait. But suddenly, from the hills, LaBour announces the appearance of a circus train, complete with a host of new animal sounds, elephant included. Green walks away, defeated.

—⚞—

The group's on-stage talk builds on country music's tradition of comedy and banter as well as the role of banter in live performance more generally, something Aimee Mann played with through her inclusion of Patton Oswalt. Standard on-stage lines include a shout-out to the site of performance—"We love you,

Houston!"—but in a compilation of some of the top banter in the music biz, "More Talk, Less Rock" (2007), the *A.V. Club* singles out David Lee Roth, lead singer of Van Halen: "The only people who put iced tea in Jack Daniel's bottles is The Clash, baby!" There have actually been whole albums devoted to this aspect of live performance, like *Having Fun with Elvis on Stage* (1974), a spoken-word compilation of Presley's between-song talk, the songs all cut.

Bluegrass, a related country genre, has a particular reputation for funny on-stage banter. In some ways, the genre's between-song gags and jokey one-liners are a continuation of the music's own comedic history, including colorful hillbilly characters and a comedic player (often the bass player, dobroist, or rhythm guitarist), as in Flatt and Scruggs, founded by guitarist Lester Flatt and legendary banjo player Earl Scruggs in 1948.[5]

In an online discussion of stage banter, hosted by mandolincafe.com, some of the participants' favorite bluegrass bits revolve around tuning issues. Musician Mike Edgerton offered, "If I can't get the mandolin in tune I'll usually make a comment about the word mandolin being Italian for out of tune." "That was an ancient Chinese melody," another discussion participant, Tavy, says while tuning. Both jokes have practical purpose—the entertainment continues during necessary points of adjustment, such as tuning or even string replacement. Edgerton also enjoys a regular laugh in the announcement of his act, instructing the MC to introduce him as "Mr. Mike Edgerton who by the age of 20 had his first top 10 pop song on the charts!" When he gets to the microphone, Edgerton clarifies, "I just need to correct that a bit, I wasn't 20, I was 25, and it wasn't in the top 10, it was in the top 100, and it wasn't on the pop charts it was on the country charts, and it wasn't me it was my brother." Introductions like this one are a favorite comedic premise, one exploited by legendary comedian and banjo player Steve Martin, a recurrent host of *Saturday Night Live* and former writer for *The Smothers Brothers Comedy Hour*.

On stage, with his bluegrass quintet Steep Canyon Rangers, he says, "Now I'd like to take a minute to recognize the band." He then turns to each player, looking at them in turn, never uttering a word.

Many of these jokes have been recycled, with lines inspired by another artist or even wholly copied. Edgerton's comedic inspiration, he explains on the forum, is legendary bluegrass musician Peter Rowan, currently performing with the group Big Twang Theory. But, for participant Ellen Tone, it's all about Riders in the Sky. (Good choice, Ellen.) "They are one of the best groups to combine music and comedy," she writes. "They are superb musicians and singers, and although everything is very tightly rehearsed, they make it all, especially the banter, seem spontaneous."

I brought up the origins of stage banter, which are admittedly hard to pinpoint, and LaBour gave me his take:

> Since I believe the fundamental rules of entertainment—timing, pace, characterization—are immutable, I think banter probably originated when one of our chimp ancestors took to the forest floor and, while explaining where he had seen a leopard to an audience perched up in the tree, realized they were drifting, and got the idea to mimic the leopard with a hilarious growl, and slink around the tree trunk like Groucho Marx. My theory is the delighted audience hooted, screamed, and rewarded him with a shower of fruit. "What th—?" I believe he said. "They're paying me to be this silly? Hmmm . . ." Thus began the long evolutionary journey leading to a seventy-one-year-old man in a huge cowboy hat, on stage at the Grand Ole Opry, parodying Eminem to the hearty laughter and applause of four thousand ticket buyers.

But LaBour also sees a basic utility in stage banter: "The purpose of banter is elemental: to keep the show moving. Nothing pains me more than a dead moment, when nothing is happening and the only sound is the energy being sucked out of the room." LaBour is not the only musician to recognize this necessity. In

2012, in an article for the *Canadian Press*, singer Barry Manilow explained, "I like telling the audience where the song came from.... I think it's interesting to an audience. I would like to see artists do more of that." He added, "Because after a while it kind of gets numbing to go from one song, to the other song, to the next song, to the next song."

Stage talk can fill a gap in this way, with announcements of the songs and other related history.[6] While classical musicians typically provide programs, a listing of the music to come, popular musicians do not. That difference in concert etiquette was part of the thrill, for me, at a performance by the Grassinators (since I'm a regular classical concert attendee). The bluegrass group, performing at World Records in Bakersfield, California, on Saturday, March 2, 2019, broke into solos, with virtuosity passed between players. After the guitar player finished his standout jam, he commented, "I think I sounded pretty good." The dobro player didn't miss a beat. "Let me put it this way," he said, "I've never heard you sound better." Hoping to drown him out, the guitar player pointed to the speaker by his feet, asking, "Can I get a little more me?" With such a long history of serious performance—concert etiquette, black dress, and quiet attention—I could not stop laughing, partly because the jokes, in between beautiful songs, surprised me. It was a welcome break from the established norms of other genres.

For Riders in the Sky, the necessity and joy of on-stage banter have become an integral part of the show's entertainment. LaBour told me, "Stage banter is critical to our success, and has been part of Riders' shows since show number one, when we performed for eight or nine semi-inebriates at a local beer joint and took delight in trying to crack each other up."

While the humor in their banter and performance is a plus for LaBour, I had to ask, "Is there a tension between being taken seriously as musicians and the comedy?" Minnie Pearl, after all, felt that tension, as did the creators of *Hee Haw*.

LaBour answered, "There can be. Early on, some audiences speculated that we were making fun of the music, as well as the whole singing cowboy persona, which we were never interested in doing." But, generally, people have responded to the group's evident joy in performing, "a quality I think is essential to our longevity." "One comment we've heard consistently through the years," LaBour shared, "is 'You guys look like you're having so much fun!' Because we are."

While humor makes for a good country show and fun for the musician, it doesn't always translate into a positive take on country music as an art form. Of course, some of the humor depends on this mismatch—the country bumpkin often pitted against the city sophisticate or the surprise of a good between-song joke. Once again, the humor both supports and depends on a hierarchy in art. The joke is inevitable in the meaning we assign country music. It's a loop at times frustrating—in the involved misunderstanding of musical genres and their histories—but also funny, in country music as well as in other genres, like heavy metal, as we will see in the next chapter. But behind that humor, in the case of Riders in the Sky, is a knowledge of country music's traditions and real musical skill and intelligence. As LaBour revealed to me, "We've always felt that the music had to be done right to make the comedy work. Interestingly, other musicians got it immediately, became fans, and have endlessly told us how we inspired them at some point to stick to their guns and do what they want to do." Like funny films about music, the Edwards act, and the PDQ ruse, it was musicians—those with musical know-how—who best understood the expertise required to clown around in country music. Their devotion to Riders in the Sky underscores the skill and tradition behind the group's humor as well as the reason some might miss the fun entirely. But, once again, with a little attention and engagement, the fun is there for everyone—whether we're talking about musical humor set in the open skies of country or, as in the next chapter, the fiery hellscape of hard rock.

NOTES

1. Quoted in Kristine Fredriksson, "Minnie Pearl and Southern Humor in Country Entertainment," in *Country Music Annual* 2000, ed Charles K. Wolfe and James E. Akenson (Lexington: University of Kentucky Press, 2014), 78.

2. For more information, see Elamin Abelmahmoud, "Rewriting Country Music's Racist History," *Rolling Stone*, June 5, 2020.

3. For more on this singular song, see Chris Molanphy, *Old Town Road* (Durham, NC: Duke University Press, 2023).

4. See John Thomerson, "Parody as a Borrowing Practice in American Music, 1965–2015" (PhD diss., University of Cincinnati, 2017), 151–155.

5. Thomas A. Adler, "The Uses of Humor by Bluegrass Musicians," *Mid-America Folklore* 10, no. 2 (1982): 18.

6. As John Bealle explains in "Self-Involvement in Musical Performance: Stage Talk and Interpretive Control at a Bluegrass Festival," *Ethnomusicology* 37, no. 1 (1993), "Speech provides the kind of 'anchoring' from which musical performance can emanate."

EIGHT

HEAVY AND HILARIOUS (METAL)

ON OCTOBER 27, 2019, I found myself among some Sunday-night hard rockers in Santa Barbara, California. In my seat at the Arlington Theatre, an indoor stage with a ceiling painted like the sky, I heard a fan shout at my friend Vanessa, "Are you ready for the D?" Shocked, it took her a second to recover, assuming the question was a sleazy come-on. And maybe it was. But it was also an enthusiastic cry, a D-voted fan waiting for the evening's headlining act, Tenacious D, with members Kyle Gass and Jack Black. Sportscaster Marv Albert inspired the band name when Gass and Black heard him commenting on a basketball game, "They're showing some tenacious D out there." But in Vanessa's defense, that defensive D is also about dick, made clear in so many different aspects of Tenacious D's art—film, music, and Jack Black's multifaceted penis sketches supporting his rock opera *Post-Apocalypto*.

The fans in Santa Barbara were distinct—their cheers guttural and low. The pitch range reflected the audience's male makeup. With dicks aplenty, the diversity was in facial hair rather than gender or, for that matter, race (the fans were mostly white). I asked one young woman, sitting next to her date, "Are you the D fan or did you buy these tickets as a present for him?" I had read that the ladies at Tenacious D concerts are often there for a male partner. I wanted to test the theory. "A present," she said, amazed at my evident psychic ability. But then there were two teenage girls, Porsche and Caprice, fans themselves. They had come for the humor, they told me, and to hear lead singer Jack Black's amazing voice. Both Gass and Black are indeed skilled musicians. With some early singing aspirations myself, I was duly impressed by Black's expressive voice—his range, both in dynamics and register, all colored by enviable vibrato and on-stage charisma. In *Good*, Penn Collins described the audience's reaction to Jack Black's singing in 2018 of the national anthem at a Los Angeles Sparks WNBA game at the Staples Center—"An earnest and powerful a cappella performance that came as a shock to fans and the unfamiliar alike." Fans often think of Black as an actor first, which is part of his voice's surprise. But based on what I heard in Santa Barbara, I am not at all shocked that Black expertly crushed the national anthem, a song notoriously difficult for even those expected to deliver the high notes.

After they performed *Post-Apocalypto*, Tenacious D introduced some of their greatest hits. The crowd was immediately on their feet, their noise climaxing during "Sax-A-Boom," a legendary showstopper that features a yellow Kawasaki toy saxophone with musical licks set off by pressing each of its eight purple buttons. Letting loose the synthetic sound, Black instructed the audience to dance. No one was too cool, too hard, he made clear, to earn an out. Check your "heavy metal attitude," Black shouted; it's time to dance. In February 2019, Black brought his saxy toy to Jimmy Fallon's show, explaining that the instrument was as "rare as a Stradivarius," a riff on the famed string instruments built by the Italian Stradivari family. In response, Twitter (now X) exploded with love for Black: "Jack Black is a national fuckin treasure and you better never forget it."

Tenacious D is a hard-rocking band with humor created around the many norms of metal—their subversion or absurd extension. Others too have offered send-ups of the heavy metal tradition. The legendary *This Is Spinal Tap* (1984) is of course the benchmark of metal hilarity. The more recent Finnish comedy *Heavy Trip* (2018) pays homage to Spinal Tap while charting its own course in heavy hijinks, with a lovable bunch of young would-be metalheads trying to secure their first major gig. Comedian Brian Posehn, a self-proclaimed "metal dork," has also made his mark on metal comedy, with the albums *Live In: Nerd Rage* (2006), *Fart and Wiener Jokes* (2010), and *Grandpa Metal* (2020), which honors Scott Ian and his metal group Stormtroopers of Death. Of his newest venture, Posehn said, "I wanted this to be the ultimate comedy/metal record, a loving record that made fun of some of the things in heavy metal." Posehn was involved with the animated series *Metalocalypse* (2006–2013) as well, which chronicles the fictitious band Dethklok and its dealings with world leaders bent on the group's destruction. In the first episode of the series, the fictitious group's chef is near death, forcing the darkly destructive Dethklok to go to the grocery store, or, as they call it, the "food library," evidently for the first time. The lead singer, unfamiliar with a meat counter, breaks the glass with his fist, aggressively grabbing the sausage he needs for his paella recipe.

But Tenacious D is one of the most prominent and longest-running metal jokes. Their humor taps into the great comedic potential in heavy metal. Not only are there serious, over-the-top clichés ripe for a humorous send-up; the genre is built on transgression. That transgression, to some, can be horrifying. But as Noël Carroll makes clear in "Horror and Humor" (1999), the line between horror and humor is fine as hell. Metal inspires humor, but the potential for humor exists in metal already. Some may assume Tenacious D is all about dick. But those dick jokes actually require real talent to realize, amazing vocal power, and an understanding of comedy, traditions of rock and metal, and the associated fandoms.

Fate framed Tenacious D in 1986, when Black and Gass met as members of the Actor's Gang Theatre troupe, cofounded by actor Tim Robbins. The two, at first rivals, became friends, and Gass started teaching Black how to play the guitar—lessons paid for in fast food. They formed their satirical band and settled on a name, thanks to one very metal sportscaster. In 2012, Black explained on NPR's "Fresh Air," "All those great '80s rock things—there's something so funny about that now. No one's really doing that particular brand of cheese, so we thought the world needed that right now."

They initially played at coffee shops and comedy clubs, seemingly low-key, but their early performances were still intense. In an interview with Simon Bland in 2019's "An Oral History of Tenacious D's Self-Titled Debut Album," Black described their whole career as "a series of fiery hoops," terrifying tests of courage, including their very first show, with Harry Shearer from Spinal Tap in the audience: "So what should have been a no-pressure coffee shop gig automatically became a fiery hoop, because of Harry Shearer's presence." The two continued to push themselves, releasing a demo tape in the late 1990s. Their first song, in 1994, was "Tribute," "the greatest song ever written," Gass told Sandy Cohen of *AP Entertainment* (2006), their "Mona Lisa." Gass explained the concept: "We thought that we could probably write the greatest song and then Jack said, 'No, we can't just write the greatest song, but we could do a *tribute* to the greatest song.'" The song itself was inspired by the epic air of Metallica as well as the absurdity of absolutes—the fastest, the greatest, the biggest, as Black explained to Bland. In the song, Black and Gass take over a mall karaoke machine, rewiring it to record their monster jam. Supported by Gass's light acoustic accompaniment, Black humbly begins, "This is the greatest and best song in the world." He then narrates the story, the two hitchhiking "down a long and lonesome road." Still speaking, Black announces the appearance on that road of a "shiny" demon, who demands in song that the two "play the best song in the world." With the demon's threat that he will eat their souls if they don't comply, the two are somehow able to do just that. Unfortunately, they can't remember their song after the fact. "Tribute" is ostensibly the next best thing, an ode to that song in an energetic lyrical story, with virtuosic guitar playing and climactic scat singing: "You've gotta believe," the two sing together.

That tape led to a show on HBO entitled *Tenacious D*, which ran from 1997 to 2000, produced by Bob Odenkirk and David Cross, of the famous musical sketch comedy *Mr. Show*, who were at the first official Tenacious D performance at Al's Bar in Los Angeles in 1994. The show chronicles Black and Gass's struggles to make it as musicians, performing at open-mic nights, regrouping in their apartment, songwriting, and stalking their only stalker fan. Playing together for over a decade and pumping out material for the show, they finally had enough songs for an album and began making their debut recording with producers the Dust Brothers, E.Z. Mike and King Gizmo, who pushed them to enlist Dave Grohl (of Foo Fighters and Nirvana fame), who they knew was a fan. Grohl agreed to play drums, but, Black admitted to Bland, "I don't think Dave knew when he came in that he was going to be playing on the whole album. Once he got into the studio we just locked the door." Gass remembers the thrill of that day in the studio: "It was like your hero walking through the door. There goes my hero—and he's playing drums on your track! It was pretty crazy." In 2001, they released the album, including their epic song "Tribute" and an ode to Ronnie James Dio, who was part of Black Sabbath and then his own metal band Dio, which formed in 1982. In the song "Dio," Tenacious D announces that it's time for Dio to "pass the torch": "You're too old to rock, no more rockin' for you." To Bland, Gass insisted the album was "magic": "Our first tour was right after 9/11 and the record might have been the healing balm that was needed. Maybe Tenacious D provided that for the nation." Looking back in 2019, Black told Bland, "18 years. It's

Tenacious D, "Tribute" (official video), screenshot from YouTube.

like our album has finally matured into adulthood. Eighteen is the age of consent in the United States. Now we can finally make love to Tenacious D."

In 2006, the magic of that first release continued with their follow-up album, *The Pick of Destiny*, a tie-in to their film of the same name, which was a box office flop. Upon release, the film was number eleven, just excluded from the weekend's top-ten list. And its domestic take was a bitter disappointment for all involved, similar to other musical-comedic films, despite its modest budget of $19 million. A heartbreaking 2008 documentary, *D-Tour*, captures Tenacious D on tour as they anticipate the film's release and then deal with its poor reception. In the film, Black reflects on the numbers, keeping it light: "Camp D was shaken." The tour as a victory lap became something else entirely. Black was still popular as an actor, having appeared in roles connected to music—in *High Fidelity* (2000), *School of Rock* (2003), and even *The Holiday* (2006)—which, in the documentary, becomes a source of frustration for Gass, especially when the two prepare to appear on David Letterman's show, only to have Gass pulled from the lineup last-minute.

But they weren't done. And, in 2012, they released the epic comeback album, *Rize of the Fenix*. They also created the animated series *Tenacious D in Post-Apocalypto*, which was the basis for their 2018 album *Post-Apocalypto*. The series' drawings are by Black himself. And the whole work marks a distinct entry for the group into the political realm. In *Rolling Stone* (2018), Christopher R. Weingarten asks the pair, "When did you guys start thinking about the apocalypse?" Black responds, "As soon as Donald Trump came down that fuckin' escalator. We were like, 'Ohhhh boy! We're going to Hell.'" Summing it up, Black explains, "So there's gonna be a lot of monsters, there's gonna be a lot of adventures, there's gonna be a lot of rad music and sex and violence and... and politics. It's all in there, bro." In early March 2020, before the full devastation of COVID-19, Tenacious D announced fall tour dates targeting swing states, "The Purple Nurple Tour—Twisting Hard to the Left," in an effort to promote voter registration and civic action against Trump.

In these various projects, Black and Gass riff on themes central to metal and music more generally, first and foremost the devil. As Black explained on NPR, "We used to make fun of the devil because the devil's influence on '80s metal is so prevalent, and now it just seems so ridiculous and hilarious." The supernatural has a long history in music, with composers looking to the divine for inspiration and virtuosic abilities. Eighteenth-century composer Giuseppe Tartini's Violin Sonata in G Minor, also called the *Devil's Trill Sonata*, combines both demonic playing and a tale of extraordinary genesis. Tartini claimed that the technically demanding piece appeared to him in a dream, the sonata played by the devil himself, to whom Tartini had sold his soul. In metal, especially the music of the band Black Sabbath, music found a similar standard of demonology. And it wasn't just lyrics, myth, and dress that supported the demonic ruse; it was also the music itself. Sabbath singer Ozzy Osbourne remembers guitarist Tony Iommi coming to rehearsal one day and saying, "Isn't it funny how people pay money to watch horror films—why don't we start playing scary music?"[1] Iommi made that happen in part by tuning down his guitar, creating the band's darker sound, and prominently featuring the tritone, an augmented fourth—a dissonant interval banned in early music as the *diabolus in musica*, or devil in music.

On the cover of their first album, Gass and Black make their own demonic connection clear by appearing shirtless and chained to the devil behind them. In their movie *The Pick of Destiny*, Black and Gass stand in a satanic circle, hoping occult forces will grant them a musical masterpiece. Eventually, they learn that true creative power has a separate source: an otherworldly guitar pick. Though they are able to fight their foes and obtain the pick, in the end they must confront the devil himself, eventually vanquishing him in song (kind of). The movie includes a cameo by Meat Loaf, as young Black/JB's father. As explained in song, JB dreams in Kickapoo, Missouri, of rocking hard, but his father punishes him, pulling off his belt. If you don't recognize Meat Loaf, you miss the joke, given Loaf's own dealings with moral outrage—his album *Bat out of Hell* was dubbed satanic. In their song "History" (2006), a mock recounting of their origins, the devil again appears as Black sings about the group's "rise to power," including a valiant ride "across the Devil's plain." And these are only some of the examples. The devil as a character is everywhere in the mythology, imagery, and music of Tenacious D. He is imposing, yes, but almost ridiculous in his overplay. And that's part of the joke.

Tenacious D also riffs on metal's supposed masculinity. Heavy metal supports the manly assumption in heavy distortion, the use of electric guitar, and sheer volume as well as man-centric topics in lyrics, album titles, and band names. Even the chaos of metal, its forceful confrontation with societal norms as well as the occult, to some, belong to a supposed male world—women being "perceived as the keepers and transmitters of order."[2] Black's voice, a true force, fits the pattern, as does the band's volume, at least when the backup players explode into view, electric guitar ramping up the duo's acoustic sound. Masculinity and a supposed related sexual prowess are also rife in their music and, again, their movie. In the film's climactic scene, an erection saves the day, prepared by training that includes a "cock pushup." The scene may seem juvenile at best, but, given the hypermasculinity and hypersexuality of metal, the film's dick focus is both an homage and a critique.

As they sing in "History," "We've run with wolves, we've climbed K2 / Even stopped a moving train." At the same time, they burst the bubble of metal's manly boasting by admitting certain supposed shortcomings in this area. In the video for "History," as they sing of their over-the-top escapades, Gass winks at a girl smiling in the audience. Her smile quickly disappears, and she turns away, effectively rejecting Gass. The two in this way hint at a softer side, their vulnerability, backed up by their choice to use acoustic guitar. Rather than the electric guitar, a man-made machine, they opt for an instrument associated with a less hard-edged sound. Visually, the acoustic guitar makes a statement as well. Rather than phallic, the instrument is round, arguably like its players. In their song "Fuck Her Gently" (2001), Gass and Black go even further, fully embracing a gentler character while calling out hypersexual, macho songs like Nine Inch Nails' "Closer" (1994). Black sets up the song while Gass lightly plucks: "This is a song / For the ladies, / But fellas, / Listen closely." Rather than fucking her "like an animal," as in "Closer," Black sweetly croons, "You don't always have to fuck her hard / In fact sometimes that's not right to do." In the ballad's chorus, Black caresses the high note on "softly," promising a tender screw, before the background strings swell.

This play with masculinity extends to Black and Gass as participants in the metal scene. Neither musician fits the image of the metal lead. In addition to their choice of guitar (and sax toy), they are at this point older than your typical popular music star—the whole music industry being often thought of as a young person's game. As Black told Bland in the oral history of D's self-titled debut album, "It's more fun now, but I do get winded a little easier. I have to pace myself. You know that song Wind Beneath My Wings? Now we have to have actual wind in the wings, like, actual oxygen tanks." "It's on our rider," Gass added. As obvious metal fans, with songs as homages to metal legends like Dio, Black and Gass also riff on notions of hard-rock audiences and devotees. Black's "Sax-A-Boom" is a direct play on those expectations—check your "heavy metal attitude." This focus highlights a recurring trope in musical comedy—the lovable metal loser. Black plays that character in *School of Rock*, and Mike Myers and Dana Carvey embody their own versions of that figure as Wayne Campbell and Garth Alger in *Wayne's World*. It was more loser than love in the MTV series *Beavis and Butt-Head* (1993–1997), with the two characters crudely insulting music video after music video as a send-up of music criticism but also a certain type of unintelligent and amoral music fan.[3] Though these characters complicate notions of the metal fan, there is also an element of punching down within this humor. And the metal fan is an easy mark, given the association with metal, which was in a 1996 study "the most disliked genre."[4]

—※—

This play on fandom, norms of masculinity, and the occult works well abroad. It's a humor that is not always dependent on lyrics, unlike so many parody songs and other examples of musical humor with gags buried in language. Anyone with knowledge of metal can get most of the jokes. Tenacious D has seen this extraverbal bent translate into international popularity, including a tour in 2012 throughout Europe, with stops in Germany, the Netherlands, and the United Kingdom, and their 2020 tour dates in Germany, Ireland, the Netherlands, and France. In "Humor in Metal Music" (2019), Deena Weinstein explains, "Although humor itself is famously known for not traveling well, even though metal itself is now fully globalized, its subculture audience shares a common set of norms and values that allow metal's humor to be a first-class world-traveler."

At the same time, with their own epic air in music and presentation, Tenacious D trades on a humor already in metal. Sure, you may not immediately think of humor in association with metal, just as you don't with rap or jazz (most music, really). As Eric R. Danton puts it, in the *Hartford Courant*, "Heavy metal has no sense of humor." Though she doesn't agree, Weinstein explains the reason: "One would have thought that a genre of music given to lyrics focusing on life's two main inexplicable horrors, evil and death, played loudly and rather expertly by musicians often dressed in black, accessorized with spiked leather, would be deadly serious." Gass and Black make use of that perception. Part of their humor is in the seeming incongruity of metal and comedy. But there has always been the potential for humor in metal, a genre based in societal rule-breaking and boundary transgression—horrifying to some and humorous to others.

Karen Bettez Halnon refers to a group of the genre's most prominent rule-breakers as "heavy metal carnival": "Noose-hanging and guillotine-executing Alice Cooper; bat-chomping, ant-snorting, and crucifix-wielding 'Satanist' Ozzy Osborne, . . . 'F*** it all' 'maggot'-inspiring, 'alienated nobodies' Slipknot; 'slave' master, blood and gore primal warriors GWAR," and others. GWAR members, for example, hose the audience in "blood" (colored water) and simulate ejaculation, body organ removal, beheadings, and the flushing of people down toilets, often within an elaborate staged story. Slipknot claims to be "anti-everything." In the chorus of their popular song "Surfacing," they scream,

> F*** it all
> F*** this world
> F*** everything that you stand for

"Heavy metal carnival," Halnon writes, "breaks through the noise of commercial culture by raising the transgression ante to the extreme and challenging nearly every conceivable social rule governing taste, authority, morality, propriety, the sacred, and, some might say, civility itself."[5] Fans take courage in the transgression—a band's ability to say and do anything—and in turn seek to liberate themselves from inhibition and concerns about judgment. One fan explained, "You get all your emotions out. It's like therapy."[6] But plenty of others have found plenty to fear in heavy metal. The Parents' Music Resource Center, formed in 1985, famously went after heavy metal, arguing before the Senate that the music, with its perceived pornography and violence, was dangerous. Several court cases were based in that fear—cases that alleged a darkness in metal, one that could supposedly incite violence, including suicide.

But one person's horror is another person's humor. Humor and horror, after all, are both built around the breaking of taboos and boundaries. The difference is contextual, benign or not; the difference is fright. As Noël Carroll writes in "Horror and Humor," "The boundary line between horror and incongruity humor is drawn in terms of fear." A red-nosed clown stands smiling against a night sky. Depending on your perspective and tricks of lighting or music, the scene is either scary or funny. Invested with fear, a situation is horrifying. Without it, maybe it's funny. For those in metal culture, the element of fear is often gone, and the upending of society's standards of behavior can be hilarious. Posehn's admiration of Stormtroopers of Death relates to that flip side, a humor he responds to in the group's work.[7] In an interview with Mammoth Metal TV in 2015, the group's Scott Ian summed up that dual and dueling reaction to his group's album *Speak English or Die* (1985) and its insider humor, explaining, "We wrote a bunch of fucking ridiculous songs that made us laugh. The whole twenty-two minutes, or whatever it is, is just a big inside joke. And it worked; it fucking worked. And people... Well, not everybody, 'cause some people hated it. Some people thought we were racist, and those people are stupid. But a lot of people got the joke all over the planet and laughed along with us, and it was fucking awesome."

Tenacious D finds the humor in certain clichés of metal, but Black and Gass also play on the humor in metal itself. The overplay of the occult and hypermasculine boasting are already a part of the humor in metal for some, along with a joy in pushing past boundaries. And with that, they have earned the appreciation of musicians firmly established in the genre. They offer up the same metal fascination with the devil, the same satanic sensibility, and tons of dicks. But the context is different. For insiders, the context helps create the humor, but the humor is there either way. Corey Taylor of Slipknot, for one, is a huge fan of Tenacious D. He even has his own tribute band, Audacious P. That's some meta-metal humor!

Tenacious D, then, has found success in cleverly flipping conventions of metal, with genre-specific metal in-jokes while trading on metal's existing humor. They have a loyal following in and outside the United States, with knowledge of metal as the only prerequisite. And these fans respond to not only the humor in metal and the band's extension of its norms but also the group's break with certain metal customs. For some, that break is inspiring. Metal's manliness is a lot to live up to for those who don't or can't. For them, there's Gass and Black—two rounder and older rockers who, in T-shirts rather than leather, don't look the part but take to the stage with unabashed joy and energy. Cohen asked, "What is the appeal of Tenacious D?" Gass considered: "A lot of people have weight problems and they still want to rock. I think they identify with us." While in 2001 Tenacious D threatened to take Dio to a "home" (insisting in song that he was "too old to rock"), in 2021 Black and Gass showed no signs of themselves honoring any supposed rock age limit. Both over fifty, they continue to rock, metal no longer being a young person's game. That break may be a secret ingredient in much of the appeal of humorous music. Yes, there's hilarity in undermining conventions of any genre. But in that subversion, there can also be a certain relief and release. There's room for musicians and fans of all types. We can all do it a different way, if we want to. And if that way includes a toy saxophone, all the better.

NOTES

1. Quoted in George Case, *Here's to My Sweet Satan: How the Occult Haunted Music, Movies and Pop Culture, 1966–1980* (Fresno, CA: Quill Driver Books, 2016), 17.
2. Deena Weinstein, "The Empowering Masculinity of British Heavy Metal," in *Heavy Metal Music in Britain*, ed. Gerd Bayer (Farnham, UK: Ashgate, 2009), 25.
3. See Andrew Dell'Antonio, "Butt-Head: A Glimpse into Postmodern Music Criticism," *American Music* 17, no. 1 (1999): 65–86.
4. Bethany Bryson, "'Anything but Heavy Metal': Symbolic Exclusion and Musical Dislikes," *American Sociological Review* 61, no. 5 (1996): 894.
5. Karen Bettez Halnon, "Heavy Metal Carnival and Dis-alienation: The Politics of Grotesque Realism," *Symbolic Interaction* 49, no. 1 (2006): 34. See also Michelle Phillipov, *Death Metal and Music Criticism: Analysis at the Limits* (Lanham, MD: Lexington Books, 2012), 89.
6. Hanlon, 44.
7. See interview in Full Metal Jackie, "Brian Posehn: I Don't Have the Energy to Front a Band for 'Grandpa Metal' Tour," *Loudwire*, March 9, 2020.

NINE

FUNNY GIRLS

IN THIS CHAPTER, METAL CAN keep the D: women take over in an exploration of humor on Broadway. In *Funny Girl* (1968), the film version of the musical (1964), Barbra Streisand says to herself, "Hello, gorgeous," announcing the distinction. She pulls down her collar and looks in the mirror, delivering that now-iconic line—brazen and funny but also a willful response to ideals of beauty that had then excluded difference. The self-greeting also marked Streisand's point of arrival—hello, stardom—the beginning of her mega-celebrity status, which has now lasted five decades long and counting. Thirty-seven years after *Funny Girl*, Jewish comedian Sarah Silverman found herself similarly launched into the cosmos with the release of her 2005 film *Jesus Is Magic*, part stand-up, part concert, with a buried reference to *Funny Girl*. During her initial musical number, Silverman too looks in the mirror. She tells her reflection, "You're beautiful," and then moves toward the mirror as if she were going in for a kiss. While Streisand as Brice sings, "'Cause I'm the greatest star," Silverman in her film confidently belts, "I've got what it takes."

In 2020, Silverman was set to have her life immortalized in a musical, based on her 2011 autobiography *Bedwetter* (another pandemic postponement). Interestingly, *Funny Girl* similarly honored a Jewish musical comedian, an earlier star, Fanny Brice. Of course, there are some big differences between *Funny Girl* and *Bedwetter*, the former being focused in part on marital distress and addiction and the latter devoted to a young girl's travails as, well, a bedwetter. But the two musicals do highlight an interesting corner of the comical musical world—Broadway—one particularly friendly to funny women, a reputation related, to be sure, to the less-than-serious reputation attached to the musical as a genre.

Indeed, musicals, unlike other music genres, have never really been taken seriously; they have instead been connected to entertainment and commerce. As Brooks McNamara wrote in 2001, Broadway does not "produce high art": "Like Hollywood and the major television networks, Broadway is involved with producing a commercial product."[1] But this dismissal has created a certain revelatory freedom. The comedy didn't flip staid perceptions of the musical, as we've seen in humorous approaches to other "serious" genres. Humor of all types was allowed and validated from the start because the musical was already considered less than true art. Without serious artistic credentials, traditional male authorities also never took complete control of Broadway. The genre suffered in reputation but was then free of certain expectations limiting other genres, a space open and able to offer up big laughs while featuring over-the-top female personalities. In his book *Place for Us* (2000), English professor D. A. Miller hinted at this intriguing flip side when he observed that "the musical was already prevented—or perhaps spared—from being an object of serious thought."

Somehow, in that space, musicals have also come to rely on women. Rather than the Python boys' club, *Spamalot*, a refashioning of the classic movie *Monty Python and the Holy Grail* (1975), boasts meaty parts for women. The movie's referenced Lady of the Lake becomes a character in the musical. According to Laurie A. Finke and Susan Aronstein in "Got Grail? Monty Python and the Broadway Stage," that change was a must. Musicals, Finke and Aronstein argue, need women. Women are "spectacle" but also representative of Broadway itself. And shows like *Funny Girl*—the "big lady shows," in musical-theater historian Ethan Mordden's wording—are the result and confirmation. Broadway's feminine association has helped create a space for women but also masculine difference more generally. As Miller puts it, Broadway lets "men in the thrills of femininity *become their own.*" With nothing to lose, the women of the musical stage can be funny too. When I was lucky enough to interview Jessica McKenna, of *Off Book: The Improvised Musical Podcast*, she confirmed this freedom, spinning it as one of the musical's assets: "I think musical theater has perhaps been ahead of the curve in allowing women to be absurd or funny." A long line of funny girls—from Brice to Silverman to McKenna herself—offers proof. In their lives and work, these women reveal the history of humor in the musical as well as the remarkable flair and ingenuity of women on Broadway. There is skill and knowledge in their work, but part of their significance is their very presence on stage. To perform, they had to be thoughtful and talented, but they also had to push past bias and sometimes create their own comedic musical worlds in platform and concept. With McKenna as this chapter's insider informant, it becomes clear that so much was required of these women, perhaps too much. A person might dismiss the musical as lowbrow, but funny women on Broadway had to do more than most musicians in the world of "serious" art: they had to confront dismissal related to gender for the very privilege of confronting dismissal related to genre, all while demonstrating undeniable star power, often in more than one area of performance simultaneously.

—⁂—

Female comedians in general continue to deal with certain stereotypes limiting who can and cannot be funny. In the mid-nineteenth century, humorist Francis Whitcher observed that it was "a very serious thing to be a funny woman." The comment concerned the decision to pursue comedy as a woman and its damage to a woman's societal standing. Cultural dictates at the time did not ignore the comedic woman but instead followed her every move closely, punishing her by way of reputation and community rank. Rather than feminine and submissive, this woman of the stage was often assumed to be loose and immoral. In 1988, in *A Very Serious Thing: Women's Humor and American Culture*, Nancy A. Walker attempted to address this wrong, discussing the merits of comedy produced by women. But, at the same time, she qualified their work as somehow different, describing women as "storytellers" rather than "joke tellers." In 1991, Johnny Carson effectively categorized show business in general as unladylike, joking on *The Tonight Show* in response to an audience question, "How does a lady make it in show business?": "It involves not being a lady [*laughter*] for a little while," he said. In 2014, much had changed, but much had also stayed the same. Comedian Jerry Lewis told a Hollywood audience that there was something of a mismatch between women making crude jokes and their miraculous ability to create life. He admitted, "I have a problem with the lady up there that's going to give birth to a child—which is a miracle." These perceptions have acted as a gatekeeper, dissuading some would-be female comics if not wholly blocking them. In a 2015 study of women in stand-up comedy, Katja Elisabet Antoine calculated that 80–85 percent of comedians performing on stage in Los Angeles are men. Comedian Aida Rodriguez told Antoine, "It's a male sport."

The Funny Music Project, "Your Online Source for New Funny Songs," acknowledged a similar divide in comedic music. In 2019, they countered the split by putting out *Madam Opus*, a collection of funny songs by women: "For years comedy has been seen as 'a boys club' and in many ways it still is. Comedy-music is no different. That's why we are proud to present *Madam Opus—Funny*

Songs by Funny Women." The effort was an attempt to fill a gap—a very real gap in funny music. At the same time, that gap does not exist in the same way in every genre of music.

On the American stage, women began appearing in musical-comedic roles in the late nineteenth century in various forms that would ultimately influence and inform the Broadway musical, including minstrelsy, revue, vaudeville, and staged variety acts. Interestingly, the earliest women to perform in this way on stage—funny and musical—appeared as men. In 1868, Annie Hindle (1840s–1897) became the first male impersonator performing in variety shows in the United States, as described in Gillian M. Rodger's *Just One of the Boys: Female-to-Male Cross-Dressing on the American Variety Stage* (2018). Two years later, Ella Wesner (1841–1917) offered her own version of the act, leaving her initial career as a ballet dancer. Their dress as men gave them the freedom to be funny—an autonomy women then generally didn't have. Rodgers writes, "The women active in this specialty had more freedom to transgress social norms than most working-class women."

Minstrelsy gave other women a similar mold-breaking platform, a chance to step out of their expected, traditional roles—though in doing so they supported the subjugation and stereotyping of Black people. In New York in the first decade of the twentieth century, Sophie Tucker (1887–1966), the daughter of Russian Jewish immigrants, found fame singing funny songs like "I Don't Want to Get Thin" and "Life Begins at Forty." She herself would push past bias against women as well as Jews at the time in her quest for success in comedic music. But to do so, she first became a "Coon Shouter," performing a repertoire filled with racist stereotypes. As Lauren Rebecca Sklaroff writes in *Red Hot Mama: The Life of Sophie Tucker* (2018), these songs "allowed immigrants to imagine themselves as truly white against the degrading image of African Americans." This example is then in line with humor's use more generally to negotiate difference—something we've seen in other contexts, including rap. Of course, the opposite coexists in this type of humor, with stereotypes potentially confirmed. In Tucker's work, the positive and negative existed together, just as it did for other comedic musicians, like Mickey Katz. While Tucker asserted her place in the United States by casting Black people as different, Katz marked himself as both a part of American culture and separate at the same time through his parodies of '50s American pop music, all with references to Jewish culture and Yiddish words and phrases.[2]

In 1909, Tucker hoped to shed the blackface routine when she joined the Ziegfeld Follies, Florenz Ziegfeld's New York revue, which began in 1907 as a combination of staged scenes, songs, dances, skits, and visual tableaux. Still, her debut once again had her "blacked-up," performing with girls barely dressed in animal prints, the number offensively entitled "Moving Day in Jungle Town." She would return to vaudeville soon after, appearing in a musical entitled *Merry Mary* and then *Louisiana Lou*. Off stage, she favored clothes that resembled menswear. Like the early male impersonators, she found in the suits "a feeling of freedom."[3] By 1916, she began including jazz in her act, performing songs like "Oh, Daddy Come Home" and "Walkin' the Dog," with banter in between, a back-and-forth with her band, the Five Kings. Her act was distinct and her voice explosive. Her popularity in the 1920s was forever commemorated in the Broadway hit *Chicago* (1975), when Roxie Hart sings, "Sophie Tucker will shit, I know / to see her name get billed below Roxie Hart."

The minstrel tradition would define the early career of another funny, musical woman, Jackie Moms Mabley (1894–1975), who was an early Black vaudeville and revue performer. Mabley initially performed as a foil, serving the male comic. But she quickly put together a solo act—according to Elsie A. Williams's *The Humor of Jackie Moms Mabley* (1995), "the first distinctive Black female comic star to run an act on her own." She performed for Black audiences but white audiences as well at the Cotton Club,

Connie's Inn, and the Savoy Ballroom. She also teamed up with writer Zora Neale Hurston, creating the Broadway show *Fast and Furious: A Colored Revue in 37 Scenes* (1931). Her career was remarkably long and, in 1974, extended to film, with the movie *Amazing Grace*. For her, the stage offered its own opportunity for self-determination, given the limited opportunities for Black female entertainers—a double bind. Williams observes, "Minstrelsy and vaudeville provided welcomed alternatives for the Black female, professional entertainer." And she was remarkably far-reaching in her comedic messaging—taking on sexuality, race, and class culture. In one of her routines, she told her audience about opera, switching into an English accent. Explaining the unexpected speech shift, she would say, "You just can't stumble up into them opera." She would then sing an aria exploring segregation and racism.[4]

The musical *Funny Girl* brought some of this history to Broadway, chronicling the life of one particular pioneer, Fanny Brice (1891–1951), who found early success, like Sophie Tucker, in the Ziegfeld Follies. She also received a career boost from legendary songwriter Irving Berlin, who wrote her the hit "Sadie Salome, Go Home" (1909), a song about a Jewish girl dancing the provocative Salome "Dance of the Seven Veils," which played on gender as well as Jewishness to get a laugh:

> Don't do that dance, I tell you, Sadie.
> Dat's not a business for a lady.
> Most ev'rybody knows that I'm your loving Mose.
> Oy, oy, oy, oy, where is your clothes?
> Sadie Salome, go home.

She appeared in musicals, like *Nobody Home*, and even film. But she found greater success with a character all her own—Baby Snooks—a troublesome toddler who gave Brice the chance to say anything. The child persona was yet another way to escape existing feminine norms. Assuming the character, she found the freedom other comedic women enjoyed in disguise, a new way to reach beyond gendered conventions toward funny ends. The ill-mannered child was central to Brice's popular weekly radio program (conceived in 1933), *The Baby Snooks Show* on CBS (1944–1951). In the early 1930s, radio programming, if comic, often included women only in a male-female comedy duo. In "Fanny Brice and the 'Snooks' Strategy" (2005), Michele Hilmes notes the exceptionality of Brice's radio broadcast—one that featured a woman alone.

But it wasn't just her performances that made headlines—it was also her romantic life, especially her relationship with Nick Arnstein, a lifelong con man. Her personal drama propelled the popularity of her song "My Man," which chronicled the pain of loving a man who brought with him nothing but trouble, a surprisingly serious song Brice took to the stage in 1921. This relationship was heavily featured in the musical adaptation of Brice's life, along with her astonishing rise to stardom. Though the song itself was not a part of the Broadway staging of *Funny Girl*, it was included in the film adaptation, with Barbra Streisand making Brice's song her own.

The depiction of fame in *Funny Girl* aligned with Barbra Streisand's real-life ascendancy, symbolically felt in a television appearance alongside another big, musical personality, Ethel Merman. Merman's huge voice and comic chops had been part of hit after hit—*Girl Crazy* (1930), *Anything Goes* (1934), *Annie Get Your Gun* (1946), *Call Me Madam* (1950), *Gypsy* (1959), and *Hello, Dolly!* (1970), among others. Always witty, Merman once joked with the crowd in an appearance at the Mann Center for the Performing Arts, an outdoor concert with the Philadelphia Orchestra, highlighting her big voice when a storm broke out: "I thought the thunder was the timpani. Look what happens when I sing! Some people break glasses. I start a storm."[5] She also did a short-lived radio show (1948–1949) called *The Ethel Merman Show* and had a hilarious cameo decades later in the 1980 comedy

Airplane! In the scene, she appears briefly as a character named Lieutenant Hurwitz who is delusional, convinced that he himself is Ethel Merman. With that, a whole new generation would learn her name. In 1963, Merman and Streisand appeared together on *The Judy Garland Show* and sang with the show's host the song "There's No Business Like Show Business," from *Annie Get Your Gun*. Merman's guest spot had not been planned. With Streisand poised to star in *Funny Girl*, Garland uneasily invited the new star on her show. The show's producer thought the addition of Merman might help Garland, who was apparently threatened by Streisand. According to Merman's biography, *Ethel Merman: A Life* (2007), "Garland's astonishment when Ethel came barreling out of the audience was 100 percent genuine." In song, the three stood together—"one former diva, one current diva, and one future diva."[6]

Producer Ray Stark and Brice's daughter Fran—the two were married—came up with the idea for the musical *Funny Girl*, and the duo responsible for *Gypsy*, Jule Styne and Stephen Sondheim, signed on to realize their vision. Frustrated with initial tensions around the casting of the lead, Sondheim left the project, to be replaced by Bob Merrill. But the eventual choice of Streisand, who had made a splash two years before in her Broadway debut, *I Can Get It for You Wholesale*, would prove the right move. Though he found some parts of the script and music lacking, Jack Gaver, in "Barbra Streisand Big Hit as Fanny Brice" (*Los Angeles Times*, March 28, 1964), maintained, "Miss Streisand should be able to carry the show to success. She has both talent and personality of a rare kind that can triumph over material." For the role, Streisand was nominated for a Tony for Best Actress in a Musical, ultimately losing to Carol Channing, but the show proved remarkably popular—with 1,348 performances. Four years later, Streisand starred in the film adaptation of *Funny Girl*, with William Wyler directing. Stanley Kauffmann, writing then in the *New Republic*, was effusive in his praise of the film and Streisand, whom he found both dramatic and comical—"in one person, Punch and Judy." And this time, she would win—an Oscar for Best Actress (tied with Katherine Hepburn).

In the role, Streisand leans into her Jewishness—that point of difference is often the backbone of her humor. In the dramatic rendition of Brice's debut with the Ziegfeld Follies, Streisand as Brice rebuffs Ziegfeld's demand that she sing the line "I am the beautiful reflection of my love's affection." Streisand is beautiful, but the scene implies that her Jewishness makes her unconventional, her looks at odds with the accepted ideal. Streisand as Brice surprises Ziegfeld, playing the part pregnant—the joke a twist on the line and a visual realization of the line's implied lust. Later, she dances as a chicken in a Yiddish take on *Swan Lake*, "Schvan Lak"—a nod to Brice's actual repertoire of stunts, which included a clumsy ballerina routine.

The story itself gave Streisand as Brice greater control and power than women customarily had in traditional staged setups. In the representation of Brice's relationship with Arnstein, Streisand takes over through humor. Rather than Arnstein lusting after Brice, Streisand as Brice stares at Arnstein, freezing him in frame as she sings, "Nicky Arnstein, what a beautiful name." Throughout a romantic dinner, she again takes the lead, deflecting Arnstein's advances with jokes: "A bit of paté / I drink it all day"; "Would a convent take a Jewish girl?" The role is both female forward (Brice, in the film, proposes marriage) and not, as Brice ultimately loses Arnstein in her own quest for professional success.[7]

In these ways, *Funny Girl* showcased Streisand's voice and humor but also a history of comedic women on the stage, especially Brice. These women found on the musical stage an independence they didn't have, in the same way, off the stage. Andrea Most describes the Broadway musical, in *Making Americans* (2004), as a sort of melting pot—a place where outsiders, especially Jews, could create their own American identities, a place where they could belong.[8] But these outsiders weren't just defined by ethnicity, race, or religion. They were also defined by gender. The musical offered a chance for women to carve out their own space while also exploring difference more generally. As Most writes, "In its songs, dances, plots, and characters, the midcentury musical theater expressed both anxiety about difference and delight in the apparently limitless opportunities America afforded for self-invention."

With this in mind, it makes some sense that one of the funniest women more recently, Sarah Silverman, would have connections to Broadway. On the radio show *Seth Speaks*, on November 3, 2011, musician and Broadway buff Seth Rudetsky talked with Silverman about her love of musical theater, nurtured by her mother, Beth Ann O'Hara, who founded the theater company New Thalian Players. Born in 1970 and growing up in New Hampshire, Silverman remembers seeing the musical *The King and I* at age six. On her own, she went to New York City and saw *Les Misérables* at sixteen. In her memoir *The Bedwetter*, Silverman describes meeting a friend, who worked the *Les Mis* show selling T-shirts: "Well before the curtain went up, my friend let me walk on the stage and I cried." In high school, Silverman acted in several musicals, including *Oliver!* and *Bye Bye Birdie*, but Rudetsky, on his show, asked the big question: "Why did you never play Fanny Brice?" Earlier in 2011, Rudetsky had actually directed a Los Angeles Actors Fund benefit concert of *Funny Girl*, with Broadway showstopper Laura Benanti and Silverman sharing the role of Brice. But why not the full role and earlier?

Silverman explained that she did dream of playing Eponine in *Les Misérables* and moved to New York City after high school graduation with some dream of Broadway. Once in New York, however, she found her way as a stand-up comic. Her early stand-up set included one musical number, a parody of the song "Memories" from the musical *Cats*, entitled "Mammories." In the song, she bemoans her slow-to-show boobs (at least until they did show): "Mammories are the glands that I need."

Her career-making film, *Jesus Is Magic*, a version of her one-woman show *Off Broadway*, finds Silverman coming up with the show's concept on the spot, explaining it as "a musical," "a real opus." In it, she darkly sings to her grandmother and considers the sorry lack of Jewish women in porn, eventually belting, "Do you ever take drugs so you can have sex without crying?" She also sings "A Love Song," filled with stereotypes: "I love you more than bears love honey / I love you more than Jews love money." On stage, she explains, "I don't care if you think I'm racist. I just want you to think I'm thin." To close, she belts "Amazing Grace," with vocal parts arranged for her vagina and butt. Silverman herself produced the film, and in her memoir, she jokes, "I didn't even have to blow me to get the job, but I did anyway."

The movie led to her own show on Comedy Central, *The Sarah Silverman Program* (2007–2010): "They offered me total creative freedom. Anything I wanted. Plus, there was the prestige of being on a network that has comedy right in its name!" Silverman ran with that independence, getting into hot water when she donned blackface to find out who has it worse, Jews or Black people. In 2017, she admitted she would not make the same joke now. On the show, she played, in her own words, "an arrogant ignorant," but with Trump as president, she told David Marchese in *Vulture*, "we have a president that's an arrogant ignorant, so it's not my thing anymore." In 2019, she revealed that "cancel culture" would not let her completely live down the ill-conceived joke, and she was actually fired from a film role after pictures of her in blackface reappeared.

Her musical *Bedwetter*, with music by Silverman and Adam Schlesinger (responsible for the music of another funny musical show featuring a woman, *Crazy Ex-Girlfriend*), was originally slated for production in April 2020 at New York City's Atlantic Theatre Company, but it was pushed back due to the COVID-19 pandemic (Schlesinger himself died of the virus). The theater shutdown was unique in Silverman's lifetime but was actually another link between her and early funny women, like Sophie Tucker, who experienced the influenza pandemic in 1918, with many theaters then similarly shuttered. But, two years later in 2022, the work would appear, focused on a ten-year-old version of Silverman, played by Zoe Glick. In the musical, we are meant to laugh at what confronts us—the obstacles, crisis, and urine-soaked mess of it all. As critic Helen Shaw notes in a review of the show for *Vulture*, Silverman is "a connoisseur of cringe and confession." But she took that facet of her work to the next level when she, cowriter Josh Harmon, and Schlesinger "decided to turn her memoir into something *totally* embarrassing . . . a musical."

During her career, Silverman has specifically targeted issues around race and gender—fun and fearless like her female predecessors on the musical stage. She sees herself as a feminist too: "My work is feminist because the things I say are coming out of the body of me, a human feminist," she said to Marchese. She has experienced some continued prejudice against female comics, in her case the expression of a perceived mismatch between a pretty girl and dirty jokes: "It kind of hurt when people would say, 'She's so pretty,'" she explained to Marchese, "'but why does she have that mouth?'" And she still sees a gender imbalance in her everyday life, including a bizarre experience with a condescending male eye doctor. But she recognizes that her current level of fame cushions her from some more overt discrimination: "Before anybody knew who I was, if I hung out with a friend who was famous, they'd go, 'Everyone is so nice!' Well, yeah. You're famous. Maybe I'm doing the same thing when I say that I feel like sexism is gone in comedy." To Marchese, she continued, "To get a more accurate answer, you'd have to ask a woman who was starting out."

I took Silverman's advice, asking newer musical comic Jessica McKenna about her experience as a woman in musical comedy.

Trained at the Upright Citizens Brigade (UCB) Theatre, McKenna isn't completely Hollywood fresh, having appeared on Fox's 2016 comedy show *Party Over Here*, produced by the Lonely Island and Paul Scheer, and in guest spots on the television series *Modern Family* and *The Goldbergs*. She has also regularly performed on the stage, with the musical improv team Magic to Do and Baby Wants Candy, as well as her own version of the premise, the podcast *Off Book*, currently with over three hundred episodes. But, born in 1987, she is part of a younger generation of female comedians—the next in a long line of musical funny girls. When asked about her Broadway influence, she cited classic musical theater and the big Sondheim ballad from *Company*, used to heartbreaking effect in the movie *Marriage Story*: "I'm just an improvisor trying to sing 'Being Alive' all the time."

Her *Off Book* podcast is a twist on her early experience, each episode an improvised musical. In the podcast, she teams up with Zach Reino, whom she met as a student at UCB. She filled me in: "He and I quickly discovered a shared sensibility and started writing musical comedy/comedy songs together." In 2014, the two worked together with the cast of Baby Wants Candy, which had been doing musical improv in Chicago since the 1990s and had casts in New York and Los Angeles as well. In 2016, McKenna found herself guesting on podcasts hosted by Earwolf, including Scott Aukerman's *Comedy Bang! Bang!* Aukerman's podcast turned show turned podcast is legendary in the alt-comedy realm connected to Los Angeles and UCB in particular. Founded in 2006, the podcast revolves around Aukerman and a host of comedic guests improvising and experimenting with various absurdist characters in an asynchronous medium with no content regulation. "It is theatre of the mind in the truest sense," writes Vince M. Meserko in "Standing Upright: Podcasting, Performance, and Alternative Comedy" (2015). With a background in musical theater, Aukerman also makes a space for music, working with musical comedians like Reggie Watts and "Weird Al" Yankovic.

In a 2017 *Forbes* interview with Danny Ross, "Scott Aukerman Talks Music and 'Comedy Bang! Bang!,'" Aukerman shared, "Essentially *Comedy Bang! Bang!* is silly and fun and I think music is a big part of what makes something fun." In 2017, Earwolf offered to host McKenna's own podcast, if she had any ideas. "*Off Book* was it," she explained to me: "It just felt like an obvious extension of what we were doing and something that felt related to other Earwolf shows but was still its own niche."[9]

The show's improvisation is nothing short of amazing. McKenna cites the episode "The Kids Are at Night" (number 55, July 30, 2018) as one of her favorites: "The scale of the story is really small and simple and even with like 140 episodes it still stands out for that reason." Guest Mary Sohn, who appeared in the hilarious movie *Between Two Ferns: The Movie* (2019), and Reino play parents while McKenna is a child, a role she has assumed elsewhere. In the part, she's not Snooks-level obnoxious. Instead, she is reflective about growing up and what that entails, singing, in a fully improvised showstopper, "I'm not ready to be a big girl." Likewise, in the song "Can I Still Like Horses?" she considers her love of ponies and its relationship to becoming an adult, or, as she puts it, "trotting into the unknown." With her clear, strong voice, she sings, "Hello, horse," holding the second note in the ascending line. The free association in these songs is hilarious, with the insertion of her favorite made-up "hoof hoof magazine." But the harmonies and layering of voice as well as the callbacks to previous songs and setups make for a remarkably cohesive musical, all improvised.

I asked McKenna, "Are there ideas (musical or otherwise) in place ahead of time?" She assured me that there aren't and explained the process—dependent on knowledge of both "traditional long-form improv" and patterns in music: "The musical improv process is no different than traditional long-form improv. Truly." Others have made a similar argument, drawing comparisons between improv in comedy and music, including jazz and rap. In the *Washington Post*'s "The Science behind Improv," the authors identify in both improvised comedy and music the importance of active listening, a loosening of mental control, and trust.[10] Focusing on process, McKenna continued, "I'm going to hit the premise in a way that feels like a pattern. That's exactly like music. I'm going to explore the premise in the verse and then I'm going to state the premise in the chorus." She downplays the effort: "Zach and I are just using the combination of our UCB training and musical theater background to find a premise and then fit it into a song structure." Her work then depends on similar structures in music and comedy—a coming together based on overlapping patterns. And despite McKenna's casual description of the process, the work itself is methodical and involved while sounding fresh and dynamic.

When I connected her work to a tradition of funny musical women, McKenna was quick to reference comical women on Broadway. The power of that female collective is reflected in the belt, McKenna's own early vocal rebellion. Describing her early roles in community theater and school musical productions, she told me, "I sort of started self-teaching and working on my belt in those shows much to the chagrin of my voice teacher." Singing with the whole power of the chest voice in higher registers, belting is potentially damaging to the voice in the long run, but it's a Broadway staple both raw and powerful in effect. How could she resist? In Oklahoma City University's on-campus newspaper, local musicologist Jake Johnson observed that "audiences believe that such guttural singing is one of the most honest sounds a woman can make." With that sound, he told me via email, "women aren't just allowed to be *funny* on Broadway but (and maybe this is paradoxical) women are taken *seriously* on the musical stage in a way that they aren't in the real world." McKenna tied this history to a need. To make it as any outsider, you often have to be more—act, sing, deliver the joke—she argued: "The reality is if you're an outsider at all you have to armor yourself with as many undeniable talents as possible so that you can break through." In stand-up comedy, more is similarly expected of women. While men can talk about their male experience, women are supposed to cater to both genders. In her study, Antoine argued, "For women to earn respect as comedians, then, they have to show that they have range beyond that expected of men, and that they can talk about things that aren't just about women." McKenna helps connect that biased expectation to the many musical women in comedy: "That may be why we've had many famous women in comedy who had to wear multiple hats to be relevant."

Broadway and musical theater in general have been generous to women. Broadway, after all, has been seen as a feminine space, a place for outsiders of all types to assert their belonging. But that progress comes at a price. While men often direct or write the music, these women are flexing many talents at once—comedy, acting, dancing, and singing. Broadway demands a lot of its women. And that's exciting but perhaps unfair.

Just as the story of *Funny Girl* is progressive and not, maybe Broadway is both. Fanny Brice is a woman who pursues her man—singing "Don't Rain on My Parade" as she goes after him by boat—but she also loses her love because he can't handle her success and the related power imbalance. It's a problematic message—women, apparently, can't have it all and may even be punished for their achievement. Broadway too has offered women a lot. However, to make it on the musical stage, women have had to do it all, in a way that men in comedy elsewhere have not. And to find fame, they have also often had to make their own platform or otherwise break with existing examples. Brice and Mabley found a way to perform without a partner. McKenna too created a unique showcase. In musical theater, funny girls have worked remarkably hard to make their way in a supposedly feminine genre, a genre already dismissed. To have it at all, they have had to do a lot. McKenna rightfully maintains, "It may be odd to root for this but I suppose I'm hoping for a world where there's enough room at the table so that people only have to be undeniable in one area. You shouldn't have to be so much more just to get the same access as someone else who maybe is bringing less." I'll be rooting right along with McKenna and, for now, celebrating the impressive women who have worked so hard to do it all, dreaming and pushing beyond accepted norms and thereby finding a way to entertain on stage in comedy and music.

NOTES

1. Brooks McNamara, "Broadway: A Theatre Historian's Perspective," *Drama Review* 45, no. 4 (2001), 125–128.

2. See Josh Kun, "The Yiddish Are Coming: Mickey Katz, Anti-Semitism, and the Sound of Jewish Difference," *American Jewish History* 87, no. 4 (1999): 343–374.

3. Quoted in Lauren Rebecca Sklaroff, *Red Hot Mama: The Life of Sophie Tucker* (Austin: University of Texas Press, 2018), 73.

4. Elsie A. Williams, *The Humor of Jackie Moms Mabley: An African American Comedic Tradition* (New York: Garland, 1995), 121–122.

5. Brian Kellow, *Ethel Merman: A Life* (New York: Penguin Books, 2007), 247.

6. Neal Gabler, *Barbra Streisand: Redefining Beauty, Femininity, and Power* (New Haven, CT: Yale University Press, 2016).

7. See Stacy Wolf, *A Problem Like Maria: Gender and Sexuality in the American Musical* (Ann Arbor: University of Michigan Press, 2002), 176.

8. Many Jewish composers responded to Christmas similarly. As *Newsweek* pointed out under the headline "The Best Christmas Songs Were Actually Written by Jews," the haunting song "White Christmas" was written by Irving Berlin, also the composer of "God Bless America."

9. In 2021, the podcast moved from Earwolf to Art19.

10. Sarah L. Kaufman et al., "The Science behind Improv," *Washington Post*, June 7, 2018, https://www.washingtonpost.com/graphics/2018/lifestyle/science-behind-improv-performance/.

PART III

HUMOROUS MUSIC BY TOPIC

TEN

HUMOR ABOUT HUMOR

IN SOME WAYS, THIS CHAPTER is about funny music on television. There are certain commonalities in this type of humor as a genre as well as its reception. For one, humorous music on television often relies on a setup conducive to musical breaks, a show within a show or a band or musical group as the focus. But with that premise, there is the potential for meta-humor, humor about humor, in the layering of fiction and reality. So, in another way, this chapter is about a certain topic in comedy: humor itself.

While musical humor collects in various genres and media platforms, it also clusters around certain topics, including the topic of comedy. In part 3, then, it isn't just music genres that cultivate expectations ripe for comedy, it's also whole subjects across different genres. To take on topics, musical comedians often have to synthesize thinking about social norms as well as various traditions of music. This fluid intelligence requires a certain mental flexibility and dexterity, including an ability to see beyond accepted standards of thought and social behavior in order to acknowledge an overlooked fact. The resulting humor can be a surprise reckoning with a hidden truth.

Kate Micucci and Riki Lindhome, folk duo Garfunkel and Oates, offer an especially rich example of humorous music on television as well as the intelligence and honesty behind comedy about comedy. And it's no coincidence that this chapter once again focuses on the work of women, with television's many connections to Broadway.

Like the art of Broadway, the musicality of television has been sidestepped in many descriptions and explanations of small-screen music. As Simon Frith observed in "Look! Hear! The Uneasy Relationship of Music and Television" (2002), "The television audience is rarely conceived as a music audience." With limits on sound quality and space, television can cut off our view of a musician's playing and dampen the effect of a musical experience, even when music is the focus of a televised event. Television, after all, is first and foremost a visual medium, and music, when it's included, often serves that sense of sight by getting our attention, eyes on the screen.

Still, television has long featured and even promoted music—*American Bandstand* and even *American Idol*. And the music of Broadway has inspired some recent TV shows—*Glee, Smash, Galavant, Crazy Ex-Girlfriend*. As Kelly Kessler, in her book *Broadway in the Box* (2020) notes, this Broadway presence in twenty-first century television actually has deeply entrenched roots, with overlap from the beginning between television and the musical. With that, television has also been home to a lot of funny women. In the 1950s, Broadway stars like Judy Garland hosted their own shows. And in the 1960s, younger stars of Broadway, like Florence Henderson, Carol Burnett, and Julie Andrews, honed their skills simultaneously on the small screen. In 1967, Burnett debuted her legendary comedic-musical television show, *The Carol Burnett Show* (1967–1979). It helped women that, by the mid-1960s, networks were experimenting with more specialized programming, as well as diversity in representation to some extent. ABC broadcast "An Evening with Julie Andrews and Harry Belafonte" in 1969, fielding bag-loads of hate-filled disapproval. And two big-voiced Black women starred in self-named shows,

The Leslie Uggams Show (1969) and *The Pearl Bailey Show* (1971). Women also worked in music and comedy on television in other ways. For example, in 1979, Sylvia Fine chronicled the history of musical comedy in a PBS television series, *Musical Comedy Tonight*, including musicals like *Good News* and *Oklahoma!* She was uniquely knowledgeable, having written music for her husband, funny actor and singer Danny Kaye, a star on stage and screen, including the small one. On PBS, she stood in front of a grand piano and said of her husband, "He couldn't afford to pay me, so he married me."

The small screen has benefited, then, from some of the autonomy that women and other diverse populations have enjoyed on Broadway. Micucci and Lindhome have built on this inheritance with their funny and musical television show *Garfunkel and Oates* (2014). And I wanted to ask them all about that experience as well as their musical influences. As a fan, I had to remind myself to ask the tough questions and not my immediate thoughts: Can we meet up for ice cream? Would you like to pet my dog? An obvious starting point was the origins of their series. Micucci and Lindhome explained that start as autobiographical inspiration: "We were touring the country every weekend and trying to figure out life as we went along. Funny and crazy things were constantly happening in our actual lives and we wanted to make a show that was just a heightened version of our own reality." Some of that self-reference would have to do with bias, in terms of both gender and musical comedy. But on *Garfunkel and Oates*, thanks in part to television's tradition of experimentation, even attention to prejudice packs a punchline. Rather than upending standards of genre, as we have seen in previous chapters, Micucci and Lindhome found a way to disrupt larger notions of comedy, women in comedy, and humorous music. Again, such meta-humor takes a certain awareness, introspection, and ability. And, to be clear, that weight and consequence, in the case of *Garfunkel and Oates*, coexists with dirty jokes about blowjobs.

"29/31," by Garfunkel and Oates, screenshot from YouTube.

Micucci grew up in Nazareth, Pennsylvania, in the Lehigh Valley. She studied piano and participated in her high school's theater program as well as in Pennsylvania Youth Theatre. Making her "heart happy," her small town also boasted special musical events like a Kazoo Parade, with the colorful toy being tooted by townsfolk on the streets of Nazareth.[1] She headed to Los Angeles to study art but also had other ambitions: "I wanted to be an actress, artist and musician," she shared with me. She credits the stability of childhood in her small hometown with giving her the strength to deal with Hollywood rejection. "When you go to Los Angeles," she told Dan Reilly of *Rolling Stone* (2014), "it's a rough city and it's hard. You drive around in your car in your own little bubble and there's tons of rejection. Being from the Lehigh Valley helped because it was something so stable." Her collaboration with Riki Lindhome offered support as well. "I had that to lean on," Micucci told Kathy Lauer-Williams. "It's good to make your own things because you can have control of your own art."

Lindhome, born in Coudersport, Pennsylvania, grew up in New York and studied at Syracuse University. There she was involved in a sketch comedy troupe called Syracuse Live before setting out for Los Angeles and, initially, a career as an actress. In our interview, she explained, "When I first moved to LA, I only wanted to be an actress. But after a while, I wanted more and started writing. I wrote funny songs on my own for almost a decade before I met Kate. Then once we met, Garfunkel and Oates became our main focus."

In Los Angeles, Micucci and Lindhome ran into each other at auditions and eventually reconnected in the lobby of UCB, both there on bad dates.[2] But they had actually come into contact earlier, at a music camp when they were young—the Mansfield Music Camp, a youth camp in Mansfield, Pennsylvania. "It's just a crazy coincidence," Micucci told me. "One day Riki mentioned going to music camp when she was a kid. I said, 'So did I!' Then we realized we had been at this small town music camp at the same time. I focused on trombone and I took a beginner drum class. Mostly I remember playing tennis and crying because I missed my parents." Lindhome apparently fared better: "I focused on flute and singing. And trying to get a camp boyfriend."

After reconnecting in Los Angeles, in 2008, they started writing songs and playing music together. Micucci recalled, "I had a show at the Steve Allen Theater called Playin' With Micucci.... Eventually when Riki and I teamed up and started writing music together, something magical started to happen," she continued. "Our sensibilities really clicked and we ran with it. We started playing shows around LA and a year later we started touring the country. Garfunkel and Oates became the thing that we wanted to focus on. We were having a blast going to different cities and playing comedy clubs and festivals. It felt new and exciting." Their first performance was "random," Lindhome told Farley Elliott of *LAist* in 2009: "A friend of mine's band was performing, and I was at my friend's house, and everyone started playing music, and I said 'well, Kate and I started writing songs,' and they're like 'alright, whatever' because we're girls." But the songs were a big hit and that band asked them to open for them. With Lindhome playing acoustic guitar and Micucci on ukulele, the two started performing shortly thereafter all over the city as Garfunkel and Oates—a tribute to two rock and roll "second bananas," Art Garfunkel of Simon and Garfunkel and John Oates of Hall and Oates. Micucci poses as Oates, an ode to her reputed ability to grow a bushy Oates-like black mustache.

Their songwriting process is involved, an extended session of brainstorming and craft: "Basically we will start with a germ of an idea and then brainstorm on that idea for a very long time ... sometimes it's months of us just writing everything we can think of on the topic. Once we find the hook of the song, we start to weed through our giant brainstorm document and shape it into verses. Then melodically we start to sing around that." The comedy depends on honesty. "Finding comedy in the truth," Micucci told Mike Hilleary, writing for *Under the Radar* (2014), "it kind of hits a little harder." But there is also a joke in the group's play on basic contrasts. Lindhome, tall and blond, and Micucci, short with dark hair, deliver some of the dirtiest lyrics you'll hear with wide smiles and big, innocent eyes. In 2009, Micucci told *LAist*, "I didn't even say the F word, ever, until like three years ago. And now our first song is called Fuck You." That song describes courtship: "I like you / And like can lead to like-like / And like-like can lead to love." But the innocence of "like-like" progresses quickly—to "fist you" and "fuck you." Lindhome especially enjoys that juxtaposition in her partner's performance: "I find Kate really funny. She says the dirtiest stuff with the most innocent face. That's the kind of stuff that makes me laugh."[3] The ukulele, one of several instruments with a humor all its own (like Weird Al's accordion or actor Will Ferrell's cowbell), ups that incongruity. Despite the instrument's current popularity, it still conjures Hawaiian kitsch, celebrated as an instrument anyone can play while dismissed as a cheap toy for kids.[4] Micucci actually discovered the instrument while in Hawaii: "I was living in Hawaii for a few months and I was missing my piano, so my grandpa bought me a ukulele. I learned some Gershwin songs on it. I moved to Los Angeles shortly after and that is when I started writing funny songs on my ukulele." While Lindhome strums the guitar, the smaller Micucci plays the smaller instrument, accompanying F-bombs and dick jokes with vacation-vibe pluck.

Along with their music, Micucci and Lindhome have had simultaneous success as actresses, appearing in multiple television shows without instruments. Highlights for Micucci include *The Big Bang Theory* and *Scrubs*, the latter with its own occasional musical interludes; and for Lindhome, *Gilmore Girls*, *The Big Bang Theory*, and *Another Period*. In sitcom comedy, Micucci enjoys a musicality, a rhythm, in delivering the punchline: "We love acting in sitcoms because it's like doing a play. You hear the laughter and wait for the right moment to land the joke." In 2014, their show, *Garfunkel and Oates*, combined the rhythm of sitcom humor with their own rhythm in song. Broadway provided inspiration: "We are just both obsessed with musical theater and have been our whole lives," Micucci shared. "One of the shows we first bonded over was *Legally Blonde*. *Book of Mormon* is another. And anything Sondheim, of course." Micucci also cites the show *I Love Lucy*, an exceptionally musical early television comedy, which popular culture professor Rosie White links to vaudeville, with Lucy often playing with gender, dressing up and cross-dressing in attempts to infiltrate her husband's show within the show. In one episode, "The Ballet" (1952), Lucy tries to win a spot on the stage by dancing, physically clowning in the episode with her foot stuck in the barre. Despite her failure, she still makes her way into the act, with a cream pie, as her husband, Ricky (played by real-life husband Desi Arnaz), sings the romantic song "Martha."[5] In an interview with comedian Tig Notaro for *Vulture* (2014), Micucci explained, "*I Love Lucy* is my favorite show, going back to when I was 4. I've watched every episode I don't know how many times. It was something to watch women being funny when I was young." To me, she added, "There were so many musical comedy moments in *I Love Lucy*. One of my favorites being the performance where Lucy and Ethel are singing a song about friendship while wearing the same dress. Also the moment where Ricky sings 'We're Having a Baby.' It's one of the best moments in TV history ... it goes from laughter to actual tears and it's perfect."

Like *I Love Lucy*, with Ricky's show a part of the series, Micucci and Lindhome had a ready-made premise supporting musical breaks in *Garfunkel and Oates*: their own musical careers as fodder and musical jumping-off point. In the show's second episode, Micucci and Lindhome audition for the fictional children's show *Pumpernickel Place*, in the office of a rather distracted higher-up, played by Tig Notaro, who is busy ordering cigarettes online. The sweetly simple song we hear, "Rainbow Connections," is part of that audition. In the show's fourth episode, "Road Warrior," we follow Garfunkel and Oates to an out-of-town show, their one thousandth performance, during which they sing "29/31," about the same woman two years apart.

Many of the best musical comedies on television settled on a similar setup for song—a musical scenario as vehicle to cut through a sitcom's typical use of music (that customary use is to call attention to a punchline, create a mood associated with a recurring joke, or help establish energy before a break in order to entice audiences to return after the commercial).[6] To this end, Fox's *Glee*, which ran from 2009 to 2015, showcased a wannabe funny girl (played by Lea Michele) in a high school glee club (Michele would become the actual funny girl in the *Funny Girl* revival in 2022 and 2023). The focus was a ready-made backdrop for song after song, all perfect for online media sharing, promoting the show and supporting a devoted fan base. As Kessler writes, "Glee coalesced into an ideal articulation of theatre fandom, teen anxiety, niche marketing, and twenty-first-century interactivity." Lindhome counts herself among *Glee*'s fans—a fandom she cemented in song, 2011's "Ain't Nuthin' but a *Glee* Thang," a parody of Dr. Dre's "Ain't Nuthin' but a 'G' Thang." In the song's video, posted on "Funny or Die," Lindhome excitedly watches the show and then argues with *Glee* actress Heather Morris and *Modern Family* actress Sofia Vergara about *Glee*'s best castmate. Lindhome sings about her favorites and what they would hypothetically do together in the library, throwing books and dancing "harder than the dewey decimal system."

The television series *30 Rock*, which ran from 2006 to 2013, likewise found a reasonable way to fold music into the show while building on earlier musical traditions, such as vaudeville and variety. The series revolved around a fictional variety show, *The Girlie Show* (*TGS*), and starred Tina Fey, also its creator, as a version of herself, a nod to her time working as the first female head writer on *Saturday Night Live*. With musical comedians like Adam Sandler, Fred Armisen, and Andy Samberg as past *SNL* players, *SNL* was an especially musical reference point with music never just reserved for the musical guest. And the show has long made use of other media platforms as promotion, especially with the digital shorts of the Lonely Island, and well before *Glee*. Micucci told me, "I've always been a fan of Saturday Night Live and how they incorporate songs into the sketches." With this touchstone, *30 Rock* could easily include a silly song, like "Muffin Top," belted by one of the fictional show's stars, Jenna, played by Broadway baby Jane Krakowski; or indulge in the hilarious "Werewolf Bar Mitzvah" (in the 2007 episode "Jack Gets in the Game"), which grew from a seeming throwaway reference to a fictional song, the eccentric *TGS* star Tracy Jordan's apparent effort to cash in simultaneously on Halloween and a Jewish rite of passage: "Boys becoming men—men becoming wolves." Showrunner Robert Carlock, in Mike Roe's 2018 "'Werewolf Bar Mitzvah' from '30 Rock': An Oral History," considers the song and what it takes to land a musical joke on television: "I think there has to be a reason for it"; otherwise, "it's jarring."

In a heightened version of their real-life musical pursuits, Micucci and Lindhome had their ready-made reason—even in less-than-musical moments, as in episode 6, when Garfunkel and Oates apply for medical marijuana, singing their song "Weed Card." But there are also fantastical musical disruptions in *Garfunkel and Oates* that depart from any reality, much like the musical segments in the HBO series *Flight of the Conchords*, which Lindhome calls "one of my all-time favorite shows." Anthropologist Kirsten Zemke compares the Flight of the Conchords' songs to arias, as a space for exploration of emotion. They also represent the characters' imagined version of their music-making—a fantasy realm divorced from their fictional struggles as musicians.[7] In an interview with Amelie Gillette for the *A.V. Club* (2007), the duo's Bret McKenzie explained of the show,

> The fact that it's a comedy helps—you get away with that strange moment when people just break into a song. But I think we thought that was funny anyway, people just starting to sing. We put a lot of care into those transitional moments, to try and make them work, because it can be a very difficult moment in a show ... We tried a variety of different methods throughout the show, whether we go into a complete other fantasy world of one of the character's minds, or there's a blurry half-reality when the rest of the world can't hear 'em.

In the third episode of *Garfunkel and Oates*, Lindhome and Micucci reveal their feelings in a sarcastic and similarly fantastic musical take. Discussing Lindhome's upcoming date, which involves watching sports with her new boyfriend and his friends, Micucci and Lindhome are obviously unenthusiastic about the itinerary. Mid-conversation, an overhead light blinks, and a booming beat begins, supporting the song "Sports Go Sports." We are suddenly in an '80s aerobic studio, and the two friends are in high-cut spandex leotards with Micucci's bangs era-perfect, hairsprayed and high. The song sung in sync with each beat is a tongue-in-cheek attempt to support the team, any team: "I promise I really totally care who wins." But the pseudo-cheering easily exposes their true feelings about sports fandom: "This is the most important thing that's ever occurred / The vicarious fulfillment of your dream that got deferred."

The song has connections to songs by other funny musicians who have mocked sports before, with little controversy: Tom Lehrer's "Fight Fiercely, Harvard" and Weird Al's "Sports Song." And yet, in an interview with Dan Reilly of *Rolling Stone*, Micucci and Lindhome revealed that their sports song has been their most hotly contested, outpacing more obvious options like "The Loophole" (previously titled "Fuck Me in the Ass Because I Love Jesus"). Lindhome said, "We're picking on sports in general and they took it so personally, like, 'How dare you? I love sports.' Didn't see that one coming."

In the show's second episode, while there is reason for the song "Rainbow Connections," reality similarly falls away when the song starts, as the office disappears and a puppet world emerges. Micucci and Lindhome become cloth creatures themselves, holding their instruments with their fabric hands, as they sing in unison accompanied by light piano playing. The screen follows two male puppets, Schubert and Sockley, as they find love: "Don't know how we found it, but we did somehow / All the moments of our lives, were leading up to now." A host of puppet friends, including bananas and sandwiches, sing together as the lovers make a promise: "If you do, then I do too." It's a touching tribute to love and an anthem in support of same-sex marriage.

Following *Flight of the Conchords*, *Garfunkel and Oates* was originally written for HBO. After Lindhome and Micucci wrote the pilot, however, HBO declined, and IFC, the Independent Film Channel, agreed to make the show. The specific network's rules conditioned content to a certain extent as well as the breadth of the show's experimentation. Television has always been experimental, which, along with its ties to Broadway, provides a space for imaginative musical innovation, such as fantastical breaks with puppets and spandex. As Lorenz Engell writes in *Thinking through Television* (2019), television is constantly changing in response to innovation. From black and white to color and so on, the rules are ever evolving, ripe for boundary pushing and creative invention. But that experimentation varies based on the mandate of each network. For example, the Cartoon Network's Adult Swim programming has a particular reputation for absurd comedic originality, more so than IFC. Eric Andre, with the network's *The Eric Andre Show*, takes full advantage, violently breaking every talk-show norm, though he did have to cut "a pro-Al-Qaeda country song": "We really have carte blanche. The network is super, super nurturing and supportive. It couldn't be a better matrimony. We're TV-MA, so we can do whatever we want."[8] IFC does not tolerate the same level of mature content, with a TV-14 rating. For Garfunkel and Oates, "The Loophole" was then out. Lindhome told Reilly, "That was the hardest part. We have so much very adult material and it's hard to tone that down." Tig Notaro asked Micucci and Lindhome, "Were you trying to show explicit sexual content or nudity?" "We wanted to, yeah," replied Lindhome. "We wanted to do all that stuff, but it was not to be." Micucci and Lindhome, however, both insist that IFC's regulation had unexpected benefits, pushing them in new directions, like the puppet montage in "Rainbow Connections." "I think not being allowed to do certain things allowed us to do other things that we'd never have thought of," Micucci said. And in a TV-14 environment, they could still take on controversial issues beyond sports, like gender, in imaginative ways, as they did to particular effect in episode 4.

In that episode, negative ideas of women in comedy and funny music provide fodder for joke after joke as our hapless heroes set out to perform their one thousandth show. In the opening sequence, Micucci and Lindhome arrive at the out-of-town venue and meet heckler Dennis, who is already out front with a sign reading, "Dames are Lame." He is mounting a lone protest: "Boycott women comics," who he insists belong "in the kitchen not on stage." The situation isn't much better inside, with owner Andrew offering a "creative note": "Please, no material about your periods." After he warns them that he is going to propose to his girlfriend during their set, Lindhome and Micucci, left alone, wonder about the assumption that female comics will talk about their periods, effectively losing the coveted male audience—which incites a funny discussion of periods, including the bloody trail that can follow a lady at the water park. They take the note but manage to play on periods for a laugh. It's another sort of loophole.

Preparing for their set, Lindhome asks the sound guy, Tom, for a second mic. Disgruntled, he does not comply, calling her "bossy" (the pre-"nasty" female pejorative), which forces the two to seek out Dennis, who is using a mic to disparage them outside. He agrees to lend them his mic if they record a video saying, "Women aren't funny." Offended, they emphatically refuse. But when Dennis counters, asking them to instead record the line "Musical comedy is an inferior form of comedy," they agree to make the recording. Lindhome says, "It kinda is." The turnaround is comedy gold, a stand against prejudice that slips into acceptance of comedic music's poor standing—a joke at their own expense.

Now with two mics, they perform their one thousandth show, singing the song "29/31." The song begins on stage but quickly becomes an imagined realm, with Micucci at twenty-nine optimistic about her marriage prospects—"I'm at the top of my game, possibilities are endless"—and Lindhome at thirty-one spiraling into depression, scream-singing, "There's nobody left! / I'm all alone!" Later in the song, in split screen, Micucci happily sings at a dinner party while Lindhome yells on her own. The song plays with the notion that women expire, an ageism that unfairly dovetails with the science of fertility. When their ride doesn't show up after the show, Dennis drives them home in his van, telling them that he's a musician—not like them, "a real musician." It's another crack at funny music and a fitting end to a terrible day—one based in reality. Lindhome told Notaro, "We took all the weird things that happened at different shows and put them into one episode." In fact, the marriage proposal actually happened at a show at Largo. Of the episode's many real-life travails, Dennis was the lone exception, instead a conglomerate of existing sexism. Micucci told Reilly, "We consider him the voice of Twitter. He's a human YouTube commenter."

Despite the success of women on television, as the episode makes clear, equality is still a work in progress. Addressing the star power of women on musical shows during the 1960s and '70s, with Carol Burnett and Pearl Bailey, Kessler cautions, "Although this string of variety specials and series driven by the stardom of the musical's women surely illustrates a gendered shift ... it would be foolish to boldly claim that the sisters were doing it for themselves." Today, the picture continues to be more complicated, with Twitter (now X) often an outlet for the most controversial takes on such issues. In the 2019 *New York Times* article "Is Peak TV Really a Bonanza for Female Comics?" Noam Scheiber insists that any notion of television's female dominance is at odds with lived reality. He cites Dan Pasternack, an IFC executive in charge of *Garfunkel and Oates*: "There's always that struggle you have with corporate people about, 'Oh, so this is a show with two women at the center of it.'" In an interview with Ruthie Feirberg, writing for *Playbill*, Rachel Bloom (of the musical show *Crazy Ex-Girlfriend*) further highlights the lack of high-profile women writing funny music, citing men like Weird Al and Mel Brooks as her own inspirations: "As a comedy songwriter, most of my influences up until recently were men because that seemed like that was what was available." The one exception she mentions is singer and comedic actress Julie Brown, known for her send-up in the 1980s of Madonna as well as funny songs like "Girl Fight Tonight" and "I Like 'Em Big and Stupid." Both gaps underscore continued thinking that women just aren't funny or aren't funny enough to entertain male audiences—the supposed prime demographic. As Sarah Silverman told *GQ* in 2018, her male comic friends insisted that the male laugh mattered most of all: "The women only laugh if their date laughs."

Many of Garfunkel and Oates's songs take on related gender issues, as in "Road Warrior." With that in mind, I had to ask, "Do you prefer comedy with a pointed takeaway?" Micucci and Lindhome answered, "We try to do a different thing with each song. 50/50 has a lot of social commentary, as do songs like The Loophole and Sex With Ducks. But other songs, like Handjob Blandjob I Don't Understandjob and College Try, are just meant to be silly and fun. We like to do a combo of both kinds of songs." While "Sex with Ducks" takes on offensive opposition to same-sex marriage, "College Try" involves a highly descriptive reaction to the vagina, including its smell: "old French dressing at a salad bar" or "a dead rotting turtle you left in your car." Just as they approach funny music in different ways, so too do they differ in their response to women in comedy and television. While "Road Warriors" mocks prejudices against women in comedy, Micucci and Lindhome have in interviews described the place of women in funny music in more positive terms, flipping the negative just as they did with the TV-14 rating. Citing their gender as a help in getting work, Lindhome explained to Elliott, "I think this may be the one case, where [being girls has] helped us. Because the comedy world is still so male dominated, even the other comedians like to have girls in there so it's not seven white dudes." Since their act is unique, they insist, they weren't perceived as direct competition. They were an easy invite. And they had certain material all to themselves. Micucci maintained, "As girls, we're allowed to say things that guys couldn't say." In *Under the Radar*, Micucci singled out one song in particular: "Even going back to one of our earlier songs like 'Pregnant Women Are Smug,' a guy couldn't write that song."

We see this optimistic bent in the series finale. "The last two episodes of the series are by far our favorite," Micucci and Lindhome revealed to me. In the final episode, "Maturity," they are both grappling with growing up, Lindhome attempting to freeze her eggs and Micucci trying to figure out how to let go of her childish hobbies. In a tribute to her lived kazoo-parade experience, Micucci in the episode attempts to organize a similar event online. The group that joins her, however, a bunch of adult men, misinterpret the event, assuming it's an orgy. After Lindhome receives bad news at the fertility clinic, the two bandmates meet up at a park bench, both dejected. They decide to have one more kazoo parade together before ostensibly moving on with their lives. A touching song then begins: "Such a Loser." As in "Rainbow Connections," unison singing, a simple melodic line, and piano accompaniment help create the emotional effect. Minimal hand-drawings support the song, with characters failing and being criticized, highlighted in an online comment (a callback to episode 4): "Go back to the kitchen." But the song's overall message is meant for anyone brave enough to try: "You're a loser, but a dreamer," they sing in the chorus. The melodic line ascends a half step on the word *loser*. Rather than an emphatic statement, there is a question in the incline. Being a loser is not what you might think. The label and song as a whole are instead a celebration of those people brave enough to fail: "You are such a loser, good for you / It's something that a lot of people can't do." After the animation fades, the screen follows Garfunkel and Oates as they dance in their own parade, playing a kazoo rendition of "Such a Loser."

—w—

In their music and show, Garfunkel and Oates reveal and build on the powerful place of women on television, with ties to a similar independence on Broadway as well as the small screen's long-standing tradition of experimentation. But that freedom is complicated, conditioned by network rules and shifting attitudes about funny women. Like their songs, Micucci and Lindhome aren't one thing, fighters for equality or victims of gendered dismissal. Instead, they are losers, in the best sense of the word—trying to create something new with echoes of past invention. The series cleverly showcases their funny music, with a reality-based musical premise. But, in the series, real life also pleasantly disappears as we experience invented worlds of puppets and animated failure. It's hard for me not to invest in Micucci and Lindhome, their on-screen characters and extra-television careers, as I myself try and fail like so many dreamers. There is much, then, to love in *Garfunkel and Oates*, a television show that upends notions of the small screen's unmusical rep, women in comedy, and comedic music more generally. That meta-humor and meta-musical humor is certainly fun, but it's also powerful, a subtle takedown of thinking both common and toxic. In this way, comedic music can play on the incongruities in notions of genre and the performance of genre. But it can also riff on wider currents of thought related to race and gender, if, that is, the comedians are clever enough to see beyond their own cultural conditioning and take a successful comedic stand. Even if unsuccessful, that attempt is worth celebrating.

NOTES

1. Kate Micucci interview in Kathy Lauer-Williams, "Kate Micucci on Growing Up in Nazareth," *Morning Call*, September 1, 2016.
2. Interview in Mike Hilleary, "Garfunkel and Oates," *Under the Radar Magazine*, August 6, 2014.
3. Hilleary.
4. Marion Jacobson, "The Rise and Fall (and Rise) of the Ukulele," *Atlantic*, January 25, 2015.
5. Rosie White, "Funny *Peculiar:* Lucille Ball and the Vaudeville Heritage of Early American Television Comedy," *Social Semiotic* 26, no. 3 (2016): 298–310.
6. See Liz Giuffre, "Music in Comedy Television from the Composer's Perspective: Getting 'the Answers You're *Not* Looking For' in an Interview with David Schwartz," in *Music in Comedy Television: Notes on Laughs*, ed. Liz Giuffre and Philip Hayward (New York: Routledge, 2017), 105–116.

7. See Kirsten Zemke, "'I Told You I Was Freaky': Gender, Genre, and Parody in the Songs of *Flight of the Conchords*," in *Music in Comedy Television: Notes on Laughs*, ed. Liz Giuffre and Philip Hayward (New York: Routledge, 2017), 117–128.

8. Quoted in Liz Shannon Miller, "'The Eric Andre Show': The Only Two Things They Can't Do on TV's Most Anarchic Talk Show," IndieWire, August 17, 2016, https://www.indiewire.com/features/general/the-eric-andre-show-hannibal-buress-adult-swim-guests-season-4-1201717792/. See also Evan Elkins, "The New Logic of the Absurd: The Eric Andre Show," in *The Comedy Studies Reader*, ed. Nick Marx and Matt Sienkiewicz (Austin: University of Texas Press, 2018), 57–70.

ELEVEN

SILLY LOVE SONGS

HUMOR ISN'T THE ONLY MUSICAL topic ripe for laughs. A more basic topic, both musical and funny, is love. Though love is often treated in sentimental or cheesy ways, love is honestly hilarious: from the obsessive overthinking ("Does he like me? Would he like these earrings?") to the awkward first crush, with its embarrassing early encounters ("Hi, I love your cat, I mean car, I mean a**"). Beating back that initial crush, we may be lucky enough to find a deeper love, what life is all about. And it's wonderful. Cupid's bow has met its mark, and two are still two, but they are better for their coupling. But try watching that mess unfold. Love is beautiful but also sticky and gross—messy both figuratively and literally, if you know what I mean. And yes, I am skirting around the issue of sex, a stand-up staple, to some related to love, to others not so much. All of this is a great premise for musical comedy. And for singer Michael Bolton, the "king of Valentine's Day," it established an easy turn from sentimental crooner to hilarious meme, first as Captain Jack Sparrow in a video with the Lonely Island and then in the laugh-out-loud *Michael Bolton's Big, Sexy Valentine's Day Special* (2017).

For some, the special may have been completely surprising, with Bolton poking fun at himself and taking part in a comical duel with Andy Samberg as Kenny G—a war over hair. But Bolton, in my opinion, had been setting up these kinds of jokes his entire career, cranking out love songs and playing with the comedy already embedded in love. Bolton's sexy special was in some ways the natural next step, but one made possible only by his existing "serious" success, the talent of his collaborators, and a willingness to look at both the love song and his own career in a new way. Once again, the comedy is silly and light but depends on a fluid intelligence, integrating notions of love and Bolton himself while astutely and honestly upending them.

Bolton's musical success was slow in the making. From a struggling rocker to a jingle writer, he eventually found fame as a songwriter and solo singer. In his memoir, *The Soul of It All* (2013), he calls his song "How Am I Supposed to Live without You" a "career changer." A ballad of love and heartbreak, the lyrics ask, "And how am I supposed to carry on / When all that I've been livin' for is gone?" It first sounded publicly in 1983 on the CBS soap opera *Knots Landing*. When singer Laura Branigan recorded it, the song went straight to number one on *Billboard*'s Adult Contemporary list. He had tapped into the long history and tremendous popularity of the love song.

As Ted Gioia writes in his *Love Songs: The Hidden History* (2015), "Most of our music-making since the beginning of time has been about love." From settings of the great poet of Lesbos Sappho to the torch songs of the 1940s and '50s, all people need is love songs, to riff on the Beatles' "All You Need Is Love." Even our ancestors would agree. Charles Darwin believed that "musical tones and rhythms were used by our half-human ancestors, during the season of courtship, when animals of all kinds are excited not only by love, but by strong passions of jealousy, rivalry, and triumph."[1] Music may then have been part of our evolution in the basic and fundamental act of partnership and procreation.

With this strong connection between love and music, Bolton was smart to stick with a winning strategy. And, in 1987, he had another big hit, "That's What Love Is All About," but this time he recorded it himself as the first single on his album *The Hunger*. A year later, *Playgirl* magazine voted Bolton one of the 25 Most Eligible Bachelors. Ladies couldn't resist his smoky vocals, long flowing hair, and perfectly square jaw. As he recalled in his memoir, magazine-listed lust became the basis of myth, and an Italian journalist confirmed, asking him if it was true that he had "found a way to bring women to orgasm" just with his singing. Comedian Whoopi Goldberg seemed to think it was. After a performance at a gala for then-president Bill Clinton, Goldberg as the event's MC told Bolton, "Not a dry seat in the house."

The critics didn't always have the same orgasmic reaction. One writer, Stephen Holden, even warned Bolton of an impending backlash, with the release of his album *Time, Love and Tenderness* in 1991. "It will be your biggest album to date," he told Bolton, according to his memoir, "but I want to give you a heads-up": "The other critics are going to crucify you." He was right and then some. By 2009, according to Guy Adams (writing in the *Independent*), Bolton was "the most reviled man in pop." With great success, there are often those who want to break with the masses, especially in music. But, in Bolton's reception backslide, the focus on love was no doubt another contributing factor. To some, despite the rebellion and power in songs about love, "this is *wimpy* music." As Gioia realized, even writing about love songs could earn an author an ill-informed dismissal. Paul McCartney wrote the song "Silly Love Songs" (1976) in response to related criticism. In 2001, McCartney told *Billboard*, "Over the years people have said, 'Aw, he sings love songs, he writes love songs, he's so soppy at times.' I thought, Well, I know what they mean, but, people have been doing love songs forever . . . So the idea was that 'you' may call them silly, but what's wrong with that?"

Bolton's particular popularity among women didn't help. As Adams wrote, "'heartbreak' song epitomized Bolton's golden era, and allowed his honey-soaked voice to capture a generation of female hearts." Unfortunately, such appeal has never been a plus among popular critics. As musicologists Ian Biddle and Freya Jarman-Ivens maintain, "supposedly 'masculine' genres such as rock musics are culturally privileged as 'authentic' and 'meaningful,' in contrast to so-called feminine genres."[2] In popular music, masculinity is power, and association with women—female fans, supposedly feminine topics or traits—is a critical mistake. This messy truth affects the reception of other musicians with heart as well, like sax-wielding Kenny G, with his own flowing locks and love-sound rep. When Kanye West gifted Kim Kardashian a Valentine's serenade in 2019—Kenny G playing for her in a roomful of roses—comedians couldn't resist. And Kenny G even helped, similarly serenading Ray Romano on *The Late Late Show with James Corden*. "It's wonderful," Romano awkwardly says during the bit, "but it's just me and him."

With his "soft" association and female fandom, Bolton was the king of cheese before he was the king of Valentine's Day. As Jason Lee Oakes writes in the book *Bad Music*, cheesy music is "overwrought, overdetermined, overemotive, overproduced, overplayed, or generally over the top." It's also associated with extreme whiteness, wrapped up in a food staple connected with the midwestern United States, imagined hyperwhite.[3] And there is nothing cool about any of that. Bolton had found success, but he was fast becoming the apex of uncool—a punchline for anyone aspiring to hipness by punching down.

With this in mind, Jack Sparrow was a significant opportunity—a chance to break with preconceived notions of love songs and those people connected with them. The song's video, which debuted on *Saturday Night Live* in 2011, begins with Bolton meeting up with the Lonely Island guys, who want a "big sexy hook" for their new track. Now working together, the group cooly sets off for

The Lonely Island, "Jack Sparrow" (featuring Michael Bolton), screenshot from YouTube.

the club, "partying with the boys" and "rolling hard." But Bolton interrupts the macho posturing and laid-back beat with his hook and, in it, pays tribute to the character of Captain Jack Sparrow, from Disney's *Pirates of the Caribbean* franchise. The Lonely Island guys appear surprised but get back to their with-it groove, rapping "back in the club." Bolton interjects again, this time in a pirate costume, and his hardly hip departure yet again does not impress. Bolton tries another movie refence, this time *Forrest Gump*. "Not better," his new buddies intone. Bolton gives them his best melodic riff, and with that an ode to various movies, appearing vocally powerful but adorably unhip.

Describing his work with the Lonely Island, Bolton explains in his autobiography, "The next thing I knew I was in a crow's nest on a pirate ship decked out like Jack Sparrow, doing Forrest Gump on a park bench, cross-dressed as Erin Brockovich, and flashing my guns as Scarface." "And that was the tamest idea they came up with," he adds. But the popularity of the video led to a whole new audience for Bolton: "Now I can't walk through an airport anymore without receiving high fives and fist bumps from eighteen-year-old guys screaming, 'Captain Jack Sparrow! Dude, you rock!'"

This video, for Bolton, was part of an image reinvention—a pivot, as Clint Worthington writes in "When a Meme Loves a Woman," from "cheesy relic to adorable meme." By guesting—a common collaborative practice in rap—he was in some ways harnessing the general power of the cameo, an appearance as a nod or tribute to another artist but also a chance to connect with a new audience in a new way. Metal's Alice Cooper had done something similar in the musical-comedy *Wayne's World* (1992). Initially, in the film, he fulfills expectations performing in front of a huge skeleton in a full leather outfit and heavy black eye makeup. But then backstage, Cooper is very polite, providing characters Wayne and Garth a thoughtful and learned history of Milwaukee. Other noteworthy musical cameos include Billy Idol in *The Wedding Singer* and Keith Richards in the third installment of Bolton's beloved *Pirates of the Caribbean*.

The video's popularity helped, a viral moment after the *SNL* short was uploaded onto YouTube. As of August 2022, it has been viewed more than 227 million times. And it turned Bolton into a popular meme, defined as an online image featuring a stock character or characters, often well-known people, with a humorous caption. The image can further be transformed by users with awareness of the other versions.[4] In one Bolton meme, he's wearing a pirate hat and sporting a big grin, with the caption: "Now Back to the Good Part!" The Bolton content was ripe for online spread, given the success, as Limor Shifman observes, of positive, humorous content and the popularity of perceived "flawed masculinity," a comic focus that can represent both rebellion against and reinforcement of traditional norms.[5] As a meme, Bolton could reach additional audiences beyond his typical fan base. Memes, after all, do not spread within a single community defined by shared interests or values but instead tend to connect people who share a "way of relating."[6]

Bolton had not played with his image and music toward comedic ends before, though plenty of others had paved the way, mining the connection between comedy and kisses. In 1953, parody songwriter and math teacher Tom Lehrer offered a great send-up of new love by dwelling on the realities of growing old together. In the song "When You Are Old and Gray," he sings, "Since I still appreciate you / Let's find love while we may / Because I know I'll hate you / When you are old and gray." And Randy Newman too responded to love, with his song "Love Story" (1968), the first track of the album *Randy Newman Creates Something New under the Sun*, which focuses on a couple with simple ambitions: "We'll play checkers all day 'til we pass away." Newman said, "It's about someone with a dream so modest that it hardly counts as a dream."[7] Frank Zappa arguably made funny love songs, or more specifically anti–love songs, a specialty. In his Zappa book, Ben Watson singles out the song "I Ain't Got No Heart" (1966), which he describes as "a deliberate upending of love-song clichés."[8] In the song, Zappa doesn't just bring romance back down to earth; he mocks love: "I sit and laugh at fools in love / There ain't no such thing as love."

The Lonely Island, partly responsible for Bolton's comedic turn, had also made their mark in this category. Their 2011 song "I Just Had Sex" is almost a love song to sex. The comedy comes in the mismatch between the cool rap, featuring Akon, and the lyrics' awkward glee: "I just had sex / And it felt so good"; "And I'll never go back / To the not having sex / Ways of the past."[9] Flight of the Conchords takes on sex too, but with far less confidence. Loveable losers in love, they list, in the ditty "Carol Brown," the many women who have rejected them. Hopefully, they sing, Carol Brown will "stick around." But in their sexy "Business Time" (2008), they get down to, well, business. "Awe yeah," Clement purrs, narrating the setup. It's Wednesday, so, you know, it's "business time"—after, of course, a little foreplay, including brushing teeth. The song is about the comfortable sex of longtime partnership, set against the highly charged sexuality of a Barry White–esque groove.

Other funny songs use love to make a gendered point. In "50/50" (2018), Garfunkel and Oates sing, "Close your eyes, make a wish, picture your perfect woman / Now open your eyes and forget about her cause / I'm here and I'm not it." Their frank assessment, in the context of a love song, is funny from the start. During the song, that honesty continues as they list their weaknesses: workaholic, driven and never home, no household abilities ("If you want food you gotta cook it yourself"), and a fundamental need for sex ("And if we stop having sex, I will leave"). Yep, as long as this works for you, "we're a perfect couple," they sing. And the many limitations make that supposed perfection seem funny. Until, that is, they pull a switcheroo. What if these realities were describing a man's needs instead? Would they seem less problematic? Even natural? They sweetly turn the screw: "Every word that I just said / Could have also been describing you." The difference? You just "don't feel bad about it." It's a funny love song with a point, advancing a true fifty-fifty partnership.[10]

Many of these examples play on honesty—a clash between delusions of love and the reality of amorous connection. With so many sublime notions of the magic of love, musical comedians clearly have a ready-made setup for the creation of comical incongruity, based in truth alone. And perhaps that in part accounts for the many examples of funny love songs: there's so much material! (The same conclusion may account for the popularity and prevalence of funny Christmas songs.[11] With the general reverence around Christmas, despite the politics, rampant consumerism, and forced cheer, truth easily collides with expectation to create humor.[12])

―⁂―

Bolton was not funny from the start, unlike many of the musicians behind the other funny love songs. And yet, he was more than ready for his comedic turn. Not only did he have the love-god persona; his memoir shows evidence of a sense of humor (or at least that potential). Describing two brothers, early bandmates, who left the East Coast with him to try their luck on the West Coast, Bolton writes of the family's decision to let the boys go: "Given that their family was in the plumbing supply business, I'm sure it was a wrenching experience (sorry)." He also makes a point to play up his playful, rebellious side: "Somewhere in my forty years as an artist and performer, I picked up a reputation for being a serious guy. Many of my fans don't realize that I was never bar mitzvahed because I was the kid betting on the dreidel in Hebrew class and smoking cigarettes during breaks." That defiant streak, he insists, made it easy for him to go along with the plan the Lonely Island had for him in 2011, a song and viral video, the third-most-viewed YouTube clip that year. Bolton loved the new attention, giving the guys a shout-out in his memoir: "Andy, Kiv, and Jorm, you can call me anytime to do another music video."

—⚡—

And then they did, kind of. The group had kept in touch after "Jack Sparrow," occasionally going out for drinks or lunch. During a get-together, Bolton mentioned that he might produce a special to coincide with the release of a new album. The guys had a very different sort of special in mind. The Lonely Island's Akiva Schaffer told *Vanity Fair*, "We started talking about his 'Jack Sparrow' character and making a comedy special as if it's from that version of Michael Bolton—very confident, very sexy, and very confident in how sexy he is. Just our dream of who Michael Bolton was without having ever met him. Then that led us to Valentine's Day, which would obviously be his holiday." Schaffer created and wrote the special with host of *Comedy Bang! Bang!* Scott Aukerman. Bolton put his faith in the pair, though he didn't always understand the show's direction. Aukerman explained in *Vanity Fair*, "Comedically, he really trusted us to do right by him. We would read the scripts, and he'd laugh and then wonder why his character would do something like that. I remember at one point he said, 'Maybe I've been hit in the head?'"[13]

The basic premise of the show is that Santa needs Michael Bolton to inspire some baby-making around Valentine's Day. As Santa tells Bolton, he has too many toys; there needs to be more kids. Bolton is initially unsure, asking what he should do, "put out another sexy single?" But another Bolton love song, no matter how romantic, would not be enough. Santa wants Bolton to go bigger, creating a whole Valentine's Day variety show. Bolton obliges in a gold jacket, showing viewers his love nest, with lots of explicit art—all made specifically for the show. In *Vanity Fair*, Aukerman recalls, "There was a lot of discussion about the nude paintings. We went through many options." "Actually," he continues, "now that I think about it, I was just looking at porn."

The first act is a direct nod to variety shows of television's past, which began in the 1950s with Jackie Gleason, Sid Caesar, and Ed Sullivan, among others, and began to fizzle out in the 1970s, after the success of shows like *The Sonny and Cher Comedy Hour*, *The Jacksons*, *The Brady Bunch Variety Hour*, and *Donny and Marie*. In early television, the variety show's combination of comedy and music (a repurposing of vaudeville and hosted radio programs) worked well, given television's earlier restrictions. As David Inman makes clear in the book *Television Variety Shows*, everything then was filmed live, and it helped if the performance took place in a studio. The Bolton special references this televised past with Sarah Silverman and Randall Park—both dressed up in groovy seventies-style duds—singing together as Misty and Blair. The performance starts out like a modern duet between Sonny and Cher in a song seemingly about the necessary compromise in coupling. However, the ditty quickly veers off course, visibly grossing out Bolton, whom we see in quick response takes: "You're Jewish / And you're Korean / Open your butt / 'Cuz I'd like to see in."

It is fitting that, with this homage to variety hours of the past, the special would draw on talent associated with variety show

Saturday Night Live. Along with the Lonely Island and Silverman, who was a writer and performer on the hit series before she was fired, Fred Armisen makes an appearance as a frustrated chocolatier, though he doesn't showcase his musical gifts. Former *SNL* star Maya Rudolph also takes part, taking full advantage of her comedic and musical powers, both a part of her tours (or "momcations," as she calls them) with her musical group Princess, a Prince cover band.[14] In the Valentine's Day special, Rudolph sings an ode to the unsung hero of the love song, the key change. This powerful modulation has been behind the climaxes of many unforgettable love ballads, including Whitney Houston's iconic "I Have Nothing" (1992) as well as her showstopper "I Will Always Love You," a cover of Dolly Parton's original version (1973). In a celebratory ode to the key change, in the *Guardian*, Glenn Waldron writes, "Yes, it's emotionally exploitative and yes, it's incredibly cheesy. But that's also the point."[15] Rudolph exaggerates the effect, expanding it beyond mere cheddar. Rather than settling for a single modulation, through a rapid succession of key changes, her song goes higher and higher until it's in the dog-only register—a remarkable vocal feat aided toward the end with technological enhancement.

The special, however, wouldn't be complete without some reference to Bolton's hair, long and luscious during his rise to fame but in recent years cropped. In the hair-centric bit, Andy Samberg as Kenny G shows up to challenge Bolton. With his short hair, Bolton has "forsaken his true nature," Samberg's G character insists. A duel between the two ensues, but the only weapon is music, with Bolton matching Samberg's saxophone licks vocally, note for note—the actual saxophone notes played by the real Kenny G, who appears in his own cameo as a janitor. To close the bit, the real G calls Samberg and Bolton "assholes." When Bolton first heard the plan for this scene, he responded, in Aukerman's wording, with "stoic resignation."

The response to the Bolton special was positive in unexpected ways. In an interview in *Vice* (2017), journalist Larry Fitzmaurice singled out Bolton, complimenting him in particular: "Michael, you're really funny in this special." "I am?" Bolton says. His expression is often unchanged during the show, as Silverman sings about pubic hair or actor Will Forte (another former *SNL* star) joins him in a rendition of "Stand by Me" as his supposed brother, Roy Fulton. Bolton is the perfect foil for the surrounding hijinks while embracing his role as the king of Valentine's Day. In so doing, he suggests that it's OK to laugh at his over-the-top, corny-love-song reputation, in effect canceling out the corn. In the movie *Office Space*, we laugh at Bolton—thanks to a character named Michael Bolton who hates having to share his name with the singer. But in this special, we laugh *with* him. He is in on the joke. As Sophie Gilbert writes in the *Atlantic* (2017), "It's Bolton who makes it work, entirely committed to his role and transforming himself from a potential punchline into a hero."

And yet, as I must again insist, Bolton had made that turn possible decades before. With his popular love songs, he had established himself as a sentimental yet serious crooner. With just a quick nod to all that is silly in love and love songs, he flips that seriousness, tapping into the comedy already in love and his reputation as the ultimate musical love god. Up for anything, he was able to enjoy the punchline lying dormant in the musical premise he had already created. And his reward? A new audience and rave reviews. As Chris Morgan writes in *Paste* (2017), "The idea of a Michael Bolton comedy special is amusing, but it's the execution that makes it so strange and wonderful."

The greatest funny love songs take on the comedy in love—the whiplash-fast rejection, awkwardness, and gross-out gagging—at the same time undermining the idealized, sanitized vision of love and the love song. In his Valentine's Day special, Bolton gets real too while exaggerating his reputation to serve comedic ends. And I can only hope Bolton sticks with this winning formula in his podcast, *The Big Sexy Interview Show with Michael Bolton*, announced in 2022, a second collaboration with Aukerman and

Schaffer. Once again, the comedy turn is funny because it's unexpected, but it's also more honest than the sincere songs associated with true love. To some, the turn may be cathartic as well. Funny songs about love, after all, can provide needed rescue from delusions fostered by traditional ballads, including the mistaken notion that the giddy feeling of new love should last forever. Frank Zappa said something similar in a 1989 interview with Arsenio Hall, insisting that love songs create "a lot of damage" with unrealistic expectations that might negatively affect "mental health." If anything's wrong with love songs, then, it's not McCartney's "soppy" tag; it's the creation of impossible ideals. Flight of the Conchords takes on that issue directly in episode 4 of their show, "Yoko," when Bret shares a love song in progress with Jemaine. In it, he promises to "climb the highest mountain" for his new love, but Jemaine counters, Would you really do that? When Bret admits that he wouldn't, Jemaine advises him to write more "realistic" lyrics. As Tom Lehrer told John Tidmarsh in a BBC interview broadcast on April 30, 1959, the dark turn in his love song "When You Are Old and Gray" isn't sick; it's "a little more realistic."

Truly silly love songs in the end get it right. And the comedic musicians behind them have the brains and bravery to make it so, overturning more traditional approaches to love in song while exploiting honesty in the creation of humor.

NOTES

1. Quoted in Oliver Sacks, *Musicophilia: Tales of Music and the Brain* (New York: Alfred A. Knopf, 2007), x.

2. Ian Biddle and Freya Jarman-Ivens, "Oh Boy! Making Masculinity in Popular Music," in *Oh Boy! Masculinities and Popular Music*, ed. Freya Jarman-Ivens (New York: Routledge, 2007), 3.

3. Jason Lee Oakes, "Pop Music, Racial Imagination, and the Sounds of Cheese," in *Bad Music: The Music We Love to Hate*, ed. Christopher Washburne and Maiken Derno (New York: Routledge, 2004), 73–74.

4. See Limor Shifman, *Memes in Digital Culture* (Boston: MIT Press, 2013), 41.

5. Shifman, 77.

6. Sverker Hyltén-Cavallius, "Classical Music Goes Viral: Memeings and Meanings of Classical Music in the Wake of Coronavirus," *Open Library of Humanities* 7, no. 2 (2021), https://olh.openlibhums.org/article/id/4678/.

7. Quoted in David Stafford and Caroline Stafford, *The Life and Music of Randy Newman: Maybe I'm Doing It Wrong* (London: Overlook Omnibus, 2016), 60. The trend of more modest depictions of love continued in 2001 with Moldy Peaches' "Anyone Else but You" (2001), a love duet for "two ugly people," set to light acoustic guitar strumming.

8. Ben Watson, *Frank Zappa: The Negative Dialectics of Poodle Play* (New York: St. Martin's, 1993), 43.

9. Spinal Tap too had an ode to sex, "Big Bottom," with comedic innuendo in every line: "My baby fits me like a flesh tuxedo / I love to sink her with my pink torpedo."

10. If you've had it with the whole genre, there's also the Australian trio Axis of Awesome, with their easy-listening 2011 hit "How to Write a Love Song," which hilariously outlines all the clichés of love songs, rhyming *breakup* with *makeup*, followed by a little a cappella harmony.

11. In a *Los Angeles Times* article by Steve Pond (December 10, 1984), "Have Yourself a Very Twisted Xmas," Dr. Demento provided some insight into this history, citing the period after World War II as the real beginning of comic Christmas songs: Spike Jones's recording of "All I Want for Christmas Is My Two Front Teeth" and Gene Autry's version of "Rudolph the Red-Nosed Reindeer." The ensuing melee of funny holiday songs included Christmas songs with animals, like "Dominic the Italian Christmas Donkey" and "Harvey, the Christmas Hippo"; jail songs, like John Prince's "Christmas in Prison"; songs bent on bounty, like Mae West's "Put the Loot in the Boot, Santa" or "Santa, Bring Me Ringo"; and drug ditties, "Frosty the Dopeman" or Phil Moore's "Chinchy Old Scrooge." See also Steve Otfinoski, *The Golden Age of Novelty Songs* (New York: Billboard Books, 2000), 197.

12. In 1989, Dr. Demento put out a compilation of some favorite funny Christmas hits, *Dr. Demento Presents the Greatest Christmas Novelty CD of All Time*. He included "Weird Al" Yankovic's take on the Christmas song "Christmas at Ground Zero" (1986), set after an imaginary atomic bomb explosion, and "All I Want for Christmas (Is My Two Front Teeth)" (1944),

written by a music teacher named Don Gardner who was urged on by the many second-graders he was then teaching—most missing their front teeth. Some more recent contributions to the funny holiday music repertoire include the exceedingly disgusting "Mr. Hanky the Christmas Poo," courtesy of *South Park* (1997), and another less-than-PG option, "Dick in a Box," the Lonely Island's gift suggestion released just in time for Christmas, on *Saturday Night Live*, December 16, 2006. In 2011, Garfunkel and Oates offered their own holiday advice while adding to the subcategory "drug songs." In "Scary Fucked-Up Christmas," Micucci and Lindhome cheerfully sing, "If you can't handle family shit, get your bong and take a hit / Christmas is much better when you're high."

13. Jane Borden, "How the Hell Did *Michael Bolton's Big Sexy Valentine's Day Special* Happen?" *Vanity Fair*, February 7, 2017.

14. Quoted in Jenna Marotta, "Maya Rudolph on Her Prince Cover Band and Mourning the Purple One," *Cut*, September 27, 2016.

15. Glenn Waldron, "Why I Love . . . Key Changes," *Guardian*, January 6, 2004.

TWELVE

POISONING PIGEONS

WHILE IT MAY NOT BE that surprising to some that love has inspired funny songs, death is surely a different story. There is plenty of music *related* to death and specifically mourning—somber funeral marches and settings of the requiem, the Mass for the dead. And some artists have recognized a commercial appeal in the topic of death, like John Fahey, who created his alter ego Blind Joe Death partly with that in mind: "I was thinking, whenever you print the word 'Death' people look at it, and I was thinking of record sales already."[1]

But funny music about death? Surely, that can't be right. Then again, humor, as we have seen, has been a part of every genre of music, covering multiple themes—from sex to holidays, politics to race. Why would humor spare death?

In her PBS special, Sylvia Fine defined opera according to its treatment of death: "In Grand opera music is alone in first place—and everybody dies. The more people that die the grander the opera. Then there is comic opera—everybody dies, but they die happy. And in those all-day Wagner operas everybody dies—including the people in the audience who forgot to bring lunch."[2]

But how can anyone laugh at music about death? How does that killer joke work? And when does it slip on a banana peel and fall flat? Via snail mail, I reached out to Tom Lehrer, whom "Weird Al" Yankovic compared to the reclusive author J. D. Salinger.[3] The composer of hits like "The Elements," a rapid-fire recitation of the elements of the periodic table, and my personal favorite, "Poisoning Pigeons in the Park," rarely grants interviews and has done little to advance his musical legacy, in writing or recording. But he's a true legend of funny music, and he has written several songs dwelling on death in comical ways—songs that, since their debut in the 1950s and 1960s, have continued to circulate and reemerge in relationship to new historical eras and events. On the Fourth of July 2020, I received a response to my long-shot letter: "I haven't done any interviews in over 20 years and don't plan to spoil that record. However, if you really want to stick to the topic (death), I'd be willing to answer a few questions." I had never felt so patriotic.

Many comedic musicians featured in this book are objectively brilliant—no surprise given the connection between humor and intelligence. Lehrer fits that pattern and then some. He initially excelled in mathematics and managed a long career teaching in academia. But part of his genius found expression and confirmation in his ability to play—comedically and musically—with the topic of death. Dark humor, after all, according to a 2017 study, has a special connection with high intelligence.[4] In dark ditties, the comedic musician has to flip not only various conventions of music but also our own responses to death—an existential exercise for some incongruous with life itself. With a hard-to-get interview by phone with Lehrer, this chapter reveals some of the ways a clever composer-comedian can exploit the surprising-to-some mirth in mortality, ensuring a laugh in music even when the topic is perceived deadly serious.

In 1959, on the album *An Evening Wasted with Tom Lehrer*, Lehrer released the song "Poisoning Pigeons in the Park." Lehrer had a picture taken of himself to accompany the song. In it, he's kneeling with his hand in a bag, one pigeon looking at him,

Tom Lehrer, "Poisoning Pigeons in the Park," screenshot from YouTube.

seemingly hopeful that he might pull out a snack. The bird's pals, some eight pigeons, lie belly-up nearby, and Lehrer looks down on their feathered corpses. Lehrer began writing songs like this one while at Harvard, where he was a student starting at the age of fifteen. Growing up in New York, he was an advanced learner, with a natural talent for complex math and logic puzzles. He also studied piano as a child, though he never gravitated toward classical music. In an interview on July 22, 2015, carried out by the Library of Congress, he explained, "I took classical music lessons, and I practiced dutifully, but as soon as I was done with the assigned pieces, I would try to pick out popular songs on my own." The two subjects, math and music, were complementary for Lehrer: "There's something mathematically satisfying about music; notes go together and harmony and all that."[5] His comical songs too were a puzzle—words fit together to serve a topic in the style of a popular song. Accompanying himself on the piano, Lehrer's funny songs were a part of Harvard's social life, and he performed as requested regularly at mixers of various sorts on campus. But, as he told Jeremy Bernstein (a friend during his Harvard days), "After about two years of this, I got tired of it—tired of singing the same songs."[6] So he decided to make a recording, renting space himself at a Boston studio and releasing in 1953 four hundred copies of *Songs by Tom Lehrer*. In a 1997 conversation with Lehrer, Paul D. Lehrman pointed out how unusual a self-made album was in 1953. Lehrer responded, "Young folks come up to me and say 'You made your own album. I want to do my own album. How do you do that?' And I have to explain to them that times have changed." It was more feasible then, he insisted: "We did it with one [mic] on the voice and piano, and an engineer. It took an hour."

The album featured ditties defined by Lehrer's dark wit, including "I Wanna Go Back to Dixie," "When You Are Old and Gray," and "I Hold Your Hand in Mine." In "I Wanna Go Back to Dixie," Lehrer put the nostalgic repackaging of the South into perspective: "I ain't seen one good lynchin' in years." And Lehrer made his point over sixty years before our recent reevaluation of that same past—the musical group Dixie Chicks for this reason reinventing themselves as the Chicks. While he wishes his beloved dead in "When You Are Old and Gray," he goes even further in "I Hold Your Hand in Mine." After killing his lover, he cuts off her hand: "And till they come to get me / I shall hold your hand in mine."

In an NPR interview on January 4, 1979, Lehrer made it clear that he saw his art as parody, not satire. "Bitterness," after all, was not the goal. And listeners well beyond Harvard responded to the album's fun, though major labels weren't willing to sign him, despite the recording's surprising underground popularity. Lehrer recalls an RCA executive explaining why: "He said, 'No, we can't do this, because we sell refrigerators and stoves. And we don't want any boycotts of any of our products.'"[7]

In 1955, Lehrer was drafted into the army, where, rumor has it, he invented the Jell-O shot. "What happened was," Lehrer told Jack Boulware of *San Francisco Weekly* (2000), "I was in the Army for two years, and we were having a Christmas party on the naval base where I was working in Washington, D.C. The rules said no alcoholic beverages were allowed. And we wanted to have a little party, so this friend and I spent an evening experimenting with Jell-O. It wasn't a beverage." After his service, in 1957, Lehrer fielded invitations to perform, and for a time he toured with his songs, visiting England, Australia, and New Zealand. By 1959, he had enough new material for a second album, *More of Tom Lehrer*. In addition to his poisoning of pigeons, he included "We Will All Go Together When We Go" and "So Long, Mom." "So Long, Mom" was a send-up of patriotic anthems like "Johnny Get Your Gun," a riff on a supposed pride in bravely fighting, or rather killing and dying, for your country: "So long, mom, / I'm off to drop the bomb." The album sold more than two hundred thousand copies. It also served a purpose for Lehrer, giving him an exit: "I didn't want to put the record out until I was ready to retire from performing. I figured that if the record was out, who would want to come and hear me."[8]

After the album's release, he returned to academic life. He attempted to complete a PhD in mathematics at Harvard but quit in 1965 before finishing his dissertation. "It wasn't something I wanted," he told Bernstein: "I kept saying to myself that if I ever get this dissertation written, I will never have to do any research again." But he continued to teach courses he had taught at Harvard, expanding his teaching to MIT and Wellesley as well. He eventually decided to seek out a break from the snow, taking a position teaching math and eventually a course on Broadway musicals at the University of California, Santa Cruz. He was a favorite instructor there until his retirement in 2001.

Explaining his career as a teacher rather than a performing musician, Lehrer told Boulware, "I didn't have the temperament of a performer, and I could see it." In other interviews, he has made it clear that he did not find pleasure in "anonymous affection." It probably didn't help that he also received anonymous animosity. In 1959, *Time* magazine categorized him among a new group of "sick" humorists, with Lenny Bruce and Mort Sahl: "What the sickniks dispense is partly social criticism liberally laced with cyanide, partly a Charles Addams kind of jolly ghoulishness, and partly a personal and highly disturbing hostility toward all the world." In 1963, critic Jonathan Miller further defined this "sick" style in the *Partisan Review* as a juvenile way of responding to "the outlines of a puzzling moral contour."[9] But was Lehrer's humor really sick?

On July 9, 2020, I called Lehrer, ready to ask him about his focus on death. At age ninety-two, he answered my call with the same voice I recognized from his recordings. For this reason, I half expected him to break into song. And I was thrilled when he almost did, humming as he went to grab a different phone. When I brought up his dark musical concentrations, he made it clear that it was all about the laugh. And, next to sex (that "little death"), "death gets a big laugh." Like the academic he is and had been, he shared his notions of humor and its relationship to mourning. And he helped me think through the topic too.

In Lehrer's estimation, first and foremost, this sort of humor relates to our attitudes toward death; many people, simply put, are "nervous" about death and "worried about what's going to happen after they die." "I'm not concerned with that myself," he told me. But death's "a very sensitive subject" for many, he said, "so you laugh it away." That response, sometimes unwanted and unexpected, explains laughter at funerals. "Oftentimes people laugh," Lehrer said: "They just can't help themselves and they laugh at funerals because they're uncomfortable."

How we generally talk about death, or don't, ups the potential for humor. While many are fascinated by death (especially on television), as folklorist Alan Dundes notes in "The Dead Baby

Joke Cycle" (1979), Americans tend to avoid talking openly about death and disease, opting for euphemisms like "passed away," "is no longer with us," or even the quasi-comedic "kicked the bucket": "It would seem obvious enough that the higher the incidence of euphemisms, the greater the anxiety about the subject matter, the direct mention of which is so scrupulously avoided." This taboo around death has been around for centuries, with fears concerning all manner of related worries: the death of loved ones, the body's decay, and the question of what happens when a person dies. Direct mention of death is left to humor, similar to our cultural treatment of sex (and part of the preceding chapter's fun), where it is effective as a surprising punchline. Like my opening monkey joke, in the introduction, the laugh is in the frank and unexpected mention of the monkey's death fall. (Hey, I did a callback.) It's a similar device in "dead baby jokes," related to the Little Willies cycle. "What's red and swings? A baby on a meathook."

Dundes ties the "dead baby" cycle to the 1960s and the many images of massacre beamed live on television during the Vietnam War. The cycle was a possible response to our forced reckoning with death in war, which many witnessed passively at home. A 1967 song by Country Joe and the Fish supports the connection, the darkly humorous "I Feel Like I'm Fixin' to Die Rag": "So put down your books and pick up a gun / We're gonna have a whole lotta fun." The upbeat sentiment, in relationship to war, is similar to Lehrer's own "So Long, Mom."

Without honest communication about death, people could deal with the topic and their discomfort in comedy and song—confronting it while at the same time softening the topic's blow through humor. As Réka Benczes and Kate Burridge recognize in *The Oxford Handbook of Taboo Words and Language*, "Flippancy towards what is feared is widely used as means of coming to terms with fear, by downgrading it." Such gallows humor has been linked to other overwhelming tragedies, like the Holocaust—with humorous performance in the concentration camps—as well as within certain professions, in medicine and emergency response, stressful jobs that necessitate some means of coping with death through release and relief. In *The Joke and Its Relation to the Unconscious* (1905), Sigmund Freud recognized the importance of humor as a means to allow society to release repressed emotions, like anger and fear, addressing related topics, like death. And humor provides that relief quite regularly, according to Sven Svebak, professor emeritus at the Norwegian University of Science and Technology, even in the face of more minor situations. In tragedy, humor can act "like shock absorbers in a car, a mental shock absorber in everyday life to help us cope better with a range of frustrations, hassles and irritations."[10]

Still, the killer joke, as Lehrer made clear, walks a rather fine line. Some jokes don't work right away, which calls to mind a commonly accepted formula: "Tragedy plus time equals comedy" (a quote attributed by quoteinvestigator.com to television personality Steve Allen). Bringing up the formulation, Lehrer mentioned Lincoln getting shot, which wasn't funny at first. "But later on," he continued, "there were all these jokes": "Apart from that, Mrs. Lincoln, how did you like the play?" Still, he observed the many memes and jokes that circulated around COVID-19, amending the issue of time somewhat: "As soon as somebody dies, online there will be jokes." He likened online culture, all too public, to a private sphere or at least a feeling of privacy in online anonymity. "We used to tell jokes right away," he explained, "but not on television, just to each other in private."

In our discussion, he added further nuance to the tragedy-plus-time adage, attaching a certain imprecision or vagueness to the formula. Think of the classic gag, Lehrer invited me: a man falls and slips on a banana peel or plummets down a manhole. An unsympathetic detail helps, Lehrer said: "It's got to be a rich person." But even with an unlikeable character, the joke's death is in the details: "He's walking along and he falls down an open manhole. Now that would be funny if Charlie Chaplin or somebody did that. That would be hilarious," Lehrer continued. "But if you then point the camera down there and show that the guy is in agony and bleeding... then it's not funny anymore." "That's the same thing, I think, with murder," he added. By ignoring the gore, we can maintain some psychological distance from the killing or death, even as we explore it to a certain extent.

Arsenic and Old Lace (1944) is a great example, what Lehrer calls "the classic murder comedy." Directed by Frank Capra, the movie stars Cary Grant as Mortimer, visiting his aunts, the Brewster sisters, described repeatedly at the start as the "sweetest" ladies, "pure kindness," "like pressed rose leaves." In search of his notes for his next book, Mortimer opens his aunts' window seat only to discover a dead body. After a double take, he says to the corpse, "Hey, mister," closing the seat again. His bubbly aunts reappear and respond to Mortimer's announcement that there is a dead body: "Yes, dear, we know," one says with surprising calm. They are forced to explain their "good deed," kindly killing lonely old men with their poisoned elderberry wine. Though the movie boasts thirteen dead bodies, the nature of the killing (no pain or bloodletting) and the sweet Brewster sisters' casual attitude toward their insane act of supposed charity make possible the hilarity as Mortimer navigates his aunts' wild world of arsenic, lace, and hidden bodies.

Some forty years later, another movie, *Weekend at Bernie's* (1989), similarly found the lighter side in a dark foundation. With lots of physical comedy, the movie basically involves a corpse, Bernie, as a character, hauled around for most of the film in order to keep a high-end party on track. That story could easily have failed to deliver the laughs. In an interview with Tim Grierson of *Mel Magazine* (2018), Catherine Mary Stewart (who played the film's love interest) recalled, "I read the script thinking, 'Oh my gosh, this is so silly. How are they going to make this work? A dead guy? Come on!'" But it helped that the dead character fit

Lehrer's comedy formulation—he was rich. He was also a criminal who had attempted to have the main characters, Larry and Richard, killed for his crimes. When Larry and Richard arrive at Bernie's house and discover he's dead, Larry misses the point, exclaiming, "Why do these things always happen to me?" It's the perfect response, a send-up of our self-involvement.

Music can support or slaughter that killer joke. Music has many connections to death and was a symbol of death itself in antiquity.[11] Music also sounds death, the death knell and funeral bells. Along with various settings of the requiem—such as Mozart's *Requiem*, rumored to have contributed to the composer's own early death—classical music boasts a long history of pieces about death or mourning, including Gustav Mahler's haunting song cycle of 1904, *Kindertotenlieder* (*Songs on the Death of Children*). In such music, we can openly express or experience feelings of loss in a way we can't or aren't supposed to in speech. The taboo around talking about death doesn't apply to music, opening up all manner of musical possibilities in death's name. There are also many legends involving death—stories of music's connection to the dead or the devil himself, who might grant a composer inspiration. In popular music, death is everywhere too. Metal music makes use of death as a part of the music's transgression against existing cultural taboos. That boundary play can be funny, as we have seen, but also erotic—"death chic," in the words of Christopher Partridge in *Mortality and Music: Popular Music and the Awareness of Death* (2015). But the effect is also often serious, with topics ranging from murder to suicide.

In funny songs about death, we combine music and humor—both used to get around the taboo of speaking death's truth. The music can work with the lyrics to deflate any weight, allowing us to laugh. While lyrics avoid focus on suffering, Lehrer told me, the "music makes it more palatable." While a dirge is "not so funny," "a particularly jaunty and funny little melody" can help. The listener doesn't reflect on the gravity of death in part because the music renders such contemplation almost impossible; the melody is major and light, free of worry. The music and rhyme pattern further remove death from our reality. Lehrer explained, "Talking about somebody who kills everybody... that's not funny at all. But if you sing it in rhymes and a jaunty melody and so on, then the audience has permission to laugh. [It's] one step away or many steps away from reality."

Lehrer cites as an example a particularly hilarious song about murder, "To Keep My Love Alive": "It's very funny," he maintained. The song was a gift to character Morgan Le Fay in the revival of Richard Rodgers and Lorenz Hart's 1927 musical *A Connecticut Yankee*, an adaptation of Mark Twain's *A Connecticut Yankee in King Arthur's Court*. In the new song, premiered in 1943, Le Fay reveals how she has kept her lovelight shining without cheating or divorce, thanks to the helpful wedding-vow tip: "Till death do us part." In short, when the going gets tough, she gets murdering. The tune, in a moderate tempo, melodiously outlines the scenario: "Sir Philip played the harp, I cussed the thing / I crowned him with his harp to bust the thing / And now he plays where harps are just the thing." There is no mention of the gory details or Philip's distress. With a cheerful tune and a reference to heavenly harp playing, we get the punchline—all meant "to keep my love alive." Likewise with Sir Thomas, who had trouble sleeping until she gave him some arsenic: "He's sleeping now all right."

The song made me think of another song, Monty Python's "Always Look on the Bright Side of Life" (1989). In it, lighthearted whistling doesn't just make death more palatable; the music becomes the punchline. For the movie *Life of Brian*, Eric Idle wrote the song as a funny means to confront impending crucifixion. Idle remembers trying to come up with the movie's ending: "But all our characters were heading for crucifixion; how do you find an end to that in a comedy? So that was my suggestion; we'll finish with a song."[12] "Bright Side" was that song, a catchy cheer-up in the face of death with some philosophical gems in the chorus and its transformation: "Always look on the bright side of death." As the song makes clear, "Life's a laugh and death's a joke," with the last laugh on you. In an interview with Judd Apatow, for his book *Sick in the Head,* Idle shared, "It's an extraordinary song. In England, it's almost the national anthem." The song is also an oft-requested favorite at funerals, one way to ensure the uncomfortable laugh Lehrer sees as understandable.

Other songs make death funny in combination, like Weird Al's "Christmas at Ground Zero." The comedy comes in the clash between Christmas and death. "Dead Puppies Aren't Much Fun," by Ogden Edsl, a favorite on the *Dr. Demento Show,* does too, working much like the "dead baby" cycle. With a wistful melody accompanied by acoustic guitar, the singer states the obvious: "Dead puppies aren't much fun." The mash-up of adorable puppies and death is part of the hilarious left turn: "They don't come when you call / They don't chase squirrels at all." Closely related is the parody "I'm Looking Over My Dead Dog Rover," a grisly description of Rover's demise by mower.

Lehrer himself found humor in an existing tie between folk song and death, sending up murder ballads like "Pretty Polly" in his "The Irish Ballad." In his introduction, filmed at a concert in Copenhagen in 1967, he mocked up front various traits of folk song—their "idiotic refrain" (in the case of his song, the repetition of "rickety-tickety-tin"), their many verses, and the involvement of, well, the folk. If anyone feels like joining in while he sings, think again; he tells them to "get out." The song itself, with a light Irish accent, introduces us to a maid who murders her family, including her baby brother: "She cut her baby brother in two / And served him up as an Irish stew." And if the song is too long, "rickety-tickety-tin," "You should never have let me begin." In Lehrer's estimation, the trappings of the folk song are fodder for humor, but they also help soften the details of each murder. "In my ballad, 'The Irish Ballad,' which is all about killing," he told me, "it's all phrased as a folk song. . . . I mean, if somebody actually did all those things, it wouldn't be funny." But as a folk song, "I guess it's funny."

In other Lehrer songs, death can serve a larger point. While the death in "So Long, Mom" is a play on attitudes toward war, Lehrer's song "Pollution" uses death to highlight the issue of pollution in the American city, seen as "very pretty." In the style of "America," from the 1957 musical *West Side Story*, Lehrer sings, "See the halibuts and the sturgeons / Being wiped out by detergents." The next line quotes the song "Can't Help Lovin' Dat Man," from the musical *Show Boat*: "Fish got to swim and birds got to fly." Rather than continuing with the musical's romantic death, "I gotta love one man 'til I die," Lehrer follows up with the gruesome death of the fish and birds from pollution: "But they don't last long, if they try." In another, "We Will All Go Together When We Go" (1959), Lehrer takes on nuclear war, finding a comedic upside in mass death—at least we'll be together: "Universal bereavement / An inspiring achievement." It's a way out of that awkward funeral, he sings: "There'll be nobody left behind to grieve."

But Lehrer's "Poisoning Pigeons in the Park" is a stand-out, at least to me. It is death at its most hilarious, with Lehrer using all the hallmarks of his own gallows-humor formula. It has a carefree melody, which makes way for the laugh. The sound, in a dancing triple meter, provides a certain context—a perspective on the lyrics. Lehrer's performance style does so as well. "So it depends on how you present it," Lehrer explained to me. In a YouTube clip sponsored by the Tom Lehrer Wisdom Channel, he performs the song with an introduction, explaining, "I'd like to sing a song about Spring and about one of the many delightful past-times which we enjoy in the United States." He then launches into the song, in a bright major key. In the first verse, he climbs to the tonic, the song's *do*, singing, "I think the loveliest time of the year is the spring." As if in intimate conversation, he asks, "Don't you?" But then, smiling and swaying as he sings, as if he is conjuring that beautiful sunny day, he drops the hammer: "All the world seems in tune on a spring afternoon / When we're poisoning pigeons in the park." The highest note of the line falls on the first syllable of *poisoning*, a seemingly joyful jump emphasizing murder. His prolific rhyming adds to the fun: notoriety, anxiety, society, impiety.

The victim, the pigeon, isn't rich, but the bird is still a generally unsympathetic character for many, a "rat with wings," which helps the joke land. On November 14, 2016, the society he mentions, the Audubon Society, considered "our misguided hatred of pigeons," crediting a loathing of the pigeon that exceeds the birds' crimes—noise, links to disease, droppings—to their invasion of urban spaces imagined the domain of people alone. Pigeons are "matter out of place."[13] But the merits of the pigeon's poor standing are of little consequence; the pigeon's established reputation is crucial to the song's humor.

The death details too are hazy, with mention of peanuts coated in cyanide as well as strychnine. In the *Poisoner's Handbook* (2010), journalist Deborah Blum insists that cyanide's effect is dramatic, with physical convulsions and redness. It also has a very dark history, including KGB assassinations and murder during the Nazi era. But in Lehrer's song, there is no description of suffering or final bird breaths. The darkness is vague, much like another ode to springtime, the song "Springtime for Hitler," from *The Producers*, which opened in 1968. "But you notice," Lehrer said of "Springtime," "there's nothing in there about concentration camps or anything like that, antisemitism. It's just Hitler." As "Poisoning" demonstrates, comedy is tragedy plus time plus only vague detail.

In 1960, Unicorn Records decided to re-record "Poisoning" as a single, with a small orchestra and a hired piano player. In a conversation with Paul D. Lehrman in 1997, Lehrer remembers the recording session as noteworthy: "I went into the booth to record, and the engineer said 'Poisoning Pigeons in the Park, take one' and the piano player said 'Whaat?' and literally fell off the bench. I had never seen anybody do that." The piano player didn't see that song coming. But once it had come, it became a classic in the world of funny music, played some 183 times on the *Dr. Demento Show* and still going strong. Dr. Demento told Boulware, "[The song's] not dated at all. Pigeons still annoy people in city streets. And that is a thought that is, if anything, more outrageous now than it was then, because now we hear so much from animal rights activists."

Lehrer's expertise and success in the area of funny songs about death is perhaps not surprising. His whole career, in some ways, has played with a humor in death. At age thirty-six, Lehrer said, "It is sobering to consider that when Mozart was my age he had already been dead for a year." While many comedians and musicians, like Mozart, die young, Lehrer simply retired from regular performance. But, to some, even early retirement is like death. In the fame game, with a career over, "You're dead in this town." In the romantic conception of the composer, who is supposedly compelled to create or perish, it's a similarly figurative death.

And yet, his songs continue to find new life, a rebirth despite his supposed death. In the 1960s, Lehrer was intrigued by a new satirical comedy show on NBC, *That Was the Week That Was*. On top of his teaching load, he contributed various songs, like "Pollution," which he insisted others on the show perform (he would not do it himself)—all released on the album *That Was the Year That Was* (1965), recorded live at the hungry i. The first was "National Brotherhood Week." The song was a takedown of uneven attempts to enforce tolerance, outlining with a lively tune the hate between groups: white folks and Black folks, poor folks and rich folks, "And everybody hates the Jews." Like many of

Lehrer's songs, this one has remained relevant. It has even taken on a life all its own, with Sarah Silverman tweeting on July 25, 2020, a clip of Lehrer singing, "And everybody hates the Jews," underscoring today's continued antisemitism. His song "I Got It from Agnes" likewise became a funny way to deal with the spread of COVID-19, although his original intent was left intentionally unclear: "I never say what it is that's being passed on." "I got it from Agnes, / She got it from Jim," he sings. Again, details can ruin the joke, despite the seeming reference to an STI. And it surely helps the humor that in the song two cultural taboos come together, sex and death.

The life and resurrection of these songs are unique in the realm of topical comedy. Typically, humor around political issues dates the song, signaling an early death. Weird Al, for that reason, tends to avoid political humor. As he told David Segal of the *Washington Post* (2003), "Things that are topical in the political arena this week would be old news a month from now, so that's probably not the kind of thing I want to have as part of my catalog." But perhaps Lehrer's recourse to vagueness helps here, especially in comparison to newer parodist Randy Rainbow, who relies on specifics in songs, as in his "How Do You Solve a Problem Like Korea?" (a take on "Maria" from *The Sound of Music*) or "Just Be Best," a dig at then–first lady Melania Trump's contradictory antibullying campaign, to the tune of "Be Our Guest" from Disney's *Beauty and the Beast*. These parodies are ideographs, defined by Tom Ballard as a subgenre of parody "that creates new messages" without "directly mocking or contradicting the messages of the originals."[14] They are not directed at the original songs (their musicians or topics) but instead at new ideological foes, most often very particular political events and politicians—so specific, in fact, that it's hard to imagine these songs resurfacing again in relationship to any other political period, the way Lehrer's have.

But it isn't just the life of Lehrer's work that has flirted with death; it's also in his work's packaging. In 1980, the musical

Tomfoolery debuted, produced by Cameron Mackintosh and featuring Lehrer's songs. The following year, in 1981, Lehrer released his songs in sheet music with piano arrangements and drawings by satirical cartoonist Ronald Searle. In Searle's cover image, a goblin-esque clown plays the piano with a large human skull at its feet. On the piano is a garland with a sash reading "R.I.P." In Lehrer's foreword to the songbook, he explains his departure from music: "What good are laurels if you can't rest on them?" He re-released his songs with Rhino Records in 2000, a three-CD box set with a fittingly macabre title, *The Remains of Tom Lehrer*.

But he had no plans of performing again. In a 2000 interview with Stephen Thompson for the *A.V. Club*, Lehrer likened seeing him in concert to visiting a dead person: it's "the Lenin's Tomb phenomenon: People want to see the actual flesh of Lenin, but it doesn't matter, because he's dead." With no new material, he sees no musical reason to attend his performance or for him to perform. Anyone interested in a Lehrer concert, he insists, is just entertaining a macabre desire to see a famous person. And he has ignored calls to write new songs. He told Bernstein, "I remember that one lady called me up and said that she loved my songs. She told me that she thought the main problem in America was materialism and that I should write a song making fun of materialism. I told her that of course I would do it—if she paid me enough money." Part of the issue, he explained to me, is the gravity of events today. Referencing his song "I Wanna Go Back to Dixie," he said, "Racism is so rampant and so ubiquitous now that to just make fun of the south because they're racist doesn't really do it anymore." And humor, he has insisted before, might not really create positive change—just "titillating the converted." In 2000, in his interview with Thompson, he added sarcastically, "I'm fond of quoting Peter Cook, who talked about the satirical cabarets of the '30s, which did so much to stop the rise of Hitler and prevent the Second World War." Oh wait. Still, to me he admitted, "It might move some people who were seeing other people laugh."

He has also avoided interviews or other related attempts to commemorate his musical legacy. He referred one reporter to "Mr. Google" rather than granting an interview. "It doesn't matter if the answer is correct—who cares?" he explained. "And I lie a lot too."[15] Ben Smith and Anita Badejo, in BuzzFeed's 2014 article "Looking for Tom Lehrer, Comedy's Mysterious Genius," wrote, "Indeed, Tom Lehrer has done everything possible, short of dying, to vanish from the American cultural scene." In fact, many assume that he is dead, which Lehrer loves. Even in 1984, he told Bernstein, "Now I see that I am often referred to as 'the late Tom Lehrer.' I have a small file of clippings like that, which I cherish, because people assume that I am dead." "I was hoping the rumors would cut down on the junk mail," he has explained elsewhere.[16]

—⚜—

Throughout Lehrer's life, he has riffed on our complex cultural attitudes toward death as well as death's connections to fame. Just as he has entertained listeners with his funny songs about death—expertly wielding his own formula of tragedy plus time plus vagueness—he has in turn been amused by our responses to his unusual course in music, an early move away from songwriting that has apparently earned him a false death and hopefully less mail. It took an especially impressive mind to mine the comedy in such a fundamental societal standard, a perceived incongruity between life and death. The mastery of his music is in part in the creativity, the knowledge of song genres and conventions of song types, as well as the flexible and fluid thinking around matters of life and death and an honesty in response. But the point, for Lehrer, is all in the laugh. He doubts humor's ability to effect change in opinions or policies. But, as Lehrer told Thomson, "Comedy is very important, yes. For one thing, it keeps you sane." In the next and final section, I consider that value, especially in times of crisis.

NOTES

1. Quoted in Steve Lowenthal, *Dance of Death: The Life of John Fahey* (Chicago: Chicago Review Press, 2014), 27.
2. Sylvia Fine, "Musical Comedy III," Library of Congress, Kaye/Fine Collection, box 829, folder 4.
3. See Stephen Thompson, "Tom Lehrer," *A.V. Club*, May 24, 2000.
4. Jamie Doward, "Black Humor Is Sign of High Intelligence, Study Suggests," *Guardian*, January 28, 2017.
5. Quoted in Todd S. Purdum, "Still a Sly Wit, Now Mostly for Himself," *New York Times*, July 16, 2000.
6. Jeremy Bernstein, "Out of My Mind: Tom Lehrer," *American Scholar* 53, no. 3 (1984): 298.
7. Quoted in Jack Boulware, "That Was the Wit That Was," *San Francisco Weekly*, April 19, 2000.
8. Bernstein, "Out of My Mind," 299.
9. See Stephen Edward Kercher, "The Limits of Irreverence: 'Sick' Humor and Satire in America, 1950–1965" (PhD diss., Indiana University, 2000).
10. Quoted in Marlene Cimons, "Laughter Really Is the Best Medicine?," *Washington Post*, June 15, 2019.
11. Kathi Meyer-Baer, *Music of the Spheres and the Dance of Death* (Princeton, NJ: Princeton University Press, 2015).
12. Quoted in Donald Liebenson, "Eric Idle Wrote 'Always Look on the Bright Side of Life' in About an Hour," *Vanity Fair*, August 2, 2019.
13. See Colin Jerolmack, "How Pigeons Became Rats: The Cultural-Spatial Logic of Problem Animals," *Social Problems* 55, no. 1 (2008): 72–94.
14. Tom Ballard, "YouTube Video Parodies and the Video Ideograph," *Rocky Mountain Review* 70, no. 1 (2016): 10.
15. Ben Smith and Anita Bedejo, "Looking for Tom Lehrer, Comedy's Mysterious Genius," BuzzFeed, April 9, 2014, https://www.buzzfeed.com/bensmith/tom-lehrer
16. See Jeffrey R. Toobin, "Tom Lehrer," *Harvard Crimson*, November 9, 1981.

CONCLUSION
Comedic Music in Crisis

WHEN TOM LEHRER CONSIDERED THE issue of tragedy and time, he addressed it in terms of what works in the creation of humor. But plenty of others have thought about the issue in terms of appropriateness and responsibility. The short-lived moratorium on humor in 2001, after the 9/11 attacks, is a case in point. On September 29, 2001, then-mayor of New York City Rudy Giuliani appeared on *Saturday Night Live* with the show's longtime producer Lorne Michaels. Michaels asked Giuliani, "Can we be funny?" Giuliani boomed back, "Why start now?" That joke gave people permission to laugh, those who thought it wasn't proper to joke in the immediate aftermath of such tragedy.[1] That same consideration resurfaced during the COVID-19 pandemic: Is humor appropriate in times of crisis? At the same time, musical humor exploded in response, especially online. So, what was the answer? And if comedy in catastrophe is somehow wrong, why has it been so popular?

Crisis has attracted a remarkably varied amalgamation of musicians. Marc Shaiman and Scott Wittman, who wrote songs for *Hairspray* and *Mary Poppins Returns*, composed a pandemic handwashing song, for those sick of the recommended "Happy Birthday" tune. In "Twenty Seconds!" the lyrics race with a jaunty accompaniment: "Twenty seconds isn't long, / Barely time to sing this song." With a political edge, Harry Shearer (of *This Is Spinal Tap* fame) released "Covid-180," mocking Trump's response to the virus. Political parodist Randy Rainbow offered up his own COVID take, a version of the heroic song "Go the Distance," written by Michael Bolton for the animated movie *Hercules* (1997): "I will break the chain / I will social distance." Summing up lockdown, Devo Spice, who describes himself as the "red-headed stepson of 'Weird Al' Yankovic and Eminem," wrote "Everything Is Cancelled," a parody of "Everything Is Awesome," written for *The Lego Movie*. Weird Al himself made it clear on Twitter that he wouldn't be contributing to this realm of comedic music-making: "Yeah, no, sorry. Not gonna do 'My Corona,'" an updating of his hit "My Bologna," itself a parody. But singer-songwriter Chris Mann, who appeared on the television show *The Voice* in 2012, filled the gap—with, you guessed it, "My Corona." Describing a stress-filled trip to the grocery store, he sings, "Guess I'm stocking up on boxed wine, Corona."[2]

And it wasn't just established musicians playing with the pandemic musically. Amateurs too created parodies, adding to a remarkably wide-ranging musical response. Erika Perzan offered, "Twinkle, twinkle little star. Look how clean my two hands are." And nurse Philip Flavin had a take on a Queen song: "We will, we will wash you."[3] On August 7, 2020, Jimmy Fallon invited still more amateur parody-making on Twitter: "Tweet out a funny song lyric parody about summer 2020." The results were all pandemic related: "And it was Fun fun fun til the 'rona took the summer away."

Addressing the outpouring of online musical humor, Rainbow tweeted on March 28, 2020, "This coronavirus got all y'all singing a whole lotta song parodies. Frankly, it's weird." Eden responded, "It's one of the primary symptoms, Randy." But Rainbow had a point. Was it "weird"? Put another way, was it right? Bo Burnham was perhaps the most reflective in this respect, at least musically.

In his 2021 Netflix special, *Inside*, created entirely by himself during quarantine, he launched into the problem of comedy, with "nothing to joke about." In song, he asks, "Should I be joking at a time like this?"

Some argue that humor is somehow inconsequential, even insulting during periods of serious loss and grave catastrophe. Not only is musical humor dismissed as less significant than "serious" art; it is also denied consequence as basic entertainment and condemned as disrespectful during and after tragedy. I get it, especially today. I'm writing this very paragraph on the fifth day of protests around the killing of George Floyd, with racism on full display in the police's response as well as the president's fascist deployment of the military against peaceful protesters, most of them masked as they demonstrate during a pandemic. In this moment, humor seems a strange subject. I have written about prejudice and discrimination before; shouldn't that be my focus today rather than musical comedy? After all, a funny song is *just* a joke, right?

For certain readers, anything I write next, an explanation or argument of sorts, will no doubt sound hollow. But, in truth, musical humor is never just a joke. While this book has argued that the craft, creativity, and cleverness of humorous music are real (and perhaps greater than those of comedy or music alone), the pandemic and its musical response highlight a final consideration: the very real purpose of musical humor, especially in times of crisis.

Humor often has a serious point. As Jonathan P. Rossing insists in "A Sense of Humor for Civic Life" (2016), "By playing with knowledge constructions and destabilizing conventional truths, humor helps audiences recognize not only the social practices and truths of our shared world but also the processes by which people collectively create, recreate, maintain and accept that reality." Comedy can challenge collective wisdom, it involves new approaches to conventional thinking, and it is endlessly inventive and inspiring. We have seen the cleverness behind this work throughout the book, with comedy addressing conventions of music, genre, and topic but also politics, gender, race, and life itself. As George Orwell observed, "Every joke is a tiny revolution."

Lehrer may suspect that humor doesn't create real change. But even a push or slight shift in thinking matters. And plenty of others believe humor can do a whole lot more than that. There can be an element of education in musical humor, just as there is in comedic political shows like *The Daily Show*. In "Getting Political Science in on the Joke: Using *The Daily Show* and Other Comedy to Teach Politics" (2011), Staci L. Beavers concludes that these shows can engage audiences who might otherwise ignore political issues. They're a sort of "gateway" to greater political involvement. They also serve a purpose all their own, helping audiences interpret, understand, and even critique the "serious" news programs.[4] In a 2019 interview with Rainbow, *Billboard*'s Alex Blynn wrote, "Arguably, independently-created political satire has helped to turn the tide of public opinion. Sometimes it takes someone other than a talking head on a nightly network news show to really put atrocities into focus."

—☙—

Musical humor has more general psychological benefits as well. When Rainbow pointed out the wild amount of parody songs posted in response to COVID-19, "debra.appling" explained, "Hey, Randy, honestly it's keeping me sane in the middle of all this crazy." Humor of all types flourished during the pandemic—created and circulated aplenty. This fad filled a need. During the pandemic, many felt out of control, unable to predict when life would reopen or if it would resume at all. Until then, we were often stuck inside, connections disrupted. But through comedy, we could regain a certain sense of power by putting our own spin on the virus, ordering and organizing our attitudes toward the disease and the many changes thrust upon us so quickly. South

London rapper Psych, who added to the COVID-19 repertoire with the darkly funny "Spreadin,'" understood, acknowledging the importance of music and humor during the 2020–2021 crisis. "It means something to a lot of people out there," he told Lanre Bakare in the article "Lyrical Lockdown: Rappers Respond to Coronavirus" (2020). "People are saying: 'Thank you for this song, I'm not coping well but this song is getting me through isolation,'" he reported. "When you see things like that it makes you realize you can have an impact on people's mental health." As one 2020 headline made clear, "'Humor is healing': Laughter soothes frazzled nerves during Covid-19 trauma."

Musical humor without a pandemic focus had value too. Through the social aspect of music and comedy, we could forge sorely needed interaction and communion with others. We could reach out with a shared joke or musical laugh—easily packaged and shared online. In an April 2020 *New York Times* profile of Weird Al, Sam Anderson wrote, "Comedy, a disembodied spark between distant people seems more crucial than ever." Circulating funny memes and silly songs of all types was a responsible way to find from afar the bond and human connection many missed. For others, musical comedy was a needed distraction and release. In a 2020 *Vulture* article, "Escape Our Current Hell with These (Good) Coronavirus Jokes," writer Chris Murphy offered an explanation: "Comedy, as frivolous and inessential as it may seem, is humanity's free coping mechanism, a medium that both distracts us from the horrors of the world while allowing us to get our best and worst thoughts out of our heads and off of our chests." Anthropologist Helen Fisher confirmed, telling Murphy, "Laughter evolved to enable us to tolerate and overcome and move beyond tough times, and it does so in many subtle ways."

Pandemic parodists were of course not the first to respond to crisis in this way. During World War II, USO Camp Shows brought plays, musical comedies, and variety acts—with comedy and music—to soldiers fighting abroad. Entertainment was seen as functional, a needed break and an essential moment of enjoyment and distraction. In this context, show programmers actively discouraged a topical focus, assuming that lighter fare was far more beneficial. To this end, the lineup often avoided contemporary issues, with programmed musicals like Cole Porter's *Panama Hattie* and George Gershwin's *Girl Crazy*. USO Camp Shows nixed one suggestion, Lillian Hellman's *Watch on the Rhine*, as "too political" and made changes to the existing norms of vaudeville based on similar thinking.[5] For one, they favored visual gags over any political chatter. Reviewing scripts before performances, they also axed mention of the president or members of Congress as well as any jokes mocking American history. As Sam Lebovic writes in his consideration of the USO, "The shows were embraced for their existence as shows." As one soldier explained in *Variety*, "I, for one, always took it for granted as a likable convenience, but 20 months have taught me—the hard way—that it is a vital part of soldiers' happiness."[6]

Humor was significant during World War I as well, as Clémentine Tholas-Disset and Karen A. Ritzenhoff chronicle in their volume *Humor, Entertainment, and Popular Culture during World War I* (2015). Likewise, during the Civil War, jokes of all kinds provided needed relief—so much so that the era has been called "the age of practical joking." The jokester-in-chief, Abraham Lincoln, explained, "If I did not laugh I should die."[7] The crisis most closely related to the COVID-19 pandemic, the 1918 influenza outbreak, also saw its fair share of music and humor. In the *New York Times* in 2020, musicologist Will Robin chronicled the musical impact of that earlier pandemic, including several different published compositions called the "Influenza Blues." In letters from the period, music was clearly valued, as was humor. A teacher in Indianapolis, Hildreth Heiney, wrote comical descriptions of life at home for her fiancé, Sergeant Kleber Hadley. On

November 21, 1918, she maintained, "And one should surely have a sense of humor."[8]

Though this book has focused on musical humor in the United States, similar use of humor has of course thrived in crises in other countries. Humor during the Holocaust is an extreme example. Satirical Yiddish song sounded in occupied lands as well—as a source of strength, release, and hope.[9] There were comical-musical responses to the pandemic in other countries too, like Hong Kong–based singer Kathy Mak's parody of Natalie Imbruglia's "Torn." In Mak's version, she's torn about how to navigate life during the pandemic—from whether or not she should use an elevator to what things she can touch. And in the Philippines, Mikey Busto created a parody of Lady Gaga's "Stupid Love": "Stupid Cough."

―✽―

Despite the obvious utility and popularity of musical humor during the pandemic, comedic musicians themselves struggled with funny music's reputation and the question of its appropriateness. Ultimately, however, many would confirm its validity and purpose. In an interview with Jesse David Fox on *Good One*, musical comedian Chelsea Peretti, promoting her album *Foam and Flotsam* (2020), insisted that comedy gives "people relief." In a *Rolling Stone* interview (April 24, 2020), Dierks Bentley admitted that he was initially unsure if he should promote his comedy country act, Hot Country Knights, but ultimately reasoned, "I'm obsessed with *Tiger King* like everyone else. More so than ever, people enjoy laughter. And the Knights, they provide plenty of laughs, usually at their own expense, so maybe it *is* the right time." Burnham, in his Netflix special *Inside*, would answer his own question—"Should I be joking at a time like this?"—in an otherworldly version of his own voice, a mock-serious technically manipulated sound: he'll be "healing the world with comedy." It's a send-up of a clichéd promotion of comedy. But, while he recognized humor's limitations, he spoke sincerely to the audience, offering his humor as a needed distraction, just as the making of comedy was for him; he has said that it distracted him from killing himself.[10]

Of course, not all musical jokes work the same way in offering such distraction, relief, and release. For those dealing with the loss of a loved one, a funny song about buying toilet paper might not have helped. Something comical could also turn dark with the passing of time—with the mounting death toll and the compounding effect of ineffective leadership. But, for many, funny songs were and are generally vital psychologically. And the topic doesn't always matter. While pandemic-parody songs addressed the situation directly, any funny song could serve to uplift in a moment of need; the topic didn't have to be especially topical. Many funny songs pose serious questions or offer pointed entertainment during periods of stress, but comical songs seemingly about nothing matter in crisis as well.

The cliché "Laughter is the best medicine" is then cliché for a reason. The COVID-19 outbreak tested that cliché in a new way. And people all over the world stepped up to make it fact. "The Cupid Shuffle" became "The Covid Shuffle," and "I Can't Get No Satisfaction" turned into "I Can't Get No (Sanitiser)." Even Haydn found new support during the pandemic. In the *Telegraph*, critic Ivan Hewett delivered the headline "Why Haydn Is the Perfect Composer to Get Us through Coronavirus" (March 30, 2020), citing his "jokiness": "Now is the time when Haydn's special qualities come into their own." Sorry, Mozart. Haydn wins again.

With so many stuck at home during the pandemic, music was an especially important chance to laugh, offering both relief and connection while people were physically isolated. And funny songs were also creative outlets for professionals and amateurs alike. As Randy Rainbow explained, "People thank me all the time for giving them some relief in this madness, and I thank them right back because it is extremely cathartic to make."[11] Like so many, I felt the weight of worry and fear during the pandemic (and still do)—responsible for two small children in a period of high anxiety and unease. Listening to funny music and writing this book was an important means for me to maintain a certain balance, finding release and distraction, which helped me stay present for my family when I couldn't afford to crumble. At certain points, I questioned myself: Could I be doing more? What's the point? But, over and over again, I recommitted, convinced that staying sane matters, and musical humor of all kinds can help maintain that sanity and balance.

Humor in music does and is so much. It offers pointed messages as well as general relief and comfort—all needed in different ways at different times. It plays on perceptions of music, creating incongruities between a funny song and any number of musical elements, associations, genres, and topics. In that clash, there is often some sort of truth, at times unmasking fictitious projections in music and revealing hidden realities in music and its histories. Music is a joke, with humor everywhere in sound, but, apparently, the joke is music too—or, at least, music as it actually is. Fluid thinking and the integration of a vast understanding of music, humor, and the world around us make possible such meta-musical humor and other humor that upends conventional thinking while opening up a wide field of musical and humorous play, one in some ways beyond the reach of humor or music alone. For all of these reasons, funny music is serious. That seriousness should in no way endanger the joke. The hierarchical divide between humorous music and serious music is based on a faulty premise. There is artistry in funny music just as music accepted as art can involve humor. The categories blur and blend until we are left with a broader understanding of music and its seriously funny points and possibilities. And comedy and music are better for it—just as we are.

NOTES

1. In "Making a Big Apple Crumble," Bill Ellis argues that humor's suppression after 9/11 along with its eventual resurgence follows a regular pattern post-tragedy: "Disaster jokes do not simply appear singly, but emerge as a cycle out of a phenomenon with a recognizable structure." See Bill Ellis, "Making a Big Apple Crumble: The Role of Humor in Constructing a Global Response to Disaster," *New Directions in Folklore* 6 (2002): 335–351.

2. Mann also parodied Adele's song "Hello" with his "Hello (from the Inside)," which he sings while pressed up against his window, desperately looking outside while sheltering in place. Legendary funny-song writer Randy Newman told the *Los Angeles Times*, "Did you see that guy who did a parody of the Adele song 'Hello'? It's funny." Newman himself broke with the parody trend, penning an original coronavirus song with a safety message, "Stay Away," which doubles as a loving tribute to his wife: "You'll be with me 24 hours a day / What a lucky man I am."

3. All compiled by Marc Silver in *Mcall*.

4. Pallas Catenella, "'I'm Not Your Normal Definition of a Rock Star': The Revolutionary Potential of Satirical Pop" (paper presented at the National Meeting of the American Musicological Society, Boston, MA, November 2019).

5. Sam Lebovic, "'A Breath from Home': Soldier Entertainment and the Nationalist Politics of Pop Culture during World War II," *Journal of Social History* 47, no. 1 (2013): 269.

6. Quoted in Lebovic, 280.

7. Quoted in Jon Grinspan, "Laugh during Wartime," *New York Times*, January 9, 2012.

8. Quoted in Jessica Klein, "A Trove of Sad, Funny, and Familiar Stories from the 1918 Flu Pandemic: A UCLA Librarian Has Built a Remarkable Collection of Century-Old Letters, Diaries, and Photographs," Atlas Obscura, May 1, 2020, https://www.atlasobscura.com/articles/letters-and-diaries-1918-flu-pandemic.

9. See, for example, David Shneer, "Is It Still Funny? Lin Jaldati and Yiddish Satire before and after the Holocaust," in *Laughter After: Humor and the Holocaust*, ed. David Slucki, Gabriel N. Finder, and Avinom Patt (Detroit: Wayne State University Press, 2020), 59–84.

10. See Alec Bojalad, "Bo Burnham: Inside's Moment of Breathtaking Empathy," *Den of Geek*, June 2, 2021.

11. Interview in Matt Grobar, "Randy Rainbow Discusses His Journey from YouTube into the Entertainment Mainstream," *Deadline*, August 21, 2019.

SELECTED BIBLIOGRAPHY

Abelmahmoud, Elamin. "Rewriting Country Music's Racist History." *Rolling Stone*, June 5, 2020.

Adams, Sam. "Farewell, Dr. Demento—and the Novelty Song?" *Salon*, June 13, 2010.

Adler, Thomas A. "The Uses of Humor by Bluegrass Musicians." *Mid-America Folklore* 10, no. 2 (1982): 17–26.

Antoine, Katja Elisabet. "'Pushing the Edge': Challenging Racism and Sexism in American Stand-up Comedy." PhD diss., UCLA, 2015.

Apatow, Judd. *Sick in the Head: Conversations about Life and Comedy*. New York: Random House, 2015.

Attardo, Salvatore. *The Linguistics of Humor: An Introduction*. Oxford: Oxford University Press, 2020.

Aylesworth, John. *The Corn Was Green: The Inside Story of Hee Haw*. Jefferson, NC: McFarland, 2010.

Ballard, Tom. "YouTube Video Parodies and the Video Ideograph." *Rocky Mountain Review* 70, no. 1 (2016): 10–22.

Bealle, John. "Self-Involvement in Musical Performance: Stage Talk and Interpretive Control at a Bluegrass Festival," *Ethnomusicology* 37, no. 1 (1993).

Beavers, Staci L. "Getting Political Science in on the Joke: Using *The Daily Show* and Other Comedy to Teach Politics." *Political Science & Politics* 44/2 (April 2011): 415–419.

Benczes, Réka, and Kate Burridge, "Speaking of Disease and Death." In *The Oxford Handbook of Taboo Words and Language*, edited by Keith Allan, 61–76. Oxford: Oxford University Press, 2019.

Bernstein, Jeremy. "Out of My Mind: Tom Lehrer." *American Scholar* 53, no. 3 (1984): 295–302.

Bessman, Jim. "Dr Demento Marks 30 Years of Funny Music with Rhino Set." *Billboard*, February 26, 2000, 11.

Biddle, Ian, and Freya Jarman-Ivens. "Oh Boy! Making Masculinity in Popular Music." In *Oh Boy! Masculinities and Popular Music*, edited by Freya Jarman-Ivens, 1–20. New York: Routledge, 2007.

Bojalad, Alec. "Bo Burnham: Inside's Moment of Breathtaking Empathy." *Den of Geek*, June 2, 2021.

Bolton, Michael. *The Soul of It All: My Music, My Life*. New York: Center Street, 2013.

Borden, Jane. "How the Hell Did *Michael Bolton's Big Sexy Valentine's Day Special* Happen?" *Vanity Fair*, February 7, 2017.

Botstein, Leon. "Laughing with and at Classical Music, in Public." *Musical Quarterly* 100, no. 2 (2017): 117–121.

Boulware, Jack. "That Was the Wit That Was." *San Francisco Weekly*, April 19, 2000.

Brendel, Alfred. *Alfred Brendel on Music: Collected Essays*. Chicago: A Cappella Books, 2001.

Bronson, Harold. *The Rhino Records Story: Revenge of the Music Nerds*. New York: Select Books, 2013.

Brown-Montesano, Kristi. *Understanding the Women of Mozart's Operas*. Berkeley: University of California Press, 2007.

Bryson, Bethany. "'Anything but Heavy Metal': Symbolic Exclusion and Musical Dislikes." *American Sociological Review* 61, no. 5 (1996): 894.

Buck, David. "Eat Them Up. Yum!" *Tedium*, July 18, 2019.

Bugler, Caroline. *The Cat: 3,500 Years of the Cat in Art*. London: Merrell, 2011.

Caldwell, Bill. "Joplin Singer Achieved Flash-in-the-Pan Fame, Devoted Following." *Joplin Globe*, March 2, 2019. https://www.joplinglobe.com/news/local_news/bill-caldwell-joplin-singer-achieved-flash-in-the-pan-fame-devoted-following/article_961c61ab-91a8-5aad-b56c-e118084e5045.html.

Campbell, Patricia Shehan. *Songs in Their Heads: Music and Its Meaning in Children's Lives*. Oxford: Oxford University Press, 2010.

Caplan, David. "Hip Hop's Sophisticated Comedy." In *The Routledge Companion to Popular Music and Humor*, edited by Thomas M. Kitts and Nick Baxter-Moore, 92–98. New York: Routledge, 2019.

Carroll, Noël. "Horror and Humor." *Journal of Aesthetics and Art Criticism* 57, no. 2 (1999): 145–160.

Case, George. *Here's to My Sweet Satan: How the Occult Haunted Music, Movies and Pop Culture, 1966–1980*. Fresno, CA: Quill Driver Books, 2016.
Catenella, Pallas. "'I'm Not Your Normal Definition of a Rock Star': The Revolutionary Potential of Satirical Pop." Paper presented at the National Meeting of the American Musicological Society, Boston, MA, November 2019.
Christensen, Alexander P., Paul J. Silvia, Roger E. Beaty, and Emily C. Nusbaum. "Clever People: Intelligence and Humor Production Ability." *Psychology of Aesthetics, Creativity, and the Arts* 12, no. 2 (2018): 136–143.
Cimons, Marlene. "Laughter Really Is the Best Medicine?" *Washington Post*, June 15, 2019.
Cusic, Don. "Comedy and Humor in Country Music." *Journal of American Culture* 16, no. 2 (1993): 45–50.
———. *It's the Cowboy Way! The Amazing True Adventures of Riders in the Sky*. Lexington: University Press of Kentucky, 2003.
Dalmonte, Rossana. "Towards a Semiology of Humour in Music." *International Review of the Aesthetics and Sociology of Music* 26, no. 2 (1995): 167–187.
Davis, Dennis. "Humor, Structure, and Methodology in Selected Works by Peter Schickele." PhD diss., University of Kentucky, 2010.
Dell'Antonio, Andrew. "Butt-Head: A Glimpse into Postmodern Music Criticism." *American Music* 17, no. 1 (1999): 65–86.
Diamond, Michael, and Adam Horovitz. *Beastie Boys Book*. New York: Random House, 2018.
Doward, Jamie. "Black Humor Is Sign of High Intelligence, Study Suggests." *Guardian*, January 28, 2017.
Dundes, Alan. "The Dead Baby Joke Cycle." *Western Folklore* 38 (1979): 145–157.
Elkins, Evan. "The New Logic of the Absurd: The Eric Andre Show." In *The Comedy Studies Reader*, edited by Nick Marx and Matt Sienkiewicz, 57–70. Austin: University of Texas Press, 2018.
Ellis, Bill. "Making a Big Apple Crumble: The Role of Humor in Constructing a Global Response to Disaster." *New Directions in Folklore* 6 (2002): 335–351.
Engell, Lorenz. *Thinking through Television*. Amsterdam: Amsterdam University Press, 2019.
Evans, Mark, and Philip Hayward, ed. *Sounding Funny: Sound and Comedy Cinema*. UK: Equinox Publishing, 2016.

Falconer, Tim. *Bad Singer: The Surprising Science of Tone Deafness and How We Hear Music.* Toronto: Anansi, 2016.

Fine, Sylvia. "Musical Comedy III." Library of Congress, Kaye/Fine Collection, box 829, folder 4.

Fitzgerald, Jon, and Philip Hayward. "Paranormal Product: The Music and Promotion of Ghostbusters." In *Sounding Funny: Sound and Comedy Cinema,* edited by Mark Evans and Philip Hayward, 92–109. Sheffield, UK: Equinox, 2016.

Fox, Jess David. "Chelsea Peretti Interview." *Good One: A Podcast about Jokes,* April 21, 2020. https://podcasts.apple.com/us/podcast/chelsea-perettis-late-with-a-coffee/id1203393721?i=1000472155103.

Fredriksson, Kristine. "Minnie Pearl and Southern Humor in Country Entertainment." In *Country Music Annual 2000,* edited by Charles K. Wolfe and James E. Akenson, 75–88. Lexington: University of Kentucky Press, 2014.

Frith, Simon. "Look! Hear! The Uneasy Relationship of Music and Television." *Popular Music* 21, no. 3 (2002): 277–290.

Gabler, Neal. *Barbra Streisand: Redefining Beauty, Femininity, and Power.* New Haven, CT: Yale University Press, 2016.

Garrett, Charles Hiroshi. "'Pranksta Rap': Humor as Difference in Hip Hop." In *Rethinking Difference in Music Scholarship,* edited by Olivia Bloechl, Melanie Lowe, and Jeffrey Kallberg, 315–337. Cambridge: Cambridge University Press, 2015.

———. "'Shooting the Keys': Musical Horseplay and High Culture." In *The Oxford Handbook of the New Cultural History of Music,* edited by Jane F. Fulcher, 245–263. Oxford: Oxford University Press, 2011.

Gervais, Matthew, and David Sloan Wilson. "The Evolution and Functions of Laughter and Humor: A Synthetic Approach." *Quarterly Review of Biology* 80, no. 4 (2005): 395–430. https://doi.org/10.1086/498281.

Gioia, Ted. *Love Songs: The Hidden History.* Oxford: Oxford University Press, 2015.

Giuffre, Liz. "Music in Comedy Television from the Composer's Perspective: Getting 'the Answers You're *Not* Looking For' in an Interview with David Schwartz." In *Music in Comedy Television: Notes on Laughs,* edited by Liz Giuffre and Philip Hayward, 105–116. New York: Routledge, 2017.

Goehr, Lydia. "'Music Has No Meaning to Speak Of': On the Politics of Musical Interpretation." In *The Interpretation of Music,* edited by Michael Krausz, 177–190. Oxford: Clarendon Press, 1993.

Goldmark, Daniel. "Anthologizing Rock and Roll: Rhino Records and the Repackaging of Rock History." Unpublished manuscript, Microsoft Word.

———. "Sounds Funny / Funny Sounds: Theorizing Cartoon Music." In *Animation and Comedy in Studio-Era Hollywood*, edited by Daniel Goldmark and Charlie Keil, 257–271. Berkeley: University of California Press, 2011.

———. *Toons for 'Toons: Music and the Hollywood Cartoons*. Berkeley: University of California Press, 2005.

Goodyear, Dana. "Largo Nights." *New Yorker*, May 19, 2008.

Gorbman, Claudia. *Unheard Melodies: Narrative Film Music*. Bloomington: Indiana University Press, 1987.

Gray, Coleman. "35 Years Later, *This Is Spinal Tap* Still Rocks Harder Than Ever." Rotten Tomatoes, March 2, 2019. https://editorial.rottentomatoes.com/article/35-years-later-this-is-spinal-tap-still-rocks-harder-than-ever/.

Green, Douglas. *Singing in the Saddle: The History of the Singing Cowboy*. Nashville, TN: Vanderbilt University Press, 2005.

Grinspan, Jon. "Laugh during Wartime." *New York Times*, January 9, 2012.

Grobar, Matt. "Randy Rainbow Discusses His Journey from YouTube into the Entertainment Mainstream." *Deadline*, August 21, 2019.

Halnon, Karen Bettez. "Heavy Metal Carnival and Dis-alienation: The Politics of Grotesque Realism." *Symbolic Interaction* 49, no. 1 (2006): 33–48.

Hamlin, Jesse. "His hungry i Helped Put S.F. on the Map as Rebel Artists' Haven." *SF Gate*, April 4, 2007.

Harrington, Richard. "Dr. Demento's Slipped Discs." *Washington Post*, September 11, 1991.

Hasty, Katie. "Hit Fix Interview: Aimee Mann on New Album, Patton Oswalt and Bummer Songs." *Uproxx*, September 28, 2012.

Henderson, George. *Blind Joe Death's America: John Fahey, the Blues, and Writing White Discontent*. Chapel Hill: University of North Carolina Press, 2021.

Hilleary, Mike. "Garfunkel and Oates." *Under the Radar Magazine*, August 6, 2014.

Hilmes, Michele. "The Evolution of Saturday Night." In *Saturday Night Live and American TV*, edited by Nick Marx, Matt Sienkiewicz, and Ron Becker, 25–39. Bloomington: Indiana University Press, 2013.

———. "Fanny Brice and the 'Snooks' Strategy." *Spectator* 25, no. 2 (2005): 11–25.

Hirsch, Lily E. *Music in American Crime Prevention and Punishment*. Ann Arbor: University of Michigan Press, 2012.

———. *Weird Al: Seriously*. Lanham, MD: Rowman and Littlefield, 2020; expanded ed., 2022.

Huizenga, Tom. "Killing Me Sharply with Her Song: The Improbable Story of Florence Foster Jenkins." NPR, August 10, 2016.

Hutcheon, Linda. *A Theory of Parody: The Teachings of Twentieth-Century Art Forms*. New York: Metheun, 1985.

Hyltén-Cavallius, Sverker. "Classical Music Goes Viral: Memeings and Meanings of Classical Music in the Wake of Coronavirus." *Open Library of Humanities* 7, no. 2 (2021). https://olh.openlibhums.org/article/id/4678/.

Inman, David. *Television Variety Shows: Histories and Episode Guides to 57 Programs*. Jefferson, NC: McFarland, 2005.

Jackie, Full Metal. "Brian Posehn: I Don't Have the Energy to Front a Band for 'Grandpa Metal' Tour." *Loudwire*, March 9, 2020.

Jacobson, Marion. "The Rise and Fall (and Rise) of the Ukulele." *Atlantic*, January 25, 2015.

Jerolmack, Colin. "How Pigeons Became Rats: The Cultural-Spatial Logic of Problem Animals." *Social Problems* 55, no. 1 (2008): 72–94.

Jones, Loyal. *Country Music: Humorists and Comedians*. Champaign: University of Illinois Press, 2008.

Kajikawa, Loren. "Eminem's 'My Name Is': Signifying Whiteness, Rearticulating Race." *Journal of the Society for American Music* 3, no. 3 (2009): 341–363.

Kaufman, Sarah L., Jayne Orenstein, Sarah Hashemi, Elizabeth Hart, and Shelly Tan. "The Science behind Improv." *Washington Post*, June 7, 2018. https://www.washingtonpost.com/graphics/2018/lifestyle/science-behind-improv-performance/.

Kellow, Brian. *Ethel Merman: A Life*. New York: Penguin Books, 2007.

Kercher, Stephen Edward. "The Limits of Irreverence: 'Sick' Humor and Satire in America, 1950–1965." PhD diss., Indiana University, 2000.

Kessler, Kelly. *Broadway in the Box: Television's Lasting Love Affair with the Musical*. Oxford: Oxford University Press, 2020.

Keyes, Cheryl L. *Rap Music and Street Consciousness*. Urbana: University of Illinois Press, 2002.

Klauber, Bruce. "Mitch Miller: The Kitsch of Mitch." Jazzlegends, www.jazzlegends.com. http://www.jazzlegends.com/mitch-miller-the-kitch-of-mitch.

Klein, Jessica. "A Trove of Sad, Funny, and Familiar Stories from the 1918 Flu Pandemic: A UCLA Librarian Has Built a Remarkable Collection of Century-Old Letters, Diaries, and Photographs." Atlas Obscura, May 1,

2020. https://www.atlasobscura.com/articles/letters-and-diaries-1918-flu-pandemic.

Kun, Josh. "The Yiddish Are Coming: Mickey Katz, Anti-Semitism, and the Sound of Jewish Difference." *American Jewish History* 87, no. 4 (1999): 343–374.

Lauer-Williams, Kathy. "Kate Micucci on Growing Up in Nazareth." *Morning Call*, September 1, 2016. https://www.mcall.com/entertainment/things-to-do/mc-kate-micucci-film-steelstacks-bethlehem-20160901-story.html.

Lebovic, Sam. "'A Breath from Home': Soldier Entertainment and the Nationalist Politics of Pop Culture during World War II." *Journal of Social History* 47, no. 1 (2013): 263–296.

Lees, Gene. *Singers and the Song II*. New York: Oxford University Press, 1998.

Lerner, Neil. "Danny Elfman: 'Funny Circus Mirrors.'" In *Sound and Music in Film and Visual Media: A Critical Overview*, edited by Graeme Harper, 524–530. London: Continuum, 2009.

Levine, Zeke. "*Lil Dicky Katz*: The Evolution of Jewish American Comedic Music." Paper presented at the National Meeting of the American Musicological Society, Boston, MA, November 2, 2019.

Lewis, Randy. "Parody Master Yankovic Stays a Step Ahead with New, Seriously Silly Moves." *Star Advertiser*, February 28, 2017.

Liebenson, Donald. "Eric Idle Wrote 'Always Look on the Bright Side of Life' in About an Hour." *Vanity Fair*, August 2, 2019.

Lowenthal, Steve. *Dance of Death: The Life of John Fahey*. Chicago: Chicago Review Press, 2014.

Marantz, Andrew. "Good Evening. Hello. I Have Cancer." *New Yorker*, October 5, 2012.

Marotta, Jenna. "Maya Rudolph on Her Prince Cover Band and Mourning the Purple One." *Cut*, September 27, 2016.

Maslon, Laurence, and Michael Kantor. *Make 'Em Laugh: The Funny Business of America*. Belfast: Bullfinch, 2007.

McCoy, Sharon. "Is a Joke Really Like a Frog?" *Humor in America*, December 6, 2011. https://humorinamerica.wordpress.com/2011/12/06/is-a-joke-really-like-a-frog/.

McGovern, Kieran. "Why Did George Martin Almost Not Sign the Beatles?" *Medium*, March 28, 2019.

McGraw, A. Peter, and Caleb Warren. "Benign Violations: Making Immoral Behavior Funny." *Psychological Science* 21, no. 8 (2010): 1141–1149.

McNamara, Brooks. "Broadway: A Theatre Historian's Perspective." *Drama Review* 45, no. 4 (2001): 125–128.
Meizel, Katherine. *Idolized: Music, Media, and Identity in American Idol*. Bloomington: Indiana University Press, 2011.
Meserko, Vince M. "Standing Upright: Podcasting, Performance, and Alternative Comedy." *Studies in American Humor* 1, no. 1 (2015): 20–40.
Meyer, Leonard B. "Meaning in Music and Information Theory." *Journal of Aesthetics and Art Criticism* 15, no. 4 (1957): 412–424.
Meyer-Baer, Kathi. *Music of the Spheres and the Dance of Death*. Princeton, NJ: Princeton University Press, 2015.
Miller, D. A. *Place for Us*. Cambridge, MA: Harvard University Press, 2000.
Miller, Liz Shannon. "'The Eric Andre Show': The Only Two Things They Can't Do on TV's Most Anarchic Talk Show." IndieWire, August 17, 2016. https://www.indiewire.com/features/general/the-eric-andre-show-hannibal-buress-adult-swim-guests-season-4-1201717792/.
Mizejewski, Linda. *Pretty/Funny: Women Comedians and Body Politics*. Austin: University of Texas Press, 2014.
Mlynar, Phillip. "We Chat with Cat Rapper El-P about 'Meow the Jewels,' a Crowd-Sourced Prank." *Catster*, February 17, 2016.
Molanphy, Chris. *Old Town Road*. Durham, NC: Duke University Press, 2023.
Most, Andrea. *Making Americans: Jews and the Broadway Musical*. Cambridge, MA: Harvard University Press, 2004.
Muir, John Kenneth. *Best in Show: The Films of Christopher Guest and Company*. New York: Applause Theatre and Cinema Books, 2004.
Mundy, John, and Glyn White. Introduction to *Laughing Matters: Understanding Film, Television and Radio Comedy*, edited by John Mundy and Glyn White, 1–20. Manchester: Manchester University Press, 2012.
Nichols, Natalie. "Largo Gets New Lease on Life at the Old Coronet." *Los Angeles Times*, May 18, 2008.
Nwanevu, Osita. "The 'Cancel Culture' Con." *New Republic*, September 23, 2019.
Oakes, Jason Lee. "Pop Music, Racial Imagination, and the Sounds of Cheese." In *Bad Music: The Music We Love to Hate*, edited by Christopher Washburne and Maiken Derno, 62–82. New York: Routledge, 2004.
Oestreich, James. "Peter Schickele Brings P.D.Q. Bach Back to the Stage." *New York Times*, December 16, 2015.
Otfinoski, Steve. *The Golden Age of Novelty Songs*. New York: Billboard Books, 2000.

Partridge, Christopher. *Mortality and Music: Popular Music and the Awareness of Death*. London: Bloomsbury, 2015.
Pecknold, Diana. *The Selling Sound: The Rise of the Country Music Industry*. Durham, NC: Duke University Press, 2007.
Pérez, Raúl. "Racism without Hatred? Racist Humor and the Myth of 'Color-Blindness.'" *Sociological Perspectives* 60, no. 5 (2017): 956–974.
Perlmutter, D. D. "On Incongruities and Logical Inconsistencies in Humor: The Delicate Balance." *HUMOR* 15, no. 2 (2002): 155–168.
Phillipov, Michelle. *Death Metal and Music Criticism: Analysis at the Limits*. Lanham, MD: Lexington Books, 2012.
Pond, Steve. "Have Yourself a Very Twisted Xmas." *Los Angeles Times*, December 10, 1984.
Purdum, Todd S. "Still a Sly Wit, Now Mostly for Himself." *New York Times*, July 16, 2000.
Ravas, Tammy. "'The Initial Plunge,' 'The Soused Period,' and 'Contrition'?: Moving Towards a Style of Peter Schickele's Funny Music in His P.D.Q. Bach Works." *Notes* 62, no. 2 (2005): 322–353.
Reich, Howard. "Mitch's New Pitch." *Chicago Tribune*, November 15, 1987.
Ritzenhoff, Karen A., and Clémentine Tholas-Disset. *Humor, Entertainment, and Popular Culture during World War I*. New York: Palgrave Mac, 2015.
Rodger, Gillian M. *Just One of the Boys: Female-to-Male Cross-Dressing on the American Variety Stage*. Champaign: University of Illinois Press, 2018.
Ross, Alex. "Why So Serious? How the Classical Concert Took Shape." *New Yorker*, September 1, 2008.
Sacks, Mike. *Poking a Dead Frog: Conversations with Today's Top Comedy Writers*. New York: Penguin Books, 2014.
Sacks, Oliver. *Musicophilia: Tales of Music and the Brain*. New York: Alfred A. Knopf, 2007.
Segal, David. "'Weird Al': Confessions of a Parody Animal." *Washington Post*, August 17, 2003.
Self, John. "Why the Funniest Books Are Also the Most Serious." BBC, November 9, 2020.
Shifman, Limor. *Memes in Digital Culture*. Boston: MIT Press, 2013.
Shneer, David. "Is It Still Funny? Lin Jaldati and Yiddish Satire before and after the Holocaust." In *Laughter After: Humor and the Holocaust*, edited by David Slucki, Gabriel N. Finder, and Avinom Patt, 59–84. Detroit: Wayne State University Press, 2020.

Simmons, Julie. "Dr. Demento: Talking Turkey about Comedy and Novelty Music." *Music Makes You Think*, November 25, 2015.
Simmons, Ted. "Run the Jewels' El-P Talks Making of Cat-Sampling 'Meow the Jewels' Charity Album and More." *Billboard*, September 26, 2015.
Sklaroff, Lauren Rebecca. *Red Hot Mama: The Life of Sophie Tucker*. Austin: University of Texas Press, 2018.
Slater, Jenny. "Aimee Mann, Michael Penn Open Tour with Romance, Cynicism, and Comedy." *MTV News*, January 26, 2000.
Smith, Ben, and Anita Bedejo. "Looking for Tom Lehrer, Comedy's Mysterious Genius." BuzzFeed, April 9, 2014, https://www.buzzfeed.com/bensmith/tom-lehrer.
Stafford, David, and Caroline Stafford. *The Life and Music of Randy Newman: Maybe I'm Doing It Wrong*. London: Overlook Omnibus, 2016.
Standley, Alessandra. "Who Says Women Aren't Funny?" *Vanity Fair*, April 2008.
Stott, Adam. *Comedy: The New Critical Idiom*. London: Routledge, 2014.
Sullivan, Jim. "What Will the Future of Concerts Look Like after the Pandemic?" WBUR.org, May 4, 2020. https://www.wbur.org/news/2020/05/04/coronavirus-pandemic-music-industry-concerts.
Taylor, Yuval, and Jake Austen. *Darkest America: Black Minstrelsy from Slavery to Hip-Hop*. New York: W. W. Norton, 2012.
Thomerson, John. "Parody as a Borrowing Practice in American Music, 1965–2015." PhD diss., University of Cincinnati, 2017.
Thompson, Stephen. "Tom Lehrer." *A.V. Club*, May 24, 2000.
Toobin, Jeffrey R. "Tom Lehrer." *Harvard Crimson*, November 9, 1981.
Wald, Elijah. *The Dozens: A History of Rap's Mama*. Oxford: Oxford University Press, 2012.
Waldron, Glenn. "Why I Love ... Key Changes." *Guardian*, January 6, 2004.
Walker, Nancy A. *A Very Serious Thing: Women's Humor and American Culture*. Minneapolis: University of Minnesota Press, 1988.
Watson, Ben. *Frank Zappa: The Negative Dialectics of Poodle Play*. New York: St. Martin's, 1993.
Watson, Cate. "A Sociologist Walks into a Bar (and Other Academic Challenges): Towards a Methodology of Humor." *Sociology* 49, no. 3 (2015): 407–421.
Weinstein, Deena. "The Empowering Masculinity of British Heavy Metal." In *Heavy Metal Music in Britain*, edited by Gerd Bayer, 17–31. Farnham, UK: Ashgate, 2009.

———. "Humor in Metal Music." In *The Routledge Companion to Popular Music and Humor*, edited by Thomas M. Kitts and Nick Baxter-Moore, 66–75. New York: Routledge, 2019.

Weiss, Neal. "The Artist Rules at Largo, the Most Vital Performance Space in Los Angeles." *Los Angeles Times*, February 22, 1998.

Weston, Paul, and Jo Stafford. *Song of the Open Road: An Autobiography and Other Writings*. Albany, GA: BearManor Media, 2012.

White, Rosie. "Funny *Peculiar*: Lucille Ball and the Vaudeville Heritage of Early American Television Comedy." *Social Semiotic* 26, no. 3 (2016): 298–310.

Williams, Elsie A. *The Humor of Jackie Moms Mabley: An African American Comedic Tradition*. New York: Garland, 1995.

Woldu, Gail Hilson. "'Don't I Look Like a Halle Berry Poster?' Humor and Irony in Women's Hip Hop." In *The Routledge Companion to Popular Music and Humor*, edited by Thomas M. Kitts and Nick Baxter-Moore, 339–345. New York: Routledge, 2019.

Wolf, Stacy. *A Problem Like Maria: Gender and Sexuality in the American Musical*. Ann Arbor: University of Michigan Press, 2002.

Yacowar, Maurice. *Method in Madness: The Comic Art of Mel Brooks*. New York, St. Martin's, 1981.

Zemke, Kirsten. "'I Told You I Was Freaky': Gender, Genre, and Parody in the Songs of *Flight of the Conchords*." In *Music in Comedy Television: Notes on Laughs*, edited by Liz Giuffre and Philip Hayward, 117–128. New York: Routledge, 2017.

INDEX

2 Live Jews, 112

Acuff, Roy, 130
alternative comedy, 24, 35
Anderson, Leona, 65. *See also* bad singing
Andre, Eric, 122, 188
Andrews, Julie, 19, 178
Ansari, Aziz, 7, 115
Apple, Fiona, 21, 22, 27, 28, 29
Armisen, Fred, 27, 185, 205
Autry, Gene, 131, 134
Aykroyd, Dan, 78

Bach, J.S., 83, 92, 95, 100, 106
Bach, P.D.Q., 92, 93, 95, 98-106. *See also* Peter Schickele
bad singing, 65-66
Bailey, Pearl, 179, 190
Ball, Lucille, 183-184
banter, 28, 127, 136-140
Barnes and Barnes, 44
Beastie Boys, 111
the Beatles, 44, 101, 126-127, 196
Belushi, John, 78
Benny, Jack, 52, 59-60
Bentley, Dierks, 131, 235
Bernstein, Elmer, 76-77, 87

Bernstein, Leonard, 6, 77, 92
Bird, Andrew, 29, 31
Black, Jack, 43, 78, 143-153, 155-156. *See also* Tenacious D
Bloom, Rachel, 190
Bolton, Michael, 195-200, 201, 202-207, 230. *See also* love songs
Bonds, Ian (or Insane Ian), 13, 47
Borge, Victor, 3, 92, 93, 99, 105, 106
Bowie, David, 25
Brasfield, Rod, 131
Brice, Fanny, 157, 158, 159, 163-164, 165, 166, 167, 173
Broadway: and humor, 157, 163, 166, 168, 172; and outsiders, 166-167, 173; and women, 158-159, 161, 173
Brooks, Mel, 76, 87, 113, 190
Brown, Julie, 190
Brownstein, Carrie, 26
Bruce, Lenny, 5, 23, 215
Burd, Dave (Lil Dicky), 113-114
Burnett, Carol, 178, 190
Burnham, Bo, 24, 26, 115, 132, 230, 235
Burton, Tim, 77

Caesar, Sid, 24, 52, 204
cameo, 200
Channing, Carol, 165

INDEX

Chaplin, Charlie, 22, 218
cheesy music, 198
Cho, Margaret, 29
classical music and humor: in the Baroque, 95; in the Classical era, 95-96; in the madrigal, 95; in the motet, 94; in the Romantic era, 96-97. *See also* P.D.Q. Bach
Clement, Jemaine, 201. *See also* Flight of the Conchords
Coen, Ethan, 78
Coen, Joel, 78
Colbert, Stephen, 122
comedy clubs, 22-24
Cooper, Alice, 20, 153, 200
Corigliano, John, 75
Country Joe and the Fish, 216
country music: and history of humor, 128-133; and humor in reception, 141. *See also* Riders in the Sky
cue sheets, 84

David, Larry, 113
Davis Jr, Sammy, 23
Debussy, Claude, 97
the dozens, 116
Dr. Demento, 36, 38-50; Basement Tapes of, 47; funny music criteria of, 43, 47, 49. *See also* Barry Hansen
Drescher, Fran, 81
Dylan, Bob, 40

Edsel, Ogden, 49, 221
Edwards, Darlene, 14, 58-65, 66-68. *See also* Jo Stafford
Elfman, Danny, 74, 76, 77
Eminem, 111, 112, 133, 135, 139, 230
Epic Rap Battles of History, 116

Fahey, John, 40, 210
Fallon, Jimmy, 43, 144, 230
Fey, Tina, 185
film music: and humor, 74, 82, 84-88; and listening, 73-74, 83; reception of, 73, 86, 88, 89
Fine, Sylvia, 179, 210
Fischer, Larry "Wild Man," 46
Flanagan, Mark, 21-22, 24, 26, 28, 29, 34, 35, 73. *See also* Largo
Flanders and Swann, 3
Flight of the Conchords, 20, 24, 25, 26, 29, 31, 86-87, 201, 207
Funny Girl, 157, 158, 163-166, 173
funny movies: and music, 78-82; and reception of musical jokes, 79-82, 89
Funny Music Project (FuMP), 38, 160
funny songs: and Christmas, 202; and COVID-19, 229-230, 232-235; and death, 210, 215-223; and love, 201-202, 206-207

Galifianakis, Zach, 21, 24, 27, 29, 31, 32
Garfunkel and Oates, 14, 24, 25, 30, 177, 179, 180, 182-184, 186-188, 190-192, 202
Garland, Judy, 165, 178
Gass, Kyle, 43, 143-153, 155-156. *See also* Tenacious D
Glover, Donald (Childish Gambino), 116
Green, Douglas B. (Ranger Doug), 126, 136, 137. *See also* Riders in the Sky
Grohl, Dave, 147
Guest, Christopher, 78-79, 80

Hall, Marcel "Biz Markie," 116
Hansen, Barry, 36, 38-50; Basement Tapes of, 47; funny music criteria of, 43, 47, 49. *See also* Dr. Demento
Hammond, Darrell, 44
Haydn, Joseph, 6, 7, 8, 11, 95, 96, 102, 236
Heidecker, Tim, 105
Hindle, Annie, 161
humor: analysis of, 5; after tragedy, 217, 229, 231, 235; as coping, 232-233, 236-237; and incongruity, 6, 12; and intelligence, 13; musical similarities,

30-33, 171; and race, 3, 9, 162-163; and reception of music in, 2-4; superiority theory of, 9; topical, 225; and women, 3-4, 159-161, 169, 173, 190-191

Idel, Eric, 220. *See also* Monty Python
Ingle, Red, 56

Jenkins, Florence Foster, 65, 91. *See also* bad singing
Jones, Spike, 39, 41, 56, 88

Kaling, Mindy, 4
Katz, Mickey, 162
Kaye, Danny, 64, 179
key change, 205
Key, Keegan-Michael, 132
Kroll, Nick, 31

LaBour, Fred (Too Slim), 14, 126-129, 130, 131, 134, 135-137, 139, 140, 141. *See also* Riders in the Sky
Lansbury, Angela, 22
Largo, 19-22, 24, 25, 26, 27-30, 31, 32, 33, 34-35, 50, 73, 190
Lavin, Christine, 44
Leggero, Natasha, 4
Lehrer, Tom, 3, 14, 23, 59, 89, 187, 201, 207, 211-215, 216, 217, 218, 219-227, 229, 232; invention of the Jell-O shot by, 214
Letterman, David, 49, 149
Lewis, Jerry, 23, 160
Lil Nas X, 132
Lindhome, Riki, 14, 25, 28, 30, 177, 179-189, 190-193. *See also* Garfunkel and Oates
live music, 20
love songs, 196-197
Luther Wright and the Wrongs, 102

Mabley, Jackie Moms, 162, 173
Madonna, 32, 82, 190

Mann, Aimee, 27, 28, 29, 30, 33-34
Martin, Dean, 23, 57
Martin, Demitri, 24
Martin, Steve, 138
Marx, Groucho, 52, 139
McKean, Michael, 78
McKenna, Jessica, 14, 159, 169-174. *See also* Off Book
McKenzie, Bret, 20, 25, 186. *See also* Flight of the Conchords
Meline, Jaime (El-P), 109, 118, 119-121, 122, 123
meme, 200
Merman, Ethel, 164-165
metal humor: and the devil, 149-150; and masculinity, 151-152. *See also* Tenacious D
Meyers, Seth, 17, 27
Michaels, Lorne, 20, 229
"mickey-mousing," 84, 86
Micucci, Kate, 14, 25, 28, 29, 177, 179-184, 185, 186-193. *See also* Garfunkel and Oates
Miller, Mitch, 53, 56, 62, 63, 69
Miller, Mrs., 65-66
Miskulin, Joseph, 126. *See also* Riders in the Sky
Missy Elliott, 117
Monty Python, 94, 134, 158, 220
Mozart, Wolfgang Amadeus, 84, 95-96, 97, 101, 103, 219, 224, 236
Mulaney, John, 31, 86

Napoleon XIV, 43
Nervous Norvus, 42
Newman, Randy, 48, 74, 87, 201
Notaro, Tig, 4, 29, 183, 184, 188

O'Brien, Conan, 26, 34, 35
O'Doherty, Claudia, 4
Off Book, 14, 159, 170-171
Oswalt, Patton, 27, 28, 29, 30, 32, 33, 34, 137

parody, 1, 7, 8, 12, 14, 19, 47, 78-79, 80, 82, 89, 93, 105, 112, 131, 133, 134, 139, 153, 167, 185, 201, 213, 221, 225, 230, 232, 235-236
Paul, Woody, 126. *See also* Riders in the Sky
Pearl, Minnie, 129, 130, 140
Peele, Jordan, 132
Posehn, Brian, 145, 154

Rainbow, Randy, 94, 225, 230, 232, 233, 236
rap and humor: and race, 111-115; and reception, 110
Reiner, Rob, 78, 80
Render, Michael (Killer Mike), 108-109, 110, 118-124
Reubens, Paul, 77
Rhino Records, 46, 50, 226
Richards, Michael, 81
Riders in the Sky, 14, 126-129, 133, 134, 135, 140, 141
Rogers, Roy, 131, 134
Rossini, Gioachino, 97, 122
Rota, Nino, 77
Rowan, Peter, 139
Rudolph, Maya, 4, 131, 205
Ruffin, Amber, 4
Russell, Anna, 91, 92, 104, 105, 106

Sandberg, Andy, 26, 78, 112, 185, 196, 205
Sandler, Adam, 26, 78, 185
Satie, Erik, 96
satire, 213
Saturday Night Live (SNL), 20, 26, 62, 86, 112, 113, 138, 185, 198, 100, 205, 106, 229
Schaal, Kristen, 4
Schaffer, Akiva, 112, 203
Schickele, Peter, 93-92, 98-106
Schumann, Robert, 4
Schumer, Amy, 4
Shaffer, Paul, 27

Shapiro, Thoedore, 14, 74, 75-76, 77, 78, 82-89
Shearer, Harry, 78, 146, 230
Sherman, Allan, 115
Silverman, Sarah, 29, 157, 159, 167-169, 190, 204, 205, 206, 225
Simmons, Russell, 115, 124
Sinatra, Frank, 55, 63
Skillet Lickers, 128
Slick Rick, 117
Smith, Kevin, 32
Snell, Christopher, 44
Snoop Dogg, 120, 124
Stafford, Jo, 14, 52, 53-65, 66-68. *See also* Darlene Edwards 14, 58-65, 66-68
Stalling, Carl, 84, 85
Streisand, Barbra, 23, 157, 164-167

Taccone, Jorma, 112
Tank, Wes, 113
Tenacious D, 43, 143-153, 155-156
The Smothers Brothers, 136, 137, 138
Thompkins, Paul F., 29, 33
Tucker, Sophie, 161-162, 163, 169

vaudeville, 22, 95, 128, 161, 162, 163, 183, 185, 204, 234

Wagner, Richard, 91, 97, 104, 122, 210
Watts, Reggie, 27, 170
Wesner, Ella, 161
Weston, Paul, 52, 55, 56, 57-59, 60, 62, 63-69
White, E.B., 4
Whitehurst, Logan, 38, 48-49
Williams, Jessica, 4

Yankovic, "Weird Al," 1, 2, 7, 14, 25, 33, 41, 44, 46, 47, 48, 74, 80, 81, 82, 102, 113, 123, 170, 182, 187, 190, 211, 221, 225, 230, 233

Zappa, Frank, 45, 201, 207
Ziegfeld Follies, 162, 163, 166

LILY E. HIRSCH is a musicologist and the author most recently of *Can't Stop the Grrrls: Confronting Sexist Labels in Music from Ariana Grande to Yoko Ono*, *Weird Al: Seriously,* and *Insulting Music: A Lexicon of Insult in Music.*

For Indiana University Press

Lesley Bolton, Project Manager/Editor
Allison Chaplin, Acquisitions Editor
Sophia Hebert, Assistant Acquisitions Editor
Samantha Heffner, Marketing and Publicity Manager
Brenna Hosman, Production Coordinator
Katie Huggins, Production Manager
Jennifer Witzke, Senior Artist and Book Designer

www.ingramcontent.com/pod-product-compliance
Lightning Source LLC
Chambersburg PA
CBHW030616230426
43661CB00053B/2015